THE SUN THAT WARMS

THEODORE CLYMER
DORIS GATES
CONSTANCE M. McCULLOUGH

CONSULTANTS
ROGER W. SHUY · Linguistics
E. PAUL TORRANCE · Creativity

GINN AND COMPANY
A XEROX COMPANY

READING 360 READING 360 READING 360 READING 360 READING 360
GINN

0-663-25207-5

ACKNOWLEDGMENTS

Grateful acknowledgment is made to the following authors and publishers for permission to use copyrighted materials:

Atheneum House, Inc., for "Cheers" by Eve Merriam. Copyright © 1964 by Eve Merriam. From *It Doesn't Always Have to Rhyme*. Used by permission of Atheneum Publishers.

Coward-McCann, Inc., for "The Great Hunt." Reprinted by permission of Coward-McCann, Inc. from *The Cave Dwellers* by Richard M. Powers. Copyright © 1963 by Richard M. Powers.

Thomas Y. Crowell Company for "I, Momolu," from *I, Momolu*, by Lorenz Graham. Copyright © 1966 by Lorenz Graham. Thomas Y. Crowell Company, New York, publishers.

Doubleday & Company, Inc., for "An Island for a Pelican." Adapted from *An Island for a Pelican* by Edward Fenton. Copyright © 1963 by Edward Fenton. Reprinted by permission of Doubleday & Company, Inc.

Farrar, Straus & Giroux, Inc., for "Pitcher." Reprinted with the permission of Farrar, Straus & Giroux, Inc. from *Pitcher and I* by Stephen Cole. Copyright © 1946, 1947, 1963 by Stephen Cole. Copyright 1946 by The Curtis Publishing Company.

Harcourt Brace Jovanovich, Inc., for "Alphonse, That Bearded One," from the illustrated edition of *Alphonse, That Bearded One* by Natalie Savage Carlson and Nicolas Mordvinoff, copyright, 1954, by Harcourt, Brace & World, Inc. and reprinted with their permission. Also for "Urashima Taro and The Princess of the Sea," from *The Dancing Kettle and Other Japanese Folk Tales*, copyright, 1949, by Yoshiko Uchida. Reprinted by permission of Harcourt, Brace & World, Inc. And for "Winter Danger," slightly adapted from *Winter Danger*, copyright, 1954, by William O. Steele. Reprinted by permission of Harcourt, Brace & World, Inc.

Harper & Row, Publishers, for "The Day They Stayed Alone," from pages 67–79 of *On the Banks of Plum Creek* by Laura Ingalls Wilder. Copyright 1937 by Harper & Brothers. Reprinted with permission of Harper & Row, Publishers.

Hill and Wang, Inc., for "The Day We Die," from *Kalahari* by Jens Bjerre. First published in Denmark by Carit Andersens Forlag in 1958 under the title *Kalahari Atomtidens Stenalder*. © Translation copyright 1960 by Michael Joseph Ltd. Reprinted by permission of Hill and Wang, Inc.

Holt, Rinehart and Winston, Inc., for "The Brontosaurus," from *Creatures Great and Small* by Michael Flanders. Text copyright © 1964 by Michael Flanders. Reprinted by permission of Holt, Rinehart and Winston, Inc.

J. B. Lippincott Company for "The Okapi Belt" from *Children of South Africa* by Louise A. Stinetorf. Copyright, 1945, by Louise A. Stinetorf. Published by J. B. Lippincott Company. And for "The Reason for the Pelican" from *The Reason for the Pelican* by John Ciardi. Copyright 1955 by the Curtis Publishing Company. Published by J. B. Lippincott Company.

McGraw-Hill Book Company for "The Mammoth," from *Odd Old Mammals* by Richard Armour. Copyright © 1968 by Richard Armour & Paul Galdone. Used with permission of McGraw-Hill Book Company.

New Directions Publishing Corporation for "In the City" (Poem starting "In the street . . .") by Charles Reznikoff, *By the Waters of Manhattan*. Copyright 1934 by The Objectivist Press. © 1962 by New Directions Publishing Corporation. Reprinted by permission of New Directions Publishing Corporation and San Francisco Review. The poem, #12 from *Jerusalem the Golden*, is here entitled "In the City" by permission of New Directions Publishing Corporation.

The Viking Press, Inc. for "Andy and the Lion" and an illustration from *Andy and the Lion* by James Daugherty. Copyright 1938, © 1966 by James Daugherty. Reprinted by permission of The Viking Press, Inc.

Henry Z. Walck, Inc., for "The Shasta Bison" from *From Bones to Bodies* © 1959 William W. Fox and Samuel P. Welles. Used by permission of the publisher.

Random House, Inc., for "The Ice Age," adapted from *All about the Ice Age*, by Patricia Lauber. © Copyright 1959 by Patricia Lauber. Reprinted by permission of Random House, Inc. Also for "Introducing Dinosaurs," adapted from *All about Dinosaurs*, by Roy Chapman Andrews. Copyright 1953

2

right 1953 by Story Parade, Inc. Reprinted and adapted by permission of Western Publishing Company, Inc.

World's Work Ltd., England, for "The Mammoth" from *Odd Old Mammals* by Richard Armour. And for "An Island for a Pelican," adapted from *An Island for a Pelican* by Edward Fenton. Both used by permission of World's Work Ltd., publisher of the British editions.

The illustrations were prepared by the following artists: Don Allbright, Willi Baum, Frances Bini, Ben Black, Mike Cassaro, Tom Cooke, George Eisenburg, Judy Sue Goodwin, Norman Laliberte, Naoko Matsubara, Tod and Judy McKie, Jack Murray, Jane Oka, Joan Paley, Jerry Pinkney, Richard Powers, Ben Stahl, Phero Thomas, George Ulrich, Dianne Winer, and Hans Zander.

The maps were prepared by Ernest Sawtelle, 268–269, 274.

The photographs were obtained through the following sources: American Museum of Natural History, 284, 335 (lower left); Christopher J. Schuberth, 284; Dr. Ralph Chaney, Department of Paleontology, University of California, at Berkeley, 275, 276, 277, 278; J. B. Collins, 124; Commissariat Général Au Tourisme, 300, 301; Thomas Y. Crowell Co., 114; Charles Michael Daugherty, 144; Shirley Eddy, 414, 415; Balden Kapoor, Free Lance Photographers Guild, Inc., 285 (upper left); Greek National Tourist Office, 404, 405, 409; Harcourt, Brace and World Inc., 124; Peter A. Juley and Son, 181; Nicholas Krenitsky, 148 (right side); Life Magazine © Time, Inc., Dmitri Kessel, 410; John Molholm, 285 (lower left); Museum of Natural History, J. B. Shackelford, 334; National Audubon Society, Inc., Dennis Brokaw, 272 (left), Lola Beall Graham, 272 (right); Préhistoric De L'Art Occidental, D'André Leroi-Gourhan, Editions D'Art Lucien Mazenod Paris-Jean Vertut, 296, 297, 307; Royal Danish Ministry for Foreign Affairs, 148 (left side); Mike Stammoulis, 419; United Press International, 335 (lower right); University of Adelaide, Australia, M. F. Glaessner, 335 (upper right); University of California, 326, 329, 330.

CONTENTS

6

THE SUN THAT WARMS

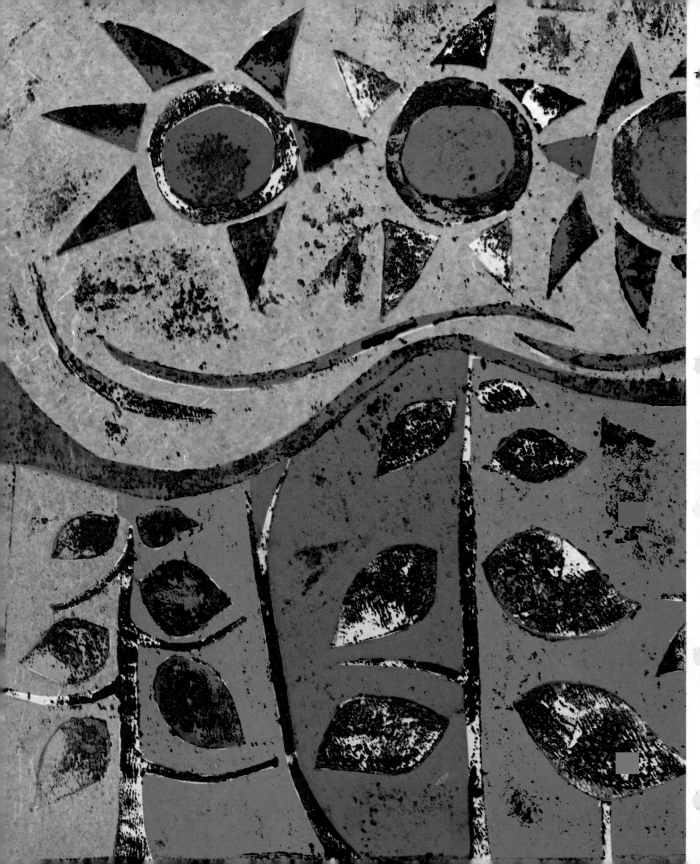

MEETING
THE
TEST

In most stories a problem must be solved in some way. The main characters in the stories of this unit face problems — some serious and some not so serious. These problems may be like the ones you or your friends have had to solve. Perhaps you would have handled the problems differently, but you will find that the main characters in these stories have "met the test."

11

THE WONDERFUL MACHINE

A pile of junk, a book, and some wild ideas—then the fun began! Pete and Orville made only one mistake, but it was a big one!

When a runaway truck dumped its load of junk on Pete McCormick's front yard, it made a mess. But Pete, who was a bright, daring boy, thought it was an interesting thing to happen.

So when the junkman threw his hands up in the air and walked away, Pete squatted on his heels to study the junk. Then his friend Orville came and squatted beside him.

12

"I have a book. . . ." Orville began.

"I know," Pete said. "But we'd better get this junk off our yard. My folks might not like it here."

Orville shook his head. "No, they mightn't."

So they carried it all around to the backyard.

"Now," said Orville, "I'll go and get my book."

They studied the book. Then they studied the junk. After a while they looked at each other and nodded.

"We can do it," Orville said.

"With no trouble at all," agreed Pete. "And we'll earn enough money for that one-man pup tent at Tinker's Store."

"We'll take turns sleeping in it," said Orville.

So they started to work.

First, they made a sign that said, "Big invention going on. Keep out! Come back later."

They tacked the sign on the gate in the backyard fence. Then they sorted springs, screens, sockets, and sprockets. They straightened pipes, pots, cotter pins, and pulleys. They untangled wires and untwisted twisted tricycle wheels. They hammered nails, screwed screws, bolted bolts, and fastened grommets, gaskets, and gauges. They put together rusty parts of a steam engine: the boiler, the firebox, the piston, the fly-wheel, and the stack.

At last they were finished. Proudly they stood back to look up at the strange machine they had made.

"The wobbliest thing I ever saw," Orville said.

"She's pretty, though," said Pete. "I like the flag on top."

Orville nodded. "Now let's get the gum stuff."

"And the jelly bean stuff," added Pete.

13

"Gum's enough," warned Orville, who was an intelligent and cautious boy. "The book says you never can tell about the Machine. It won't stand for too much."

"Oh, it'll be all right," Pete said quite fearlessly.

So they went to the store to buy the stuff.

A big crowd of curious children gathered at the gate as Orville made a fire in the steam engine. Pete climbed to the top of the Machine and poured the gum stuff and the jelly bean stuff into the hoppers.

"She's all ready!" he called, climbing down. "I'll let the customers in now!"

He opened the gate and hundreds of children burst into the yard. At that moment the steam engine's wheel began to turn. The Machine shook and shuddered. Balls bounced; springs sprang; lights lit; pipes jerked, jumped, and gurgled. Buzzes, clinks, and rumbles became *whizzes, clanks, and roars.*

The children watched with eyes as big as pie pans.

Suddenly, colored balls of bubble gum shot out of a spout with a *pink, pink, pink*. The children squealed with delight; and Pete and Orville sold the gum balls for a penny apiece.

Then out came jelly beans with a *floop, floop, floop*. They sold these too.

And sure enough, they earned enough money for the one-man pup tent at Tinker's Store.

"If we make some pop too," said Pete, "we'll earn even more money and buy the *two*-man tent. Then we could both sleep at once."

"Gum and jelly beans are enough," warned Orville. "There might be trouble. The book says you never can tell about the Machine. . . ."

"Oh, it'll be all right," Pete said, and he went off to get the pop stuff.

A little later, cherry pop was squirting from a faucet on the puffing Machine. It was a nickel a glass. Pete and Orville soon had enough money for the two-man pup tent.

"We need popsicles too," said Pete. "We'll earn more money and buy the big center-pole tent with the bug-proof door flap."

Orville looked worried. "The Machine is already making funny noises. The book says you never can tell . . ."

But Pete, who didn't mind taking chances, went for the popsicle stuff.

15

By late afternoon the Machine was shaking, gasping, and groaning. From its spouts and faucets came pop, popsicles, popcorn, bubble gum, jelly beans, and gingerbread cookies.

But that wasn't enough for Pete. "There aren't any pretzels," he said.

"You'd better watch out," Orville warned. "The Machine is shooting sparks, and it has an awful bend in the middle. The book says . . ."

"If we make pretzels," observed Pete, "we can buy the super-standard bungalow tent with the roll-up sides. All of our friends could sleep in it at once."

Orville frowned. "The Machine's making some terribly funny noises. . . ."

But Pete, who was a daredevil, got the pretzel stuff. He *never* should have poured it into the hopper. But he did. And then . . .

An eggbeater began to go the wrong way. The bubble gum

went *pwack!* instead of *pink*. The jelly beans went *brrt!* instead of *floop*. Popsicles squirted, and bolts rained down on the crowd.

Children screamed and ran for the gate. And then — Ka-POOM!

A fiery cloud of smoke roared into the sky! The Wonderful Machine rose in the air and came down in a million and one pieces.

From the back porch, Pete and Orville gazed at the mess. "Well," said Pete, "we earned enough money to buy the medium-standard wall tent with the canvas floor. One or two of our friends could sleep with us, and . . ."

He stopped. A big lump of bubble gum was bulging in the middle of the flattened Machine. The bulge grew bigger . . . then *pwack-zing!* Something shot across the yard. It thudded against his stomach and fell to the porch.

Orville picked it up and his eyes grew wide with wonder.

"Well, what do you know," he grinned. "A *pretzel!*"

—Eda and Richard Crist

THINKING IT OVER

1. Tell about the part of the story you enjoyed most. Why was it your favorite part?
2. Find the places in the story where Orville warned Pete about the Machine. How many places were there?
3. What lesson do you think the boys learned?

THOUGHTS AT WORK

1. Think of a <u>question</u> to go with this answer: They used springs, screens, sockets, sprockets, pipes, pots, cotter pins, pulleys, wires, tricycle wheels, nails, screws, bolts, grommets, gaskets, gauges, and the rusty parts of a steam engine.
2. In what places do you suppose the junkman found the junk?
3. Have you ever built something out of a pile of junk? Tell about it.
4. How do you think the Machine made gum and jelly beans?
5. Why did Pete keep insisting that they make more kinds of "stuff"?
6. Find the "made-up" words in the story. Make up other words the author might have used instead.
7. Write about a wonderful machine you'd like to make. Describe how it is made, how it works, and what it does.

CHEERS

The frogs and the serpents each had a football team,
and I heard their cheerleaders in my dream:

"Bilgewater, bilgewater," called the frog,
"Bilgewater, bilgewater,
Sis, boom, bog!
Roll 'em off the log,
Slog 'em in the sog,
Swamp'em, swamp'em,
Muck mire quash!"

"Sisyphus, Sisyphus," hissed the snake,
"Sibilant, syllabub,
Syllable-loo-ba-lay.
Scylla and Charybdis,
Sumac, asphodel,
How do you spell Success?
With an S-S-S!"

——*Eve Merriam*

19

BADGE 53

Ricky, the main character in this story, has his problems. And he has a "smart-aleck" friend who doesn't help any. In the end, Ricky's ability pays off, but in a way you may not expect.

Coming home from school, the boys—and some of the girls too—always went the long way around past the Arena. The sign on top of that bare, block-size building said: ENTER THE WORLD OF SPORT AT THE ARENA.

On each side of the wide front doors and the glass ticket office were pictures of sports stars as big as life. There were tennis players slamming balls over the net; hockey players cutting a spray of ice with their skates; riders on sleek horses jumping fences.

Here was the world of sport indeed! Every week the pictures were changed to show the stars of new events going on inside.

The boys and girls always stood a long time looking at the new sets of pictures. Everybody—the boys especially—wished to be a sports star someday.

20

"My picture is going to be right here in front of the Arena," Alec said, talking big. "I'm going to be a champion hockey player. Or maybe a tennis champion."

"My picture is going to be here too." Kathy did a happy little hop. "I'm going to be a famous ice skater."

"Me too," said Sandra. "I'll wear a stick-out skirt and whirl on my toes. Like this." She showed them but nobody looked.

Billy said, "I'm going to play basketball here when I'm grown up. Why don't you be a basketball player too, Ricky?"

"Ho-ho," Alec laughed. "Ricky can't even hit a baseball."

"That won't matter in basketball," Ricky said, hoping he was right.

"It will so! It means that you'll never be good at *any* sport." Alec wagged his head as if he knew everything. "Not if you can't bat a baseball."

"I don't hit the ball lots of times. Does that mean I can't ever be a fancy ice skater?" Sandra asked.

21

"Sure does," Alec said. "It means you don't have the right kind of muscles for sports."

"But Ricky can run fast," Kathy said. "He's good at that."

"Running isn't a sport!" Alec hooted at the very idea.

"Why isn't it?" Ricky asked.

"Running is the same thing as walking, only you move faster," Alec said. "There's no sport to *that*."

"It's fun anyway," said Kathy. "Let's race home."

"I'll beat all of you," Ricky shouted. "Last one to Moskin's is a pickled pig's foot!"

Around the corner they went, and around the next one, till they came panting down their own block. Ricky reached the delicatessen store first. He went inside. "I'm home from school, Mrs. Moskin," he said to the lady cutting cheese behind the counter.

She smiled at him. "Your mother just called to ask about you. She said to tell you to change your shoes if you are going to play ball."

"Mmm hmm." Ricky had heard this so many times that he didn't pay much attention.

"And she said if I made cheesecake today, would I save two pieces for your supper," Mrs. Moskin went on.

"Did you?" Ricky was all ears at once. "Can I take it with me now?"

She shook her head. "I didn't bake today."

Ricky poked around in the little box underneath the counter. He took out a key with a tiny plastic submarine tied to it. This was his mother's door key. She always left it here for him when she went to work.

"Be sure and bring it back," Mrs. Moskin called after him.

Ricky and his mother lived in a large apartment building next to the delicatessen. Billy lived on the floor above them with his parents and big brother and sister. While Ricky was putting on his old shoes, he heard Billy running down the stairs and stopping at the door to shout, "Hurry up, Rick! I'll meet you down in front."

Ricky didn't take time for his usual snack. He hurried out to the street. He wanted to start some other game before Alec got the teams to play baseball.

He found a ball game already going. Kathy had just landed on second base. "You're on our side, Ricky. You bat next," she called to him.

"What do you mean—*bat*?" Alec asked. "You know he can't."

First base was the water plug near Moskin's Delicatessen. Home plate was the manhole cover in the middle of the street. Ricky picked up the bat Kathy had dropped. There was nothing for him to do but try once again to hit the ball. He went to the plate.

Billy was pitching. He signaled to Ricky, "I'll send over some easy ones."

Even with this help Ricky missed every ball.

"Ho, you'll never play baseball in the Arena. I can see that!" Alec yelled from third base in front of the bakery.

"Neither will you!" Ricky snapped back. "The Arena isn't big enough for baseball."

Billy pitched the next one. Alec burst out laughing at the way Ricky swung the bat so hard he sent himself into a spin. "Ho-ho, and you never even touched the ball!"

Billy said, "Try to watch the ball coming at you, Ricky. And then *wham* it."

"I do try," Ricky said. He was sure he did.

"Well, try harder this time." Billy threw a soft one.

Ricky struck out.

While this was going on, Alec stole home. Sandra, who was catching, forgot to tag him.

"I just scored a run, and I bat next," he said, taking the bat from Ricky. Alec knocked the ball halfway to the corner on his first swing. He ran the bases and stepped on home plate wiping his hands on his pants. "That shows you how to do it, boy!"

Ricky grumbled to himself, "*He* doesn't have to try hard. It's easy for him. Why can't I find a sport that's easy for me? Then I could show *him* how to do it—for a change."

He thought about the different sports he knew, wondering which one he might be good at.

Ricky decided he would watch the pictures in front of the Arena more closely than ever. Maybe there was a sport he never heard of which would be the right one for him. *If I could only go inside and watch*! he thought. There was no chance of that. Tickets to sports events were high in price, he knew. Besides, he wasn't allowed to go there without his parents. His father was away in the Navy. His mother worked all day at the office. At night she was too tired or too busy at home to go anywhere.

Ricky's thoughts were interrupted.

"Hey, Ricky!" he heard Alec yell. "Don't just sit there! Get up and try to bat. It's your turn again."

"Please hit it this time and move me off first base," Kathy called to him. "I want to make another run before my mom calls."

"Watch Billy give Ricky another baby's pitch. He should clobber this one," Alec yelled so everybody could hear. Then— "What do you know! He couldn't even hit it."

There was nothing for Ricky to do but go sit on the curb again, wishing his same old wish. If he could only get to be good at some other sport, he wouldn't mind looking like such a fool at baseball! He thought of all those sports at the Arena. Surely there must be one which he could master easily. And in a hurry.

But what chance did he have of finding it? He'd never get in the Arena.

"Are you sitting on the sidelines again, Ricky?" Mrs. Moskin called from the door of her store. "Ai, ai, don't they ever let you play?"

"I have a hard time hitting the ball," Ricky answered.

"Don't let that worry you. As soon as you get on base, you'll show 'em," she said. "You can run faster than anybody."

"He can't get on base till he hits," Alec shouted from first.

Mrs. Moskin went back into the store. After a while she came

to the door again. "Are you still sitting there, Ricky?" she asked. "Maybe you can run an errand for me. To the Arena."

"To the Arena!" Ricky couldn't believe he'd heard it. He jumped up. "You mean—the *Arena*?"

"Sure, sure." She sounded as if it were any old building and not the place where you entered the world of sport. "Will you take this over there for me?"

She put a small white bag into his hands. He was so excited he almost dropped it.

"Gosh, it's heavy! What's in it?" he asked.

"Five hundred pennies," she said. "My brother is the boss at the Arena. He just phoned to say they ran out of pennies to make change at the ticket window. The banks are closed now. So he wants to borrow some from us. Take good care of them till you get there."

"Oh, I will!" Ricky held the bag tightly to his chest. He already had one foot in the air, ready to start.

"Leave them at the ticket office," Mrs. Moskin said. "Tell the man they are for Mr. Farber. Mike Farber."

Ricky put both feet on the ground long enough to ask, "Hadn't I better give this bag to—to Mr. Farber himself? Don't you want me to take it *inside* to him?"

"Just make sure the Arena gets the pennies," Mrs. Moskin said.

Ricky ran so fast he was gasping for breath when he reached the ticket window. But he went on past it, heading for the door.

"Hold on there, boy!" the man behind the glass shouted. "Where do you think you're going?"

"Inside," Ricky panted. "I-I-I have to g-g-give this to Mr. F-F-Farber."

"Are you bringing the pennies?" He looked at the bag in Ricky's hands. "I'll take them."

"They are for Mr. Farber," Ricky said over his shoulder. As he started through the door, another man stopped him.

29

"I have to give this to Mr. Farber," Ricky said. He ducked under the man's arm and kept going. Now he was actually *inside* the Arena. He didn't have time to look around. He ran down a wide, shadowy hall with the ticket taker after him.

"Mr. Farber!" Ricky shouted with all the breath he had left. "MR. FARBER!"

A door opened. A head like a snapping turtle's popped out. "*Now* who wants me?"

"If you're Mr. Farber . . ." Ricky began.

The short, square, bald-headed man bellowed, "Who else would I be? What do *you* want?"

Ricky shoved the bag of pennies at him. "Here. Mrs. Moskin sent me."

The man chasing Ricky now grabbed the boy by the shoulder. "This kid sneaked past me," he began, "and before I could catch . . ."

"Let him go. He's okay," Mr. Farber said. "He brought us this sack of pennies. Take it out to the ticket window, will you? And then trot around and tell Sax to put up two more bull's-eyes. In a hurry."

"Let this kid do it. He likes to run. I have to get back and stand guard at the doors." The ticket taker started off, jingling the pennies. He said over his shoulder, "I can't see why those bow-and-arrow nuts need two more bull's-eyes anyway."

"They just sent word that they'll need ten targets to shoot at," Mr. Farber called after him. "That means Sax has to put up two more. And I'm too busy to hunt him up and tell him."

"I'll tell him," Ricky said, ready to start at once. "Two more bull's-eyes—who is Sax? Where do I find him?"

30

Ricky heard a loud buzz. "That's my telephone," Mr. Farber said, turning back to his office. "Just follow this hall till you come to the big open doors. Ask anybody inside for Sax."

The office door slammed shut. Ricky started toward the glimmer of light far down the dim hall. Now that he was inside, the Arena seemed every bit as mysterious to him as it did from the outside. He could feel his toes tingling with excitement as he hurried along until he came to the open doorway. He entered, blinking in the bright light.

"Wow!" he exclaimed. "You could put our whole apartment in here. And Moskin's too, I'll bet. What a place!"

The shining yellow floor was nearly big enough for a football game. Around it went the rows of seats, higher and higher. At the other end of the floor he saw some men working. He ran toward them. They were building a wall with large blocks of straw.

One man looked up, saw Ricky, and asked, "What are you doing here?"

"Me?—Oh, I have a message for Sax. Is he around?"

"He's not here, but I can hear him." The man laughed as if he thought he had made a joke.

Ricky listened. He heard only a faint clink-clink of metal. It grew louder. "There he comes," the man said, pointing to the doors.

Ricky saw that the clatter came from a pair of overalls loaded with tools. Screwdrivers and hammers hanging from loops, front and back, clanked together. A file drummed upon an oil can slung from one hip. Nails and tacks tinkled in the pockets. The man inside the overalls yelled, "Snap into it, fellows! The archers are already coming in to practice. They must have targets to shoot at. Hurry and fasten those paper bull's-eyes to the straw."

Bull's-eyes. Ricky snapped to attention. "Say, are you Sax? Mr. Farber sent me to tell you . . ."

"Now what's the boss got on his mind?" Sax frowned at Ricky.

"He says for you to put up two more bull's-eyes," said Ricky.

"Since when is Mike Farber sending orders by a strange boy?" Sax pointed a screwdriver at Ricky. "How do I know you aren't playing some kind of trick on us?"

"I'm sure he isn't, Sax."

Ricky looked around at the sound of this new voice. He saw a man with a round, friendly face, a coat on his arm, and a pencil behind his ear.

"Oh, it's you, Fritz. Greetings," Sax grunted. "What do you know about this kid?"

"Never saw him before." The newcomer smiled at Ricky. "But I have just been downstairs in the dressing rooms talking to the archers. Their captain told me they would need ten targets for this match."

"That's what Mr. Farber sent me to tell you," Ricky said to Sax.

34

"Hmff," Sax answered with a grunt. Then he yelled, "Mike says to put up two more targets. Snap into it, fellows! Set up one at each end of your row. If you need more straw . . ."

Ricky didn't wait to hear the rest. He hurried to the office to report that he had carried out his orders. He got lost in the long dim hall. When he finally opened the right door, Mr. Farber was putting down the phone.

He looked more like a snapping turtle than ever. He sounded like one too. "Well, boy, who are you?"

"I'm . . . I'm . . ." Ricky froze in the glare from those beady black eyes. "I'm . . ."

"You should know who he is, Farber."

Ricky turned to see who had spoken. In the doorway stood the same friendly man who had helped him before.

"Come in, Fritz," Mr. Farber greeted him. "What did you say?"

"I said *you* should know this young fellow. You hired him as your errand boy, didn't you?"

"I did no such thing, Fritz."

"But he certainly carried an order from you to Sax. I heard him. He did an excellent job, actually. Delivered your message

35

and came back as if he were running the 50-yard dash,'' Fritz
said. "If you haven't already hired him, you should. Then
you wouldn't have to chase all over this place to give an order
to Sax or somebody. You could send the boy.''

"I've had kids running errands here before.'' Mr. Farber gave
Fritz a fierce look. "And they're all alike. They don't keep
their minds on what they are asked to do. This one wouldn't
be any different.''

"Try him,'' Fritz urged. "You wouldn't have to pay him for
the time he spends here. Most any kid would be happy just to
get inside the Arena and see the sports shows for free.'' Fritz
smiled at Ricky and asked, "You would, wouldn't you?''

"I sure would!'' said Ricky.

Mr. Farber paid no attention. He was looking at some papers
on his desk. "You stick to your newspaper writing, Fritz,'' he
said. "I'll run the Arena.''

Ricky felt it was time to go. "Good-by, Mr. Farber. If you need any more pennies, I'll be glad to bring them," he said.

Mr. Farber made no answer. Then, as Ricky left, he said, without looking up, "On your way out, boy, tell Sax to be sure all the straw is swept off the floor."

"What did I just tell you, Farber?" Fritz slapped his knee and laughed. "Actually, you *can* use this kid. Right now. Later on, you'll have tennis matches in here. He would be a big help collecting the balls."

Ricky crossed his fingers and wished very hard for Mr. Farber to do as Fritz said. He thought it might help if he showed how fast he could carry a message. So he said, "I'll go tell Sax about the straw, Mr. Farber."

Ricky really put on the steam. He was back almost at once, saying, "I told Sax. Do you have any more jobs for me to do, Mr. Farber?"

"Say, 'Yes,'" the newspaperman urged again. "Remember what I am always telling you, Farber. It would be a great thing for you to let the boys in this neighborhood grow up with sports here in the Arena. Besides, did you notice how fast this lad can run? I think he could be a winner in some sport or other."

To Ricky's surprise, Mr. Farber laughed. "You're always seeing a great sports star in some kid, Fritz."

"Even the greatest begin as kids, don't they?" Fritz asked. "We know this boy can run fast. We know he can deliver a message correctly. Give him a chance to show what he can do. You need a good errand boy here."

Fritz gave Ricky a friendly smile. He smiled at Mr. Farber too.

Ricky held his breath, hoping for the right answer.

"Okay, boy," Mr. Farber said. "Stop in after school on Friday."

"I will. I will. Thank you, Mr. Farber," Ricky said quickly, before the man could change his mind. "And thank you too, Mr. Fritz."

"Wait!" Mr. Farber called Ricky back as he started out the door. "You'll need this to get you past the ticket taker."

He took something from his desk drawer and handed it to Ricky after looking at the number on it. "Fifty-three," he said as he wrote in a notebook. "Badge 53 to—What's your name, boy?"

"Richard Richards," said Ricky. "Same as my father. I don't think you need to put Junior after it because Dad is away in the Navy. So I'm the only Richard Richards at home."

Fritz laughed. "Does anyone ever call you Double Dick?"

"They call me Ricky."

"Badge 53 to Ricky. What's your address? Do you have a telephone number?" Mr. Farber wrote Ricky's answers in the notebook, then put it in a drawer. "That's all for today, boy."

Ricky hurried along the dim hall. He held the badge so tightly it pricked his finger. He did not stop to look at it until he came out into the sunlight of State Street.

"Oooooh!" he said. There in his hand lay a silver map of the world no bigger than a half dollar. On it were the words: ENTER THE WORLD OF SPORT AT THE ARENA.

It was like magic, he thought. It would take him inside the Arena any time he wished. It would spread before him all the sports in the world. He could take his choice. He had Fritz's word that he could be a winner at *some* sport. Which would it be, he wondered.

How soon could he master it and show the whole block that baseball isn't the *only* sport?

——*Marion Renick*

THINKING IT OVER

1. What was Ricky's problem? Do you think he really solved it? Why or why not?
2. Which boy would you rather have as your friend—Ricky or Alec? Tell how you feel about these two boys.
3. Do you think Alec's remarks had any effect on Ricky's baseball playing? Why or why not?

THOUGHTS AT WORK

1. Could you say that Mrs. Moskin, the lady in the delicatessen store, was Ricky's "substitute" mother? Find some examples to back up your answer.
2. Find places in the story where Alec teased Ricky and write them under the heading, Teasing. Find places where Alec boasted of his hitting powers and write them under the heading, Boasting.
3. Ricky was good at some things, but not at others. What things can you do well? What things can't you do very well?
4. An artist paints pictures with paint. An author paints word-pictures with words. What was the author describing in each word-picture below?
   - a. bigger than our whole apartment
   - b. one foot in the air, ready to start
   - c. a round, friendly face, a coat on his arm, and a pencil behind his ear
   - d. a silver map of the world no bigger than a half dollar
   - e. a head like a snapping turtle's
5. Ricky's mother worked, and she probably didn't want him to go far from home to play. If you had been Ricky, how would you have avoided being teased by kids like Alec?
6. Why do you think Ricky was given the badge? Do you think he deserved it? Why or why not? How many different kinds of badges can you think of?

The Milestone Group

Milestone is a word with an interesting history. In olden times when there were no road signs, the miles were marked off by large stones set by the side of the road. These stones were called milestones. What does the old word *milestone* have to do with a modern story about people who live in a large city?

THE PLAN

Mom seemed unusually grumpy this evening, Lucy decided, as she set four plates on the kitchen table and slid four forks toward them. Mom turned from the stove with a steaming pot in her hand and Lucy stepped back to let her serve up their supper.

The kitchen was small and there wasn't room for all six of them to sit down to supper together. But it didn't matter, really. Dad wouldn't be home from his night job until morning, and the boys ate almost on the run. Now they came noisily into the kitchen to gobble up their food and return to the teeming street.

"You, Dennis," cried Mom, grabbing her eleven-year-old by the back of his T-shirt, the steaming pot still in her right hand. "You go wash yourself. You too," she added, darting a look at Dennis' younger brother Christopher. "Come, Bonnie," she said more gently to the small girl beside Lucy. "Come, baby. Time to eat."

Bonnie slid into a chair and pulled her plate toward her. Mom put the pot back on the stove but didn't join her children at the table. There was only room for four.

"Take my place, Mom," said Lucy suddenly. Mom worked in a small factory and she seemed very tired tonight.

"No," said Mom wearily. "You go ahead. I'm going to stretch out for a little while before I eat. Right now I'm just too downhearted to think about food."

Bonnie, with a forkful of food halfway to her mouth, suddenly put it down and called to her mother, about to leave the kitchen.

"Look, Mom. Look a-here." She put two small fingers into her mouth and took hold of a front tooth. "Look, Mom. It's loose. It's gonna come out any day now."

"Don't I know it," said Mom. "It's been haunting me day and night. Here I been planning on a bright and

43

smiling picture of my littlest and by the time I get the money saved up, she's gonna be gap-toothed."

The boys giggled and Mom threw them an angry glance. "Go right ahead and laugh," she told them. "I got pictures of you at her age. Lucy too. But not one picture of my Bonnie and she the prettiest of the whole shootin' match."

Mom went heavily from the room and the four at the table looked at each other with sudden soberness. It was not like Mom, dear, good-natured Mom, to lash out at them in this way. Sure she got tired and grumpy, but she never said mean things like now. Mom must be more upset than they had ever seen her.

When she was sure Mom had gone into her bedroom and could not hear her, Lucy said, very low, "I been thinking about something." The other three fastened interested eyes on their big sister, and the boys stopped chewing to listen.

"Next month is Mom's birthday."

"So what!" exclaimed Dennis. "I ain't fixin' to get her anything. Birthdays don't mean nothin' in this family. Where would we get the money for 'em?"

Lucy ignored the question. "This birthday's real important to Mom. She says it's a milestone. She says she aims to live to eighty and this birthday puts her halfway there. Forty! Right in the middle. A milestone!"

Mom forty! It seemed a great age and they considered it in silence as they cleaned up their plates.

Finally Christopher said, "You fixin' to do something for Mom?"

Lucy nodded. "In a way," she said. "I got an idea, that's all." She looked around the table. "You want to come in on it?"

Dennis' eyes grew cautious. "What you got in mind?"

"I want to have a picture taken of all of us together, and I want it right now before Bonnie's tooth comes out."

"You got money for that?" demanded Christopher in an astonished whisper.

Lucy shook her head. "That's the trouble. We got to get the picture first and the money later. Bonnie's gonna lose her tooth before we can get the money together."

"Why not just a picture of Bonnie by her own self? It might not cost so much," suggested Dennis.

"No," said Lucy. "This is the milestone picture. I want Mom should have us all together just the way we looked when she got to be forty. A 'Group', that's what they call a picture with lots of people in it."

"The Milestone Group," said Dennis slowly. "I can see it on the wall now. Mom would like that. You got a good idea there, Lucy."

"Then you'll come in on it?"

"What you mean 'come in on it'?"

"You'll help get the money to pay for it?"

"How?"

"Any way but stealing. Or begging," Lucy said. "Stop hanging around the schoolyard after school and running up and down the alleys on Saturday. Go look for something to do. You'll find something if you look hard enough. Christopher can look along with you."

"What you gonna do?" demanded Christopher.

"Oh, I got several good leads," said Lucy confidently.

"I want to do something too!" said Bonnie in a loud wail that surely reached the bedroom.

"Shoosh," hissed Lucy fiercely. "You're only six. You can help me here at home so I can get to my jobs quicker. Helping me is just the same as helping at a regular job. See?"

Bonnie nodded a bit uncertainly, but seemed satisfied.

Before leaving the table, they agreed they would have the picture taken. Then the conspirators picked up their plates and stacked them in the sink. They'd get around to washing them after Mom had eaten.

Next day Lucy hurried home from school, taking the three flights of stairs without a stop. Bonnie, she knew, would be there waiting for her, she hoped, bathed and in her best dress. The boys would be along soon, and she must lay out clean shirts for them—if there were clean shirts. It wouldn't matter about their jeans because the Milestone Group would picture only their heads and shoulders.

"Bonnie," she called guardedly, entering from the dark hall into the small living room. Above everything, they better not wake Dad.

Bonnie came out of the other bedroom, grinning purposefully.

Lucy's face lit. "You still got it, Bonnie!"

Bonnie nodded delightedly, enjoying the sudden drama of her loose front tooth. She was dressed neatly and cleanly in a pink cotton print that hugged her smooth brown throat. It was small for her but this wouldn't matter, any more than the boys' worn jeans.

"Let me braid your side hair and put a ribbon on," said Lucy, "and then I'll change into a clean blouse. The boys should be here by that time."

She had hardly finished with Bonnie's braids when the boys came in. "Your clean shirts are in the bedroom," Lucy informed them. "Put 'em on quick. We got a lot to do before Mom gets home."

PUTTING THE PLAN TO WORK

A few minutes later, four very clean and quietly-behaved children descended the dark stairs and emerged onto the street. Letting the boys go in front of her where she could keep an eye on them, Lucy seized Bonnie's hand. "It's Greenberg's across the street in the next block," she said.

"Yeah. We know," Dennis called over his shoulder, and he and Christopher were off, dodging in and out among the people on the crowded sidewalk. Lucy hurried after them, pulling Bonnie along at a trot.

A buzzer sounded as they opened the door of Greenberg's Studio, and Mr. Greenberg, himself, emerged from the area beyond the small showroom in which they stood. Behind him they could see lamps on tall

48

stands surrounding a lone chair which had all the importance of a throne.

Mr. Greenberg was round—round bald head, round cheerful face, round belly, round-toed shoes on his feet, and round steel-rimmed glasses over his eyes, which were round and dark and wise.

"Something I can do for you?" he asked, looking from one anxious face to the other.

Lucy drew in a long breath. "Do you ever take pictures on credit?"

Mr. Greenberg smiled at her. "Not knowingly," he said gently.

Lucy pushed Bonnie in front of her. "Show him," she said, and Bonnie dutifully wiggled her front tooth for Mr. Greenberg.

"You want I should take out the tooth?" he demanded in some surprise.

"No!" cried Lucy. "But it's on account of the loose tooth we're here." And in a rush of words she explained about Mom's milestone and their great desire to have a group picture to present to her on that important day.

"Your mama sent you?" inquired Mr. Greenberg.

"Oh, no," said Lucy. "It would spoil everything if she knew."

"I see," said Mr. Greenberg, slowly, thoughtfully.

"And if I go ahead and take this picture, how will you plan to pay?"

"We'll all go out and find something to do. Already I have two baby-sitting jobs for next week. The boys

can wash cars, or run errands to the grocery store——oh, anything," explained Lucy rather desperately.

"But how do I know you will bring me the money?" Mr. Greenberg went on. "Sometimes people get a picture and forget about the money."

Lucy shook her head. "You don't understand. We won't take the picture away. We'll leave it right here and every time we get a quarter, even a dime, we'll bring it in to you."

"Then why not save up the money and *then* have the picture taken?" Mr. Greenberg flung out his hands as if he had hit upon the only answer.

"We already told you," said Lucy, her voice rising with exasperation. "We got to get this picture before Bonnie's tooth comes out. Don't you see?" She shook Bonnie's shoulder. "Show him again, Bonnie." And Bonnie did.

A light dawned on Mr. Greenberg's face and he lifted his eyes to the ceiling. "Ah, yes. Now all is clear. I didn't get it at first." Again he looked from one to the other as if trying to make up his mind, and all four returned his gaze, their brows wrinkled with anxiety.

At last he whirled about.

"Come," he said. "Come in," and he led them toward the tall lights and the waiting chair.

The next few days were worrisome for Lucy. If the others shared her concern, they didn't let on. Her worry was their father. What would he say? Had they dared too much? What would he do when he found out that

they had actually paid eight dollars and ninety-five cents for a picture?

"We won't tell him. It will be safer that way," declared Lucy.

"You can say that again," returned Dennis. "He'd skin us if he knew we weren't bringing that money home."

Would he, Lucy wondered? They hardly knew their father; they rarely saw him.

"Yeah, and when he does find out, he's gonna want us to go on a-diggin' up all the dimes and quarters we can," offered Christopher.

"Well, I intend to go on working anyway," said Lucy stoutly. "Nothing wrong with work. Within reason," she added. "Besides, when I baby-sit, I can watch TV."

It wasn't easy that first week. Only three dollars and a quarter went into the little box under Mr. Greenberg's counter in the front room of the studio. Three weeks to go, about. It seemed a very short time in which to earn five dollars and seventy cents.

But the three were eager to work and the news got around. Slowly the value of the coins in the studio box grew, until on the day before Mom's birthday, they added up to eight dollars and seventy cents. Just a quarter to go. It might as well have been ten dollars! What could they do?

That night at supper, Bonnie's tooth came out.

"Look, Mom," she cried, holding it out on her small palm. "My tooth!"

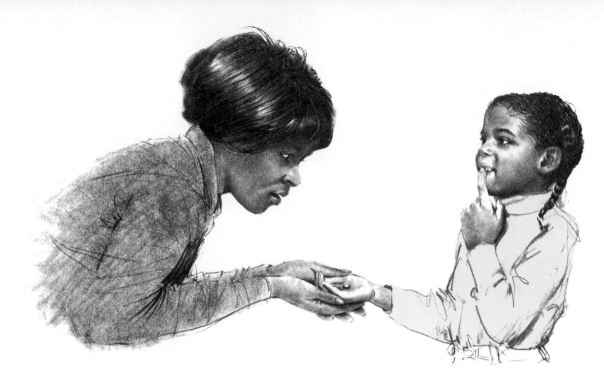

Mom gave one horrified look at Bonnie's hand, then at her gap-toothed mouth and burst into sobs. "It happened!" she wailed. "It happened just like I knew it would. My baby's gone and I never got a bright and smiling picture and she the prettiest of the lot."

The "lot" looked into each other's joyous faces, pleased that Mom was too upset to notice their secret smiles.

Then their faces sobered. Tomorrow was Mom's birthday, and though a Saturday when they were free to find jobs, they couldn't be sure that they would get the needed quarter.

It was Bonnie who saved the day. Soon after Dad had had his breakfast-dinner and gone to bed, and Mom had picked up her string bag and gone out to do the weekly shopping, Bonnie sprung her surprise.

"I got something to show you," she whispered as the four were gathered together in the living room.

"What you got?" demanded Christopher.

Again, as on the night before, Bonnie held her hand out straight. On her palm lay a shiny quarter!

"I put my tooth under the pillow last night and this morning the good fairy took it and left me a quarter."

"You kiddin'?" asked Dennis.

Bonnie shook her head. "It happened to a girl at school, and now it's happened to me."

"How come the good fairy would know about this place?" demanded Lucy, who had never found a quarter under her pillow.

Bonnie shrugged. "Maybe Dad told her."

The others exchanged quick glances.

"Did you tell Dad about the good fairy?" asked Lucy.

Bonnie nodded. "When he started to bed, I followed him and I showed him my tooth and told him I needed a quarter to pay for Mom's birthday and maybe the good fairy would leave it. And he said the good fairy wouldn't leave nothin' if I stood around. So I went away and when I came back, the tooth was gone and the quarter was under my pillow."

"Then you gave away our secret," said Lucy. "Did you tell about the Group?"

"No," said Bonnie. "When Dad asked me how much we spent on Mom's birthday, I told him and said we all worked together. And he said what could a little runt like me do? And I said nothin' until my tooth came out,

but now I could get a quarter with it, maybe. And so I did."

"And he didn't act mad?" asked Dennis.

"No, he didn't," said Bonnie. "He said we were good kids to remember Mom's birthday. And he gave me a hug."

"Mom was right," said Lucy softly. "This is a milestone." Suddenly her face lit with a wild joy. "Come on," she said, still remembering not to wake up Dad. "Let's go and get the Group. The Milestone Group."

Moving quietly, they made for the door.

——*Doris Gates*

THINKING IT OVER

1. Bonnie's loose tooth caused the problem, but it also "saved the day." Explain how it did both.
2. Even though Mom was grumpy, how did the family feel about her and what made them feel that way?
3. Why do you think the author ended the story where she did? Write an ending of your own.

THOUGHTS AT WORK

1. What Lucy planned for her mother seemed very difficult. Do you think she was right to try? Explain your answer.
2. You can read people's feelings by the way they act. How did Mom show her grumpiness? Why did she act this way?
3. We never meet Dad, but we learn something about him from the children. How did they feel about him during most of the story? Did their feelings change at the end? If so, how?
4. Why do you think the children didn't ask Dad to be in their picture?
5. Show how Dennis changed his mind about Mom's birthday by telling how he felt when he said:
     a. "So what. I ain't fixin' to get her anything."
     b. "What you got in mind?"
     c. "Why not just a picture of Bonnie by her own self? It might not cost so much."
     d. "The Milestone Group. I can see it on the wall now."
6. Why do you think Mr. Greenberg agreed to take the Milestone picture on credit?
7. Tell about a time when you worked hard to do something special for someone you liked very much.

In the City

In the street I have just left
the small leaves of the trees along the gutter
were steadfast
in the blue heavens.
Now the subway
express
picks up speed
and a wind
blows through the car,
blows dust
on the passengers,
and along the floor
bits of paper—
wrappers of candy,
of gum, tinfoil,
pieces of newspaper . . .

——*Charles Reznikoff*

IS BLACK YOUR COLOR ?

Listen!
You should be
Proud of your color.
Don't let people
Make fun of your color.
Be proud.
Say to yourself,
I am black
And I am proud.

—V.H., Age 10

58

soul

Soul is power
Soul is happiness
Soul is beautiful
Soul is love.

Soul is singing
Soul starts the bell to ring
Soul makes you dance
Soul makes you jump with joy.

—L.D., Age 10

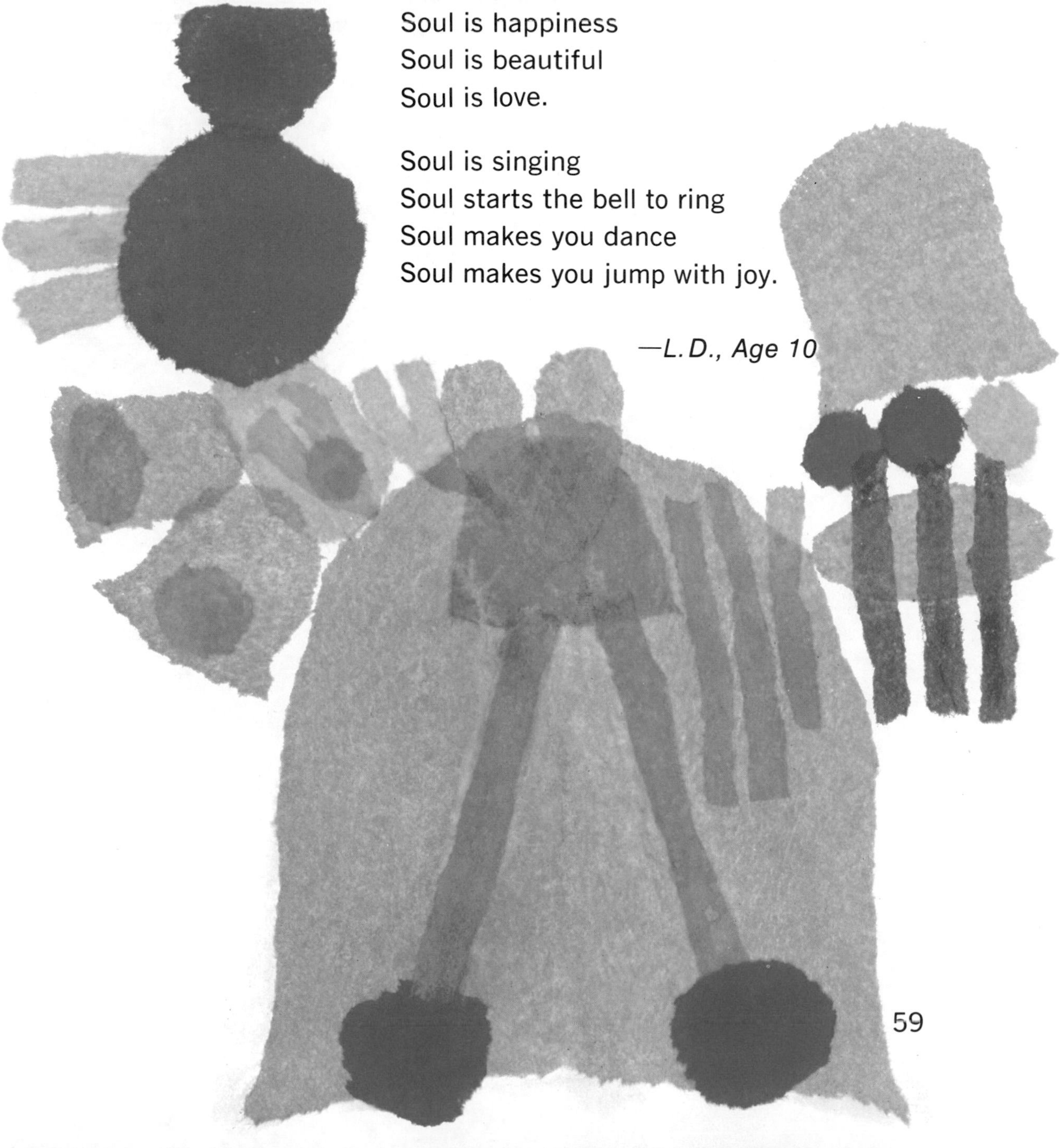

59

Here is one of many stories Glen Rounds has written about a young cowhand who was nicknamed Whitey because his hair was almost white, like the color of pale straw. The ranch country out West where Whitey lived was big. So big that the mailbox was two miles away from his house. And the blizzards! The storms were so fierce that a person walking through the snow could see nothing but white before his eyes. As you read, you'll see what part such a snowstorm plays in this story.

THE NEW SPURS

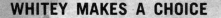

WHITEY MAKES A CHOICE

When Whitey woke up and looked out of his bedroom window, he saw it was snowing. Well, Uncle Torwal had been correct yesterday when he predicted snow. Now here it was, coming down steadily. There was no wind; so the flakes lay where they fell, piling high on the tops of the fence posts and along the poles of the corrals.

After Whitey and Uncle Torwal had finished breakfast, they put on their sheepskin coats and went out to do the chores.

It was while they were splitting some firewood that a horse-man rode up to the gate and climbed stiffly out of his saddle.

"Looks like Highpockets, Bearpaw Smith's hired man," said Uncle Torwal, and they hurried to the gate.

It was Highpockets, all right, and he had ridden over for help. His boss had met with an accident and had a broken leg.

"He's got to get to a doctor," said Highpockets, "and with all this snow on the ground, it would be a rough ride in a wagon. Thought maybe you could haul him in your bobsled."

"Let's get started then," said Uncle Torwal. "You go back and get Bearpaw ready and I'll be along later."

The old bobsled was in the shed where it had been stored all summer. After they'd put half a dozen bricks in the oven to heat, Whitey and Uncle Torwal piled robes and quilts on top of a deep layer of hay in the bottom of the box. By the time they'd finished that and harnessed the team, the bricks were ready to be wrapped in gunnysacks and put down in the pile of hay.

"Now mind what I say, Bub," Uncle Torwal said as he arranged his big buffalo coat around him on the seat of the bobsled and gathered up the lines. "Don't go far from the buildings here unless it clears up some. The way the barometer is falling, this snow could turn into a blizzard without half trying! You look after the ranch, and I'll be back tonight or sometime tomorrow. So long, now."

Whitey closed the gate after him and went back to the chores.

By the time he'd finished, it was almost noon, so he got a hammer and the big butcher knife and chopped a steak off the quarter of beef hanging frozen outside the door. After he'd eaten and washed his plate and skillet, he sat down to work a little on the fancy hackamore noseband he was braiding from rawhide and old boot leather.

But he soon gave that up and got out the mail-order catalogue, turning to the picture of the spurs he'd ordered two weeks ago. He'd saved his money for a long time waiting to send for those spurs. They had long gooseneck shanks and dollar rowels, with a bright chain that went under the instep. But the finest thing about them was the two little bells that hung just by the outside buckle on each spur.

They would be fine to wear when he and Uncle Torwal went into Lone Tree on a Saturday. They would jingle wonderfully when he walked on the wooden sidewalks, or when he went into the stores.

The more Whitey thought about it, the more certain he was that those spurs were over in the mailbox right now. The mail carrier made his trip twice a week, and yesterday had been mail day. But he and Uncle Torwal had forgotten to go after the mail last night.

Whitey scratched a hole into the thick frost on the window and looked out. It was a little over two miles out to the main road where the mailbox was, and Uncle Torwal had told him not to go far away unless the weather cleared.

However, it looked to him like the snow was already thinning just the least little bit. Rattlesnake Butte[1], less than half a mile away, was just a faint blur through the snow, but he was sure he could see it a little plainer than he had when Uncle Torwal was leaving. Of course, that wasn't exactly clear weather, but on the other hand, Uncle Torwal hadn't said just how clear the weather should be before he went out, and there still was no sign of wind.

The more he thought about it, the more sure he was that it'd be all right for him to go out to the mailbox to get his spurs. He'd have to walk, because Old Spot, the horse, had slipped on some ice the day before and was a little lame. But if he took his .22 rifle, he might get a couple of rabbits or maybe even a coyote on the way.

Each time he looked out of the clear place he'd scratched in the frost on the window, he thought the snow was thinning a little more. So at last he made up his mind to go.

In almost no time he had his heavy sheepskin coat on and a scarf tied over his ears. At the last minute he decided to

[1] Butte (būt)

64

put his big four-buckle overshoes on over his boots. Then he picked up his rifle and started out.

As soon as he walked away from the house, Whitey saw that the snow was still falling steadily after all, and it lay on the ground almost boot-top deep. It fell softly as feathers, muffling all sounds. A few yards off, fences and buildings seemed to melt into the soft gray and there was no difference between ground and sky.

But this didn't bother Whitey, for he felt perfectly able to find his way. And the way the snow and the light changed the shapes of things gave him the feeling of exploring strange country no one had ever seen before.

Whitey almost ran the last quarter of a mile, stumbling and sliding through the soft snow, in his hurry to see if his spurs were really there. He got to the mailbox without difficulty and threw down two rabbits he'd shot on the way.

When he opened the big wooden box standing on its posts, he saw the mail sack with Uncle Torwal's name stenciled on the side. It didn't seem to be bulging as it should if his spurs were in it, but he untied the string and started taking the mail out to be sure.

In the very bottom he felt a little package. It seemed too small to be spurs, but when he got it out of the mail sack, he found it was addressed to him, after all.

He stuffed the rest of the mail back in the sack, along with the two rabbits, and slung the sack over his shoulders so he'd have his hands free as he started back toward the ranch. Carrying his rifle under his arm, he broke the strings and tore the paper wrappings off the box.

Inside, nested in crumpled paper, were the spurs, looking even more beautiful than they had in the catalogue. The straps were rich brown leather with a handsome design stamped on them, and the bells, when he shook them, had a fine silvery tone.

BLIZZARD

Whitey had been stumbling along through the snow for some time, with eyes for nothing but his fine new spurs, when he suddenly noticed the wind was blowing against his face. He stopped to look around. The snow had thickened until he could see only a little way in any direction, and the wind was already picking more off the ground and whirling it into the air in blinding clouds. The mailbox behind him was already hidden and, as he stood watching, his tracks filled with blowing snow and disappeared.

This was the thing Uncle Torwal had warned him about. However, Whitey wasn't worried, for all he had to do was walk straight ahead and he'd soon come to the pasture fence, and he could follow it right on around to the corrals. But he felt it wasn't a good idea to waste any more time; so he stuffed the spurs back into the mail sack and hurried ahead, bowing his head to protect his face from the beating of the snow.

Before he'd gone any great distance, the wind was blowing full force and seemed to push and shove at him from all sides. It roared and cracked until his ears rang with it. His breath froze on the edges of his coat collar and gathered in white frost on his eyelashes and brows. The powdery fine snow whipped into his eyes and nose until it was almost impossible to see or breathe.

But there was no shelter near. There was nothing for him to do but keep walking, and hope he could keep his direction by the feel of the wind on his face. He'd heard of people lost in storms who'd wandered around in circles without knowing it.

He had been walking a long time and was just beginning to wonder if maybe he had somehow missed his way, when he ran right into the barbed wire. He walked against it without seeing it, and the shock threw him off balance so that he fell floundering in the snow, dropping his rifle. Picking himself up, he felt around until he found the gun, then held onto the wire while he caught his breath.

Turning his back to the wind, he took off his mittens to warm his nose and cheeks, feeling pretty well pleased with himself for getting safely to the fence. It would never have done to have gotten lost in the blizzard right after Uncle Torwal had warned him against that very thing!

Just before he turned to start hand over hand along the wire, the driving snow thinned enough for him to see that this wasn't the pasture fence after all. It was only a small stackyard fence, one of several built out on the open flats to keep range stock away from the stacks of wild hay the ranchers cut for winter feed. He knew then that he was lost.

68

69

If there had still been hay in the stackyard, he might have burrowed into it and waited out the storm. But the ground inside the fence was bare; so there was nothing for him to do but go on.

By keeping the wind in his face as he walked, he would still be able to find the pasture fence. The trouble was to tell which direction the wind was coming from, for it whipped and eddied until it seemed to come from first one way and then another.

However, he would freeze for sure if he stayed where he was; so he started out again. This time he took care to walk straight ahead, but after a long time he knew that in spite of himself he had drifted off his straight line.

He had a hard time then, keeping himself from getting panicky and running to find some landmark that looked familiar. This was one of the things that the cowboys had always spoken of that a lost person must avoid at all costs. So every

70

little way he made himself stop and stand still, swinging his arms to keep warm while he caught his breath.

Starting ahead after one of these stops, he suddenly felt the ground give way under his feet, and the next thing he knew he had fallen several feet, landing up to his neck in soft snow. Overhead he could see a circle of light and when he felt around, he found solid walls of earth on two sides of him.

He'd fallen into one of the deep narrow washouts common in that country. The walls were higher than his head and too steep to climb, while the head-high drifts blocked his way in the other directions.

He got out his pocketknife and, after some difficulty getting the blade open with his numb fingers, he started trying to cut steps in the steep bank. It was hard, slow work, digging at the frozen dirt with the small blade, and when he had gotten a couple of steps cut, he found that the bank sloped inward. He slipped and fell back when he tried to climb up.

Getting to his feet, he bumped against the rifle which he had dropped when he fell. Now it occurred to him that if he could brace it across the gully, he'd have a step to climb up on.

He found that the rifle was considerably longer than the distance between the walls; so he dug another hole on the opposite side from the steps, and about level with the highest one. He jammed the muzzle in one hole and wedged the butt in another on the other side. Carefully trying his weight on it, he found it was solid enough to hold him; so all he had to do was get his feet up on it, if he could.

That took some doing, however, in the narrow space, bundled up as he was and with the mail sack still slung over his shoulders. But he managed to get his chest across the rifle; then by squirming and twisting he got a knee across, and finally braced his foot on the gun stock against the wall. After that he carefully straightened up, supporting himself against the sides with his hands until he had both feet firmly braced on either end of the rifle.

With his shoulders above the level of the ground, it was no great job to pull himself up and roll out onto the snow.

72

He took a few steps and felt a deep, worn cattle path under his feet. The chances were good that it led either to shelter or a fence he could follow.

After what seemed ages, the trail suddenly dropped, spilling Whitey into a draw and smothering him in snow. He picked himself up and dusted off some snow. Now he was off the flats and out of the wind. He started walking down the draw.

When he bumped into a big cottonwood tree standing squarely in his path, he stopped and leaned against it to rest and catch his breath. It wasn't until he straightened up, ready to move on, that he noticed the pieces of board nailed to the trunk; and then for the first time he knew where he was. This was the old Owls' Nest Tree. Somebody years before had nailed boards to the trunk to make a ladder to the nest where the pair of great horned owls raised two young ones every year. And less than a hundred yards down the draw there was an old shack the hay crews sometimes used.

Now that he was close to shelter, Whitey forgot his tiredness. He went confidently ahead, keeping close to the bank of the draw and counting his steps so he'd know if he passed the shack without seeing it in the swirling snow.

Feeling his way along the wall, he floundered through the deep drifts until he found the door of the shack, hanging crookedly from one hinge, and squeezed his way inside.

Some snow had sifted into the shack and in places was several inches deep. But after his long struggle against the beating of the wind and the smothering swirling snow, this place seemed safe and comfortable. Even so, he realized he would quickly chill, now that he wasn't moving, unless he managed to get a fire started.

Against one wall there was a litter of old broken pieces of lumber and wooden boxes. Using one of the boards for a shovel, he soon scraped a patch of the dirt floor clear in the most sheltered corner. Then he got his jackknife opened and started whittling kindling sticks, setting them in a teepee-shaped stack. His matches were in an empty shotgun shell he always carried in his sheepskin pocket.

As soon as the fine feathery shavings caught and began to blaze, he carefully added larger sticks, one at a time, until his little fire was burning well. Some of the smoke found its way out through cracks and holes up near the roof, but most of it eddied about inside, making his eyes smart, and gusts outside occasionally sent fine snow sifting down inside his collar. But they were small things and he didn't mind them too much. With shelter and wood enough to last the night, he was in no real danger. But he was hungry.

That reminded him of the rabbits in the mail sack. Getting his knife out again, it took only a few minutes to skin and dress them. Now all he needed was a piece of wire to broil the meat on. Searching carefully, he found a length of old baling wire and proceeded to cook the rabbits. After he'd eaten the meat and sucked the bones, the warmth and the sound of the storm made him drowsy.

Pulling an old canvas close about him, he huddled over the tiny fire. He roused now and again to add small scraps of wood or to pull forward the old fence post the shack had yielded, one end of which he had placed on his fire, Indian fashion. Occasionally he dozed, but cold always woke him before the fire went completely out.

It was sometime near morning when he realized he was no longer hearing the wind. Getting stiffly to his feet, he shoved the door open a crack and looked out. The storm had stopped and the stars were shining. Quickly gathering up the mail sack, he squeezed outside and floundered through the drifts between the shack and the top of the draw.

Once he was out of the draw and up on the flats, the walking wasn't difficult, and the starlight on the snow was bright enough to make traveling easy.

After Whitey had gotten back home and rebuilt the fire in the stove, he took the new spurs out of the mail sack and tried them on. Tired as he was, he spent a while walking about the warm kitchen to hear the tinkling of the little silver bells.

By the time full daylight had arrived and Whitey had fixed himself some breakfast and started on the morning chores, Uncle Torwal drove in.

"Everything go all right here?" he asked, as they unhitched the horses.

"Yes, sir," Whitey told him. "And I got my new spurs in the mail yesterday."

"Good," said Uncle Torwal.

There was certainly more than that to tell, but Uncle Torwal asked no more questions, and that suited Whitey just fine. Later on he would tell Uncle Torwal the whole story. But just now didn't seem to be the right time. Besides, he'd learned his lesson.

——*Glen Rounds*

76

THINKING IT OVER

1. Uncle Torwal told Whitey, "Don't go far from the buildings here unless it clears up some." Do you think Whitey disobeyed his uncle? Explain your answer.
2. Why do you think Whitey decided to wait until later to tell Uncle Torwal the whole story? Explain what you would have done.
3. What kind of person do you think Whitey was?

THOUGHTS AT WORK

1. Tell the main things that happened to Whitey during the blizzard. When do you think he was most worried?
2. When did you begin to think Whitey might get home safely? How did you feel then?
3. Whitey's feelings changed many times. How did he feel when
    a. he saw snow falling on the way to the mailbox?
    b. he saw his new spurs?
    c. he realized the fence wasn't the pasture fence?
    d. he fell into the washout?
    e. he reached the deserted shack and built a fire?
    f. he saw Uncle Torwal drive in?
4. What lesson do you think Whitey learned?
5. What things did Whitey do that you can't do or aren't allowed to do? What things can you do that Whitey couldn't?
6. Reread pages 65 and 67 to 70. Find the sentences that describe the wind and snow. Copy the sentences you like best under the headings Wind and Snow.
7. In what way was Bearpaw Smith important? Could the author have written the same story without including him?

A story about baseball? Don't let the title fool you. "Pitcher" takes place in a boarding school. There the students live in dormitories rather than at home. Boarding school can be fun but students are on their own, especially the new ones, who often face some rough times before being accepted.

Robby Armstrong tells this story in his own words and you will feel that he is talking just to you. If you had been in Robby's place, would the story have been any different?

PITCHER

THE NEW BOY

When boarding school opens in the fall for a new term, the smart thing to do is to get there early in the morning. Then you can grab the best bureau and the lower bed in your double room. You just pile your stuff on them and they're yours for the year, and then spend the rest of the day fooling around with the other old boys, watching the scared new ones come in. I hope I didn't look lost and lonely the way they did when I was a new boy, but maybe I did.

Anyway, last fall we—that's me and Monk and Horseface and Geezil[1] and a few other guys I don't remember—were sitting on the stone wall in front of the dormitory watching the new boys come in. They'd walk past us, stiff and shy in clothes you could tell were new and uncomfortable, carrying shiny suitcases. They wouldn't really look at us except out of the corners of

[1] Geezil (jē′zl)

78

their eyes while they hurried past us into the building. We'd sit there and keep quiet while they walked by, but after they'd gone inside, we'd talk about them, trying to decide about what kind of people they'd turn out to be.

In the middle of the afternoon, a funny little character walked up the path with great big horn-rimmed glasses perched on a nose that looked kind of punched in and ears that stuck out like flags. Only he didn't hurry past us like the others. In front of us he put his suitcase down and smiled. It was a stiff smile, like the ones people had in pictures taken about forty years ago, but it was a smile. I guess he was trying to be friendly.

"Hello," he said.

"Hello, boy," said Monk, without much interest.

The new boy smiled wider, wriggling like a puppy when you pat him. "Hello," he said again. Then he waved his arm around. It was the longest and skinniest arm I've ever seen on a kid his age. "I guess this is the school." He bobbed his head and batted his eyes when he said it. You could tell that he really knew it was the school, that he was only trying to be nice. But Monk's too sharp to let a simple remark like that get past him.

"The school?" Monk rubbed his chin. "What school, boy?"

"Why, *the* school." When this new boy wrinkled his forehead, he looked more like a bewildered owl than before. "The school where you all go."

Monk scratched his head and turned to us. "Do you fellows go to school?"

"I haven't been to school today," said Horseface, which wasn't exactly a lie.

"And neither have I," said Geezil. "Do you go to school, son?"

The new boy laughed. It was a squeaky sound and showed he knew he was being kidded. "You fellows sure are funny," he said. "I think I'm going to like it here." With that he picked up his suitcase. "So long. See you later." At the foot of the steps he turned to wave his hand, but that was a mistake. I can see him now, smiling under his horn-rimmed glasses as he looked at us while his foot reached for the steps behind him. Then, he fell sprawling up the stairs.

"Somebody's in for a bad time," Monk said.

"Huh?" I asked.

"Somebody has to room with him, you dope," he explained wearily.

"That's right," I admitted. "Say, I wonder when my roommate is going to show up. It's beginning to get late."

Monk gave me his glassy stare that makes you think he's a moron until you learn that he's as sharp as the next guy. "Maybe he has," he said.

"Huh?" I said again.

Monk nodded his head toward the door. "That last character rooms with *somebody* in there," he said. "You might be the lucky one."

"Oh-oh," I said, and I got up. A few seconds later I was standing in the doorway of my room, and Monk was right.

The new boy had his coat and shirt off by now and was over in front of the long mirror, trying to make a muscle with his left arm. His back was to me, so for a minute he didn't see me. He stood there —I could see the smile on his face in the mirror—with one of his pipe-stem arms bent at the elbow. It had the poorest excuse for a muscle in it that I've ever had the misfortune to see on a human being. Then he caught sight of me in the mirror. Even through the dust on the glass I could see him blush. But when he

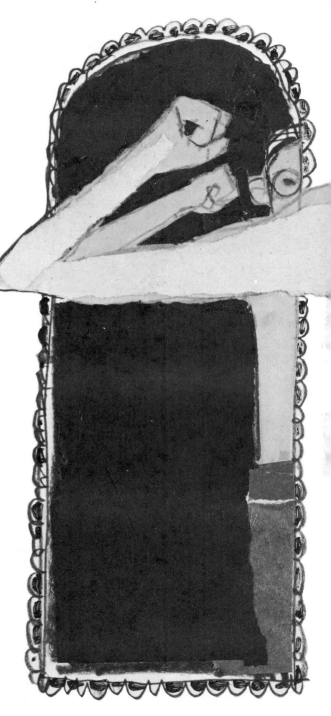

turned around, he was still grinning.

"Dynamic tension," he said.

Honestly, I didn't laugh. Right then I think I liked the kid for trying to carry it off with a laugh on himself. I think I was glad he was going to be my roommate, but all the same I did a mean thing. I went over to the window, stuck my head out, and signaled Monk and Horseface and Geezil to come up. You can bet they came running. I hardly had my head back in again before they were in the room.

"Why, hello again," said the new boy. "Come on in."

"Thanks," said Monk, meaning by his tone of voice that any fool could see that he was in already. He sat down on the bed. "What's your name, boy?"

"My name's Robert," said the new boy. He smiled all over.

Monk shook his head. "It won't do," he said firmly. "That's Robby Armstrong's name"—he pointed to me—"and he was here first." He turned to us. "Anybody got any ideas?"

"Handsome?" Horseface suggested. The new boy winced, but smiled.

"Four-eyes," said Geezil. The new boy blinked, still smiling.

Monk snorted. "You guys have no imagination."

"Of course you could do better," said Horseface scornfully.

"Sure," bragged Monk. "I named *you*, didn't I? This guy is Pitcher."

Geezil nodded. "Turn your head, son," he said to Pitcher.

Pitcher showed us his profile. To this day I haven't gotten used to his punched-in nose and his flappy ears.

"See what I mean?" asked Monk. "You know, little pitchers have big ears. Maybe someday he'll be a great baseball pitcher too, or even a tackle on the football team. Who knows? Funny things happen."

"Right," said Geezil. "Well, what are we waiting for? Let's initiate him."

So we put Pitcher into the shower the way we do with all the new boys around here, and Pitcher didn't mind it a bit. He grinned all the time, except when he fell over the soap and sprawled flat on the tile floor. Then he laughed. He was such a good sport that I began to feel mean. I hope you believe me when I say I was glad when Monk and Horseface and Geezil got tired and left to look for some more new boys. I wanted to get Pitcher alone so I could have a chance to talk with him. You see, already I was coming to like him!

When the first bell rang, I took him to the dining hall right away, so I'd have ten minutes to show him the ropes —I mean, where to get water and milk in case his table ran out—and we bumped into Coach. So I introduced Pitch.

"Coach, this is Pitcher, my new roommate," I said. They shook hands, both smiling.

"It's a good name, don't you think?" Pitcher asked, putting his hands over his ears.

"Yes. . . ." said Coach slowly. "And I'm glad you like it, because that helps." Then, maybe to keep the conversation going, he asked, "Are you coming out for football tomorrow?"

Pitcher's eyebrows went up. "Me?"

"Certainly. Why not?"

"Gosh, I didn't know that I could. I mean, I'm not very big. . . ."

Coach put his hand on Pitcher's shoulder. "We have

a couple of teams especially for the smaller boys," he said, "because we've noticed that they don't stay small very long. How about sitting at my table tonight — we'll talk about football."

"Gee, can I?" Pitch looked as pleased as a boy can be.

"Sure," I put in, maybe to show that I knew my way around. "On the first night you can sit anywhere. After that they assign you a table."

So we sat at Coach's table, Pitch on his right and me on his left, talking football. Coach was telling Pitch how everybody in school is almost as interested in the Brat team (that's what they call us) as in the varsity, and how all the boys come down to cheer the Brat games even louder than they cheer the big team.

Well, Pitch managed to live through the first night of school with all its devilishness, and the next afternoon we all went out for football. Perhaps if Pitcher had been a big athlete he wouldn't have made such a bad start. But the trouble was, he was just the opposite. He was terrible, as we learned at the first practice. He was the *tryingest* person I ever saw, but he couldn't do anything right. Sometimes I thought the poor guy was left-handed all the way through. He missed more tackles than all the rest of us put together. He'd dive at the ball carrier—dive like crazy—but the ball carrier wouldn't be there anymore. When he ran interference for me—I'm quarterback—half the time he'd get tangled in his own feet and fall down just in the right place for me to fall over him.

I lost my temper a few times over things like that. After all, a guy wants to have his team win, and you can't hate me for liking to make a few good gains myself now and then, but the other Brats were worse than I was toward him. Because, after all, I liked Pitcher. The others didn't,

and they rode him to death. I don't need to tell you how they did it. You know how boys can be when they've found somebody to pick on. Chickens aren't a patch on boys when it comes to pecking at the weaklings.

Of course, I could tell from the way Pitcher acted in our room that his unpopularity was beginning to get under his skin. But it was nearly a month after school started before I learned just how badly he felt. I'll say this for Pitch, he could keep his feelings to himself. It wasn't until I woke up one night and heard him crying, that I had any real idea of how much he'd been hurt inside. I listened to him for a while, wondering what I could do to make it easier for him, when he started to moan and talk out loud.

He gasped words out, and then I heard him beating his fist on the pillow. "I can't take

it! I can't take it another day!"
The way his voice sounded
made my hair stand on end.
Then he went on. "And I can't
run away. I just can't quit and
run away, that's all. What'll I
do . . .?"

But I didn't hear any more.
I stuck my fingers in my ears.

COACH TAKES OVER

The very next afternoon I
went down to see Coach, to
tell him the whole story. Coach
listened. He didn't interrupt
once. Toward the end he got
up and stuck his hands in
his pockets and then started
looking for his pipe over behind where I was sitting. When
I got through, he sat down
quietly for a few minutes,
looking out the window and
blowing smoke rings the way
he does when he's got something on his mind. After a
while he laid down his pipe
suddenly, put his hands on

his knees, and looked hard
at me.

"Go get Pitcher," he said.

"Yes, sir," I said, and I got
out of there without asking
any questions. Lots of times
with Coach you don't ask any
questions out loud, but you
can bet that I was wondering
plenty while I ran up to the
room.

When we got back, Coach
had a football in his hands.
He turned it over once or twice
before he said anything.

"Pitcher," he said at last,
"I sent Robby for you because
I want you and him to learn a
private play. A play that nobody else is going to hear
about until we use it in your
Brat game this Saturday."

"Yes, sir," said Pitcher. His
voice sounded kind of eager,
and sad too.

Coach turned to me. "You
understand me, Robby? No-
body is to know this play but
you and Pitch."

I nodded. The Coach was up to something.

"It's simple," Coach said. "So simple that it might do the trick. Especially against boys who haven't had much football experience. Robby, who plays right end against your team?"

"Monk does," I said.

"Perfect!" Coach smiled happily. "If we have to make an idiot of somebody, it might as well be . . ." All of a sudden he got brisk in his manner. "Well, let's get down to business. Robby, you take the ball." He tossed it to me. "Now bend over and move to the right as if you were going on an end run — exactly as you do in play eighteen. That's right. Now, Pitch, stand over here in the wingback position. Right. Okay, Robby. Come over in this direction again on your end run, and give the ball to Pitcher as you go by him. He'll be starting in your direction."

"Yes, sir," I said.

As I remember, we practiced that movement for half an hour, until we had our timing perfect. Pitch almost never dropped the ball when I put it in his hands, and that is very good for Pitch. Coach stood there criticizing us and coaching us; he had me bend over farther and slip the ball to Pitch until finally I hardly knew myself that I had given it to him as he went past me. He had Pitch hold the ball behind his hip with one hand, until you couldn't see it from the front. I think he worked over us harder than he does with the varsity backfield. Finally he seemed satisfied. He tossed me the ball again and sat down.

"Do any of the varsity backfield men live up in your dormitory?" he asked me.

"Yes, sir," I said. "Washburn lives on the first floor, and Star Collins lives on the second, right down the hall from us."

"Collins is the man," Coach said, sort of to himself. He looked at us. "I'm going to change my mind about nobody knowing this play but yourselves. I want Star to help you practice, because, after all, both of you are rather inexperienced."

"Yes, sir," I said. That suited me fine, because Star is a good guy besides being a classy backfield man.

"So take this ball to your room and keep things quiet," Coach told us. "Every night this week you two are to practice what we've been up to, with Star watching you. I'll tell him myself what I want him to look for. Get that play perfect, understand?"

"Yes, sir," said Pitch. I nodded.

"Then Friday you'll come down here for a last workout with me. If I can see that ball

pass between you, or if Pitch drops it, I'll skin you both alive. Understand?"

"Yes, sir," I said. Pitch nodded. Coach has a habit of meaning what he says.

Well, we practiced with Star watching us. We practiced up in our room in front of our mirror, until we ourselves couldn't see the ball slip out of my arms into Pitcher's. And we didn't say anything to anybody. Then on Friday we showed our stuff to Coach and he was satisfied. When we had done it for him half a dozen times without a slip, he made us sit down and then he told us what to do in the game the next day.

You should have seen that game! Of course, the whole school was there, the way they always are for Brat games, and of course they were cheering and hollering the way they always do. The first half was full of good football too—I mean, as good as we can play—and plenty exciting. Most of the time our two teams rolled back and forth, up and down the field, but finally Monk—he's the captain of the Blue team— caught a pass and scored. But they didn't convert, so when I slipped around right end later on and scored, we had them tied. We didn't convert either, so the half ended 6-6.

All this time the big guys in the bleachers were yelling and hollering and pleading and advising, while Coach was sitting quietly on the bench with Pitcher beside him, not saying a word. Once, during a time-out, I noticed that Pitch was biting his nails, but except for that he seemed all right. Even at the half he didn't say anything except, "Nice going, fellows. Let's beat 'em this half." Only nobody noticed him. I'm afraid that most of the fellows were hoping Coach would never send him into the game, because they figured with him in the game we'd never beat Monk's team. Maybe I felt the same way myself, even with that trick play up our sleeves. I remember I began to wonder whether Pitch would hold on to the ball if we had a chance to try the trick in a real game. Then the second half started and I had to use all my wondering trying to figure what Monk's team would pull next.

Halfway through the last quarter the score was still tied when we took over the ball on our forty-yard line. I was trying to decide what plays to use when I saw Pitch come galloping out onto the field. So did the rest of my team back there in the huddle, and they groaned.

"There goes the ball game," said Horseface, completely disgusted.

"And how," said Geezil.

Then Pitch tripped over a blade of grass or something and fell flat on his face before he had gotten halfway to us, and nobody said anything more.

Even I was feeling worried until Monk called across to us, "Oh, you lucky fellows!" When I looked up and saw him grinning at me, I made up my mind to fix his wagon like it had never been fixed before.

So, the way Coach had told me, I called play eighteen, a right-end run, with me carry-ing the ball and Pitch on the wing. It didn't work worth a darn, because I fell over Pitch on the line of scrimmage, but that was all right because it wasn't supposed to work. Back in the huddle I called the same play again. This time it went for a couple of yards, because I managed to get out of Pitcher's way. In the huddle I hollered "Eighteen!" again, good and loud.

"Quiet, you dope, they'll hear you!" Horseface whis-pered fiercely to me.

"Well, let's run it anyway," I said, and I didn't even smile.

Horseface wasn't supposed to know that part of the idea was to have Monk hear me call the play.

So we ran it, and how I got smeared! Even Monk was in on the tackle, because he'd run behind the line of scrimmage all the way around from his end to get me. Which was what Coach had figured he would do.

"Play eighteen," I said in the huddle, good and loud.

"Have you gone crazy, Robby?" Horseface was part mad, part worried too. "Are you out of your feeble mind?"

"Eighteen!" I said again, loud and clear.

"It's fourth down," said Geezil. "Coach will kill you if you don't kick on fourth down."

"Eighteen!" I repeated. "Me in the tailback, Pitch on the wing."

"Buddy, you asked for it," said Horseface, plenty grim. He walked up to the scrimmage line, because Coach gets mighty sore if anybody but the quarterback tries to run the team, but I had an idea he was planning to murder me after we lost the game.

91

I was kind of worried myself, but then the ball came back at me and I stopped worrying in order to get down to business.

Just as if we were in our locker room practicing in front of the mirror, I started off to the right and Pitch started toward me. We passed each other behind our right tackle, and even I didn't know when I slipped Pitch the ball, it went so slick and easy. I was still doubled up, pretending I had the ball, when Monk sailed into me from the side and knocked me out of bounds. But I got up again as if I'd been made out of rubber, because I was about to see if our naked-reverse was going to work. Brother, I saw!

Way out there across the field Pitch was galloping toward the goal line, the ball held off behind his hip exactly the way Coach had taught

him, and there wasn't a soul near him. Even the halfback and the safety man on Monk's team had pulled way over to the right to get me. Coach's naked-reverse had worked.

It had worked so fine that even the guys in the stands hadn't followed the play. You could tell because they weren't making a sound. They were just looking all over for the ball. And then they found it. Boy, you should have heard the yelling!

"Pitch has it!"

"Pitch—he's got the ball!"

"Look-it the rascal run!"

"How'd he get it?"

"Run, Pitch! Run with that ball, Pitch!"

I've heard noise on a ball field, but none like that. I've seen guys stamp their feet and jump up and down and throw their hats in the air, but not the way they did that day when Pitcher went racing down the left-hand sideline—

the ball hugged to his chest now, the way Coach had told him in order to prevent accidents—and not a soul near him. Everybody was hollering, "Pitch! Pitcher!" and pounding each others' backs.

Mind you, I wasn't sitting on the ground with Monk in my lap all this time. As soon as I could, I'd pushed him away and taken off after Pitch, not that there was any blocking to do but just because I wanted to be somewhere around when he crossed the goal line. Even running as hard as I could, I heard the shouts for him, and I could see his white teeth flashing the world's widest grin.

And then, of course, he tripped. On the two-yard line he caught one toe behind his ankle and went sprawling in every direction at once. So did the ball. It squirted out of his hands like wet soap. That didn't matter. It squirted over the goal line, and I was there to fall on it. That counts six points in any league.

When I sat up with the ball, Pitch was still lying flat on the ground.

"Hey, Pitch!" I hollered. I was worried. "Are you all right?"

Pitch sat up then and batted his eyes. He looked at the other guys on the team running toward him, yelping, clapping, and laughing. He listened to the guys in the stands screaming his name while they jumped up and down. Then he smiled, the biggest smile I've ever seen on a human being his size.

"I'm all right," he said as he got up. He took a deep breath, smiled wider, and just before the team swamped him to beat him on the back, I heard him say, "I'm the happiest boy in all the world!"

——*Stephen Cole*

THINKING IT OVER

1. What was Pitcher's problem and how was it solved?
2. Did you find a deeper meaning in this story? What do you think the author wanted you to think about?
3. In what ways did you like or admire Pitcher? In what ways would you not want to be like him?

THOUGHTS AT WORK

1. Why did the other boys pick on Pitcher during that first month of school?
2. How do you think Monk and the boys treated Pitcher during the rest of the school year? Explain your answer.
3. How did the naked-reverse play help solve the problem? Try to explain what happens in this play.
4. Which people tried to help Pitcher solve his problem? What did each one do to help?
5. Choose one or two characters you liked best in this story and tell why you liked them.
6. How did the author make you think the story was written by Robby Armstrong?
7. Your feelings probably changed several times as you read this story. Tell the part where
       a. you wanted to laugh.
       b. you felt sad or unhappy.
       c. you felt a little worried.
       d. you wanted to groan.

BASE STEALER

Poised between going on and back, pulled
Both ways taut like a tightrope-walker,
Fingertips pointing the opposites,
Now bouncing tiptoe like a dropped ball.
Or a kid skipping rope, come on, come on,
Running a scattering of steps sidewise,
How he teeters, skitters, tingles, teases,
Taunts them, hovers like an ecstatic bird,
He's only flirting, crowd him, crowd him,
Delicate, delicate, delicate, delicate — now!

———*Robert Francis*

96

BIBLIOGRAPHY

The Empty Schoolhouse, by Natalie Savage Carlson.
Lullah refuses to give in, even when threatened with violence, and wins more than the right to go to the school of her choice.

The Mailbox Trick, by Scott Corbett.
How do you get back letters you're now sorry you mailed? Before Kerby solves this problem, there are some awkward moments.

The Stone-Face Boy, by Paula Fox.
How would you like to rescue the family dog only to be thanked with a growl? This is the way life is for Gus, the third child squeezed in a family of five.

The Ghost of Five Owl Farm, by Wilson Gage.
In this exciting and funny mystery, you'll read about suspicious happenings in an old abandoned barn.

A Trainful of Strangers, by Eleanor Hull.
After eight children spend forty-five minutes in a subway car stalled beneath New York City, their feelings about themselves and others are changed.

Jennifer, Hecate, Macbeth, William McKinley, and Me, Elizabeth, by E. L. Konigsburg.
Want to become an apprentice witch? Elizabeth learns that you begin by eating raw eggs for a week.

While Mrs. Coverlet Was Away, by Mary Nash.
Strange and funny things happen when three children try to keep it secret that they are living alone all summer.

The Jazz Man, by Mary Hays Weik.
Zeke, left alone for most of the day in a Harlem tenement, eagerly watches a certain window across the court.

WHERE DO STORIES COME FROM?

Authors are often asked, "Where do you get ideas for your stories?" As is true with most interesting questions, there are many answers. An author may write about events of his childhood. Sometimes story ideas come from people an author meets and places he visits. Some authors base their stories on events in history. Other authors use fanciful events and characters from tales told long ago. As you can see, authors get story ideas from many sources.

In this unit, you will find how authors have used these ideas to write many kinds of stories. Perhaps you, too, have ideas for a story. The last three selections in the unit will show you that children's experiences can be turned into stories.

99

This story comes from a series of books called *The Little House Books* written by Laura Ingalls Wilder. These books are filled with exciting events from Mrs. Wilder's childhood in the 1870's, when she traveled West with her pioneer family. Mrs. Wilder is the Laura in the next story. You will see why she remembered this day.

The Day They Stayed Alone

Before you begin to read, you should know that the family, which includes Pa and Ma and the three girls, is living on the prairie in a one-room dugout built into the side of a hill. Their only cow is called Spot.

Alongside their farm is another owned by the Nelson family. The Nelsons raise cattle and they have a boy, Johnny Johnson, working for them. His job is to watch the cattle to prevent their straying off.

Near the end of the story, Laura refers to a wolf. There is no wolf in this story, but in an earlier home on the Kansas prairie, a pack of fifty wolves closed in around Laura's father while he was out riding. The wolves did nothing but trot along side of him. But Pa wasted no time getting home that day. Laura was grateful toward all wolves ever after. Now go on with the story.

100

Summer was gone, winter was coming, and now it was time for Pa to make a trip to town. Here in Minnesota, town was so near that Pa would be gone only one day, and Ma was going with him.

She took Carrie, because Carrie was too little to be left far from Ma. But Mary and Laura were big girls. Mary was going on nine and Laura was going on eight, and they could stay at home and take care of everything while Pa and Ma were gone.

For going-to-town, Ma made a new dress for Carrie, from the pink calico that Laura had worn when she was little. There was enough of it to make Carrie a little pink sunbonnet. Carrie's hair had been in curl-papers all night. It hung in long, golden, round curls, and when Ma tied the pink sunbonnet strings under Carrie's chin, Carrie looked like a rose.

Ma wore her hoopskirts and her best dress, the beautiful chailis with little strawberries on it, that she had worn to the sugaring-dance at Grandma's, long ago in the Big Woods.

"Now be good girls, Laura and Mary," was the last thing she said. She was on the wagon seat, with Carrie beside her. Their lunch was in the wagon. Pa took up the ox goad.

"We'll be back before sundown," he promised. "Hi-oop!" he said to Pete and Bright. The big ox and the little one leaned into their yoke and the wagon started.

"Good-bye, Pa! Good-bye, Ma! Good-bye, Carrie, good-bye!" Laura and Mary called after it.

Slowly the wagon went away. Pa walked beside the oxen. Ma and Carrie, the wagon, and Pa all grew smaller, till they were gone into the prairie.

The prairie seemed big and empty then, but there was nothing to be afraid of. There were no wolves and no Indians. Besides, Jack stayed close to Laura. Jack was a responsible dog. He knew that he must take care of everything when Pa was away.

That morning Mary and Laura played by the creek, among the rushes. They did not go near the swimming-hole. They did not touch the straw-stack. At noon they ate the corn dodgers and molasses and drank the milk that Ma had left for them. They washed their tin cups and put them away.

Then Laura wanted to play on the big rock, but Mary wanted to stay in the dugout. She said that Laura must stay there, too.

"Ma can make me," Laura said, "but you can't."

"I can so," said Mary. "When Ma's not here, you have to do what I say because I'm older."

"You have to let me have my way because I'm littler," said Laura.

"That's Carrie, it isn't you," Mary told her. "If you don't do what I say, I'll tell Ma."

"I guess I can play where I want to!" said Laura.

Mary grabbed at her, but Laura was too quick. She darted out, and she would have run up the path, but Jack was in the way. He stood stiff, looking across the creek. Laura looked too, and she screeched, "Mary!"

The cattle were all around Pa's haystacks. They were eating the hay. They were tearing into the stacks with their horns, gouging out hay, eating it and trampling over it.

There would be nothing left to feed Pete and Bright and Spot in the wintertime.

Jack knew what to do. He ran growling down the steps to the foot-bridge. Pa was not there to save the haystacks; they must drive those cattle away.

"Oh, we can't! We can't!" Mary said, scared. But Laura ran behind Jack and Mary came after her. They went over the creek and past the spring. They came up on the prairie and now they saw the fierce, big cattle quite near. The long horns were gouging, the thick legs trampling and jostling, the wide mouths bawling.

Mary was too scared to move. Laura was too scared to stand still. She jerked Mary along. She saw a stick, and grabbed it up and ran yelling at the cattle. Jack ran at them, growling. A big red cow swiped at him with her horns, but he jumped behind her. She snorted and galloped. All the other cattle ran humping and jostling after her, and Jack and Laura and Mary ran after them.

But they could not chase those cattle away from the haystacks. The cattle ran around and around and in between the stacks, jostling and bawling, tearing off hay and trampling it. More and more hay slid off the stacks. Laura ran panting and yelling, waving her stick.

104

The faster she ran, the faster the cattle went, black and brown and red, brindle and spotted cattle, big and with awful horns, and they would not stop wasting the hay. Some tried to climb over the toppling stacks.

Laura was hot and dizzy. Her hair unbraided and blew in her eyes. Her throat was rough from yelling, but she kept on yelling, running, and waving her stick. She was too scared to hit one of those big, horned cows. More and more hay kept coming down and faster and faster they trampled over it.

Suddenly Laura turned around and ran the other way. She faced the big red cow coming around a haystack.

The huge legs and shoulders and terrible horns were coming fast. Laura could not scream now. But she jumped at that cow and waved her stick. The cow tried to stop, but all the other cattle were coming behind her and she couldn't. She swerved and ran away across the ploughed ground, all the others galloping after her.

Jack and Laura and Mary chased them, farther and farther from the hay. Far into the high prairie grasses they chased those cattle.

Johnny Johnson rose out of the prairie, rubbing his eyes. He had been lying asleep in a warm hollow of grass.

"Johnny! Johnny!" Laura screeched. "Wake up and watch the cattle!"

"You'd better!" Mary told him.

Johnny Johnson looked at the cattle grazing in the deep grass, and he looked at Laura and Mary and Jack. He did not know what had happened and they could not tell him because the only words he knew were Norwegian.[1]

They went back through the high grass that dragged at their trembling legs. They were glad to drink at the spring. They were glad to be in the quiet dugout and sit down to rest.

All that long, quiet afternoon they stayed in the dugout. The cattle did not come back to the haystacks. Slowly the sun went down the western sky. Soon

[1] Norwegian (nôr wē′jen)

106

it would be time to meet the cattle at the big grey rock, and Laura and Mary wished that Pa and Ma would come home.

Again and again they went up the path to look for the wagon. At last they sat waiting with Jack on the grassy top of their house. The lower the sun went, the more attentive Jack's ears were. Often he and Laura stood up to look at the edge of the sky where the wagon had gone, though they could see it just as well when they were sitting down.

Finally Jack turned one ear that way, then the other. Then he looked up at Laura and a waggle went from his neck to his stubby tail. The wagon was coming!

They all stood and watched till it came out of the prairie. When Laura saw the oxen, and Ma and Carrie on the wagon seat, she jumped up and down, swinging her sunbonnet and shouting, "They're coming! They're coming!"

"They're coming awful fast," Mary said.

Laura was still. She heard the wagon rattling loudly. Pete and Bright were coming very fast. They were running. They were running away.

The wagon came bumpity-banging and bouncing. Laura saw Ma down in a corner of the wagon box, hanging onto it and hugging Carrie. Pa came bounding in long jumps beside Bright, shouting and hitting at Bright with the goad.

He was trying to turn Bright back from the creek bank.

He could not do it. The big oxen galloped nearer and nearer the steep edge. Bright was pushing Pa off it. They were all going over. The wagon, Ma and Carrie, were going to fall down the bank, all the way down to the creek.

Pa shouted a terrible shout. He struck Bright's head with all his might, and Bright swerved. Laura ran screaming. Jack jumped at Bright's nose. Then the wagon, Ma, and Carrie flashed by. Bright crashed against the stable and suddenly everything was still.

Pa ran after the wagon and Laura ran behind him.

"Whoa, Bright! Whoa, Pete," Pa said. He held onto the wagon box and looked at Ma.

"We're all right, Charles," Ma said. Her face was grey and she was shaking all over.

Pete was trying to go on through the doorway into the stable, but he was yoked to Bright and Bright was headed against the stable wall. Pa lifted Ma and Carrie out of the wagon, and Ma said, "Don't cry, Carrie. See, we're all right."

Carrie's pink dress was torn down the front. She snuffled against Ma's neck and tried to stop crying as Ma told her.

"Oh, Caroline! I thought you were going over the bank," Pa said.

"I thought so, too, for a minute," Ma answered. "But I might have known you wouldn't let that happen."

"Pshaw!" said Pa. "It was good old Pete. He wasn't

running away. Bright was, but Pete was only going along. He saw the stable and wanted his supper."

But Laura knew that Ma and Carrie would have fallen down into the creek with the wagon and oxen, if Pa had not run so fast and hit Bright so hard. She crowded against Ma's hoopskirt and hugged her tight and said, "Oh, Ma! Oh, Ma!" So did Mary.

"There, there," said Ma. "All's well that ends well. Now, girls, help bring in the packages while Pa puts up the oxen."

They carried all the little packages into the dugout. They met the cattle at the grey rock and put Spot into the stable, and Laura helped milk her while Mary helped Ma get supper.

At supper, they told how the cattle had got into the haystacks and how they had driven them away. Pa said they had done exactly the right thing. He said, "We knew we could depend on you to take care of everything. Didn't we, Caroline?"

They had completely forgotten that Pa always brought them presents from town, until after supper he pushed back his bench and looked as if he expected something. Then Laura jumped on his knee, and Mary sat on the other, and Laura bounced and asked, "What did you bring us, Pa? What? What?"

"Guess," Pa said.

They could not guess. But Laura felt something crackle in his jumper pocket and she pounced on it. She pulled out a paper bag, beautifully striped with

tiny red and green stripes. And in the bag were two sticks of candy, one for Mary and one for Laura!

They were maple-sugar-coloured, and they were flat on one side.

Mary licked hers. But Laura bit her stick, and the outside of it came off, crumbly. The inside was hard and clear and dark brown. And it had a rich, brown, tangy taste. Pa said it was hoarhound candy.

After the dishes were done, Laura and Mary each took her stick of candy and they sat on Pa's knees, outside the door in the cool dusk. Ma sat just inside the dugout, humming to Carrie in her arms.

The creek was talking to itself under the yellow willows. One by one the great stars swung low and seemed to quiver and flicker in the little wind.

Laura was snug in Pa's arm. His beard softly tickled her cheek and the delicious candy taste melted on her tongue.

After a while she said, "Pa."

"What, little half-pint?" Pa's voice asked against her hair.

"I think I like wolves better than cattle," she said.

"Cattle are more useful, Laura," Pa said.

She thought about that a while. Then she said, "Anyway, I like wolves better."

She was not contradicting; she was only saying what she thought.

"Well, Laura, we're going to have a good team of horses before long," Pa said. She knew when that would be. It would be when they had a wheat crop.

——*Laura Ingalls Wilder*

THINKING IT OVER

1. Why do you think Laura Ingalls Wilder remembered this day?
2. In what ways did the characters in the story show courage?
3. Put yourself in Laura's place and tell how she felt when
     a. she saw the big red cow running toward her.
     b. she found Johnny asleep in the grass.
     c. she saw the oxen running away with the wagon.

THOUGHTS AT WORK

1. Laura knew differently when Pa told Ma that it was really Pete who kept the wagon from going over the bank. Why do you think Pa said this if it wasn't true?
2. Why was it so important that Laura and Mary chase the cattle from the haystacks? What might have happened to the family if the haystacks had been destroyed?
3. Find some words such as hoopskirt to show that this story took place long ago.
4. Why do you think the hoarhound candy Pa brought from town was such a treat for the girls?
5. After Pa and Ma left for town, "The prairie seemed big and empty . . ." to Laura. Why do you think she felt this way?
6. Pa said, ". . . we're going to have a good team of horses before long." Why do you think the family didn't have horses? How could horses have made their lives easier?
7. Tell about a time you stayed alone while your parents were out.

WESTERN WAGONS

They went with axe and rifle, when the trail was still to blaze,
They went with wife and children, in the prairie schooner days,
With banjo and with frying pan—Susanna, don't you cry!
For I'm off to California to get rich out there or die!

We've broken land and cleared it, but we're tired of where
 we are.
They say that wild Nebraska is a better place by far.
There's gold in far Wyoming, there's black earth in Ioway,
So pack up the kids and blankets, for we're moving out today!

The cowards never started and the weak died on the road,
And all across the continent the endless campfires glowed.
We'd taken land and settled—but a traveler passed by—
And we're going West tomorrow—Lordy, never ask us why!

We're going West tomorrow, where the promises can't fail.
O'er the hills in legions, boys, and crowd the dusty trail!
We shall starve and freeze and suffer. We shall die, and tame
 the lands.
But we're going West tomorrow, with our fortune in our hands.

——Rosemary and Stephen Vincent Benét

113

Lorenz Graham

Next is a story based on an author's experiences in a foreign country. As a young man, Mr. Graham, wanting to help the people of his race, became a teacher in Liberia, Africa. Momolu, the boy in this story, is like many of the boys he knew there.

With the author's help, put yourself in Momolu's place as he sees for the first time the strange sights in a city.

I, MOMOLU

Trouble had come to Momolu's jungle village, and all because of a misunderstanding. Soldiers of the Liberian Government had marched in one evening just as the village women were preparing their families' suppers. The soldiers came in peace and so the villagers welcomed them and made them feel their friendliness even though they spoke a different language.

Momolu was impressed with the soldiers, their uniforms, their guns. Then one of them, noting Momolu's interest, dressed the boy in his own uniform, even to the round red cap on his head. Momolu felt proud in the fine government uniform— until his father saw him. Flumbo hated all soldiers because he felt they were evil men who kill. He didn't want, even in

114

play, his son to love the feeling of being a soldier. Enraged, he ripped the clothes from his son's back and in minutes he and the soldier were at combat with each other. More soldiers and villagers joined the conflict and soon a riot threatened.

When the captain of the troops had finally brought the situation under control, he ordered Flumbo to be brought before him. Because Flumbo had destroyed the soldier's uniform which was government property, he was sentenced to take ten sacks of rice down the jungle river to the large city, Cape Roberts, and there surrender the rice to the government officials. It was a hard sentence, for ten sacks of rice would be half the crop from Flumbo's harvest.

The next morning Flumbo and Momolu set out by canoe from the jungle village. After several days on the river they came to the city of Cape Roberts. There they stayed with a former village man, Jalla-Malla. He had settled in Cape Roberts, had learned the American way of speaking, and had traveled to far countries, working on ships. Jalla-Malla was a man of the world.

Momolu, who had hardly been outside his own village, thought he never would come to the end of the wonders of Cape Roberts. One of his most unforgettable adventures was his first ride in a truck. Here is Mr. Graham's account of that ride.

One day as Momolu was walking with Jalla-Malla along the street of open-front shops, Jalla-Malla stopped to talk with a man leaning against a truck. Standing still, the truck seemed to hold no danger, and Momolu considered it. In the flat, box-like part of the body, enough rice could be carried to feed a family for the space of a year. Momolu felt it and looked carefully to see its different parts, the wheels under it, the seats, the shiny glass parts like eyes.

To amuse Momolu, Jalla-Malla's friend showed him how the lights could be turned on and off.

"The voice?" Momolu asked. "How does it know when to make a roar?"

Jalla-Malla repeated this to his friend in his own speech. The man reached inside, and the wild noise, like no animal Momolu had ever heard, came forth from the front. They laughed, the men, at the country boy's fright, but once Momolu

saw the place to touch, he pressed his own hand there again and again, and then he lost his fear.

"Would you like to ride?" Jalla-Malla asked. "Our friend will take us in his truck."

When they had seated themselves inside the part that was like a small house with Momolu between the two men, he tried his best to see what the friend would do. He wanted to remember so he could tell the boys in Lojay, his village.

The driver touched some things with his hands and some

other things with his feet. The truck seemed suddenly to be a live thing wakened from sleep. It was made, Momolu knew, of iron and wood, but under him the soft seat trembled like an excited animal.

Momolu wanted to get out, but the truck had begun to move. The awful noise sounded. People jumped from the truck's path. The driver turned his wheel first to one side and then to the other. At the end of the street where the government house stood, the truck turned and started up a hill. Momolu had never seen this part of Cape Roberts.

Few people were on the road. The houses were large, and they stood far apart. The truck was moving swiftly and smoothly. Momolu had never traveled so fast. The seat under him bounced, but the feeling was not as though the thing were angry. Riding was good, and Momolu was no longer afraid.

Over the hill and down again, and along a level stretch of road they rolled, moving faster and faster. Then it seemed that the truck was not moving but that all the world was flying past them, trees and shrubs and houses slipping along with the land. Ahead the scene would move toward them at first slowly, then faster, and suddenly it whizzed by. How would he ever be able to make the village boys understand it? There were no words to tell about it. The truck slowed as it climbed a long, steep hill. When they came over the crest, Momolu saw stretching below and far beyond the land, the wide sweep of unending, sparkling sea.

The truck shook off the struggle of the climb and, lowering its nose, it rushed faster and faster with each moment, rushing toward the sea with those inside. The truck seemed angry

now and anxious to destroy the men it bore. It was taking them out to drown them in the water. It was going too fast ever to stop.

Momolu looked sideways at the driver. He was crouched over with his hands holding fast to the wheel. His jaw was set in a hard line. His teeth were clenched. It was as if he, too, was holding on in terror.

"Stop! Stop!" Momolu shouted. "We will die in the water!"

Jalla-Malla laughed. Momolu tried to climb over him to get out, but Jalla-Malla held onto him. Momolu turned to get out the other side, but the driver's hands still clutched the wheel, and he was laughing too.

"Crazy!" Momolu shouted. "Now these men are crazy! Pa, come and save me! Mommy! They are crazy! Now I die! Now I die! O my little Mommy!"

He covered his face to shut out the sight of death and sobbed into his hands.

The movement slowed and the truck stopped. Jalla-Malla put his arm around Momolu's heaving shoulders. "Never mind, Momolu boy! Never mind!" he said.

Momolu lay back, his eyes closed, his breath coming in short gasps. "Sick," he finally muttered. It was the one word that he could utter.

Jalla-Malla stepped out and helped Momolu to follow. It was none too soon. Momolu vomited.

Sometime later, Momolu sat beside the road and looked at the truck. It had stopped far short of the water. The man, Jalla-Malla's friend, stopped it. The truck was a thing that the driver had made a slave. He could make the truck work

120

for him. He could make it carry himself and his friends, and in the back the truck could carry more bags of rice than many canoes could.

Momolu was still afraid of the truck, but Jalla-Malla and his friend were standing by it, leaning against it as they talked. The driver was the master. He was not afraid because he understood. The man who had mastered the truck was not afraid because he understood.

"I, Momolu, will understand," he said softly, speaking only to himself. "I will understand these mysteries someday, and I will have no fear."

121

"Come," Jalla-Malla called, "we must go home now."

Momolu would rather have walked. Although he had said he would have no fear, he knew he still did not understand, and so his legs became so weak that Jalla-Malla had almost to lift him to get him back into the seat.

He watched again the movements of the driver. The man's two hands and both his feet moved together. It was too much for one pair of eyes to know everything that was done, but as the truck was backed and turned and headed up the hill again, one thing seemed clear. When the driver wanted the machine to move toward the right, he turned the wheel in that direction. When it was to go straight ahead, he held the wheel still. This much Momolu could see. This much he learned.

"If I learn one thing today," he told himself, "I can learn something else another time. Then by and by I will understand and I will have no fear."

——*Lorenz Graham*

Momolu and his father at last returned to their village. During his stay at Cape Roberts, Flumbo had learned that not all soldiers were to be feared and hated. Momolu came home more than ever determined that someday "I, Momolu, will understand."

THINKING IT OVER

1. Why was Momolu afraid of the truck? Why wouldn't you be afraid of it?
2. Pretend you are Momolu telling the boys in the village about your ride. What part would you keep to yourself? Would you exaggerate anything?
3. Momolu promised himself that he would not always be afraid of the truck. Find on page 122 his plan for losing his fear.

THOUGHTS AT WORK

1. Momolu was frightened when the truck first started but he soon began to enjoy the ride. What made him less frightened?
2. We say an airplane roars because the noise of the motors makes us think of the sound an animal makes when it roars. Find words or phrases that tell what Momolu thought of the truck.
3. Momolu saw that the driver was not afraid of the truck. Find the sentence on page 121 that explains why Momolu felt the driver had no fear.
4. What did Momolu learn about the truck that helped him understand it better?
5. How was Momolu like other boys?
6. Think of something you were afraid of until you understood it better. What helped you understand it?
7. What problems are caused in this world by people who are fearful because they don't understand? What can you do to help solve these problems?

Winter Danger

Did you ever wish you were a pioneer traveling with Daniel Boone and living in the vast wilderness? William O. Steele did when he was a boy living in the mountains of Tennessee. As he grew older, he realized that the past was all around him in old log cabins, in Indian arrowheads he found, and in the way his neighbors spoke. His stories "come alive" because they are based on facts and on events that really took place. This kind of story is called historical fiction. As you go back almost two hundred years in the story, ask yourself if you could have survived the "winter danger."

Caje[1] and his father had come to spend the winter in the cabin of the Tadlocks, relatives of Caje's dead mother. Jared,[2] his father, was a woodsy. He had no home except a hollow tree and he scraped a living by hunting animals for their hides.

[1] Caje (kāj)   [2] Jared (jār'əd)

124

When this story begins, Jared had returned to the woods, leaving Caje behind. The boy resented his father's going. But even more he resented having to stay, a guest of the Tadlocks. Not that they didn't make him feel welcome. All of them, except possibly Sam, one of the Tadlock boys, had been kindness itself. But food was getting low and Caje imagined that Uncle Adam and Aunt Jess would be glad of one less mouth to feed, especially after the accident which had almost killed his Uncle Adam.

Caje knew the ways of the woods. Ever since his mother's death he had shared his father's woodsy life. He could hunt and shoot almost as well as Jared. He was strong too. So, one night he decided to leave the warm cabin and face the wilderness and the cold on his own. He would not be a burden any longer on the kindly Tadlocks.

The Bad Winter

Caje made a neat bundle of his stockings and the piece of flannel. He laid it on the fireboard and beside it he put all but three of the lead balls he'd found in his pouch. By the dim light of the fire Caje wrapped the rabbitskins Jared had given him around his feet and tied his moccasins. He pulled his shirt tight about him and looked around the room once before he opened the door and silently slipped out.

The stars were bright over his head. The cold was terrific. The air stung his hands. His teeth chattered a little as he hurried down the hill.

At the foot he turned and looked back. He remembered the day he and Jared had come here. He'd had high hopes then of spending a winter under a snug roof with a warm fire and enough to eat. But he and Jared had brought their bad luck with them. It was a good thing he was leaving.

Well, it was what he got for trying to be something that he wasn't. A woodsy was a woodsy. He couldn't be a farm boy. As long as he might have lived with the Tadlocks, he would always have been taking what he couldn't return.

He set off through the poplar trees across the frozen creek. He hated to leave them, just the same. They were good folks. Maybe someday he'd come to see them and bring them skins and deer meat to pay for his stay with them.

It was lighter now. The snow squeaked under his moccasins. He kept moving his rifle from hand to hand so that he could warm his free hand in his shirt. Sam would be up by this time, feeding the horse and the cow.

A flock of little birds scattered like dark specks on the snow.

But as the pale sun rose higher in the sky, he began to doubt that he'd live to see it set, much less to last the rest of the winter. He found a slippery elm tree and slashed off long strips of the thick bark with his ax. He pulled off the slick white inner bark and ate it. It was better than dried **corn** for filling him up, but it didn't stick to his ribs for **long. He** stuffed some of the bark in his shirt.

Halfway through the morning, his feet bothered him so much he stopped and took off his moccasins. His feet were bright red and the veins stood out purple and thick along the tops and sides of them. But his toes were turning white. He rubbed them gently for some time before he put his moccasins back on. Then he jumped up and down and stamped his feet to get some feeling back into them, but it did little good.

He'd have to build a fire, he decided. He couldn't risk getting his toes frostbit the first day. He looked around for a sheltered place where he could make a fire.

Something caught his eye, something that made him forget

his feet for the moment. Halfway up a hillside a little ledge of rock stuck out from the snow. And over it hung a little puff of white smoke. The puff drifted away and another came to take its place.

His hands trembled as he picked up his rifle. He knew what was up there. Many a time he'd heard Jared tell of hunting bear by the white puffs their breath made in the cold air over their dens.

Quietly he made his way up the hillside. Jared always said a bear didn't sleep any sounder during his winter sleep than any other time. He'd have to be careful. Oh, he hoped it was a young bear, still fat. But even if it was an old one, tough and strong tasting, it would keep him from starving.

He knelt and swept the snow away from around the entrance to the den. The smell of bear, heavy and harsh, rose up around him. He checked his gun carefully. Faintly he could hear the beast's regular breathing. Picking up a fallen branch, he jabbed it into the hole and felt it ram into something solid. There was

a growl from the den. Hastily Caje stepped back, dropping the stick and raising his rifle. He heard a scuffling sound and then the great brown face and little eyes of a bear looked out from the hole, sticking almost straight out of the snow.

Caje sighted down his rifle barrel at a spot right between the bear's eyes and pulled the trigger. The bear stared around at Caje for a minute and then it slumped forward. Caje loaded his rifle. It was hard work, for his fingers were stiff and numb with cold. He poked at the great head with his foot, holding his rifle ready. The bear was dead.

He set to work clearing away a space at the den entrance. Finally he had made enough room so that he could skin the bear. He was delighted to see that it was a young one, fat and plenty big enough to feed ten Cajes. Big enough to feed a family.

It was big enough to feed the Tadlocks! He stood there, staring down at the brown coarse fur. If he could get this bear back to the cabin, it would save the Tadlocks. It would save Uncle Adam and old Brit, the horse. It would feed them all for

the three weeks till help came from Salisbury. They wouldn't have to kill old Brit for food.

He took off his moccasins and rubbed his feet up and down the bear's warm hide, until the feeling came back in them and his toes began to tingle. The big body gave off almost as much heat as a fire. Then he began to skin the bear.

Oh, he'd be glad to go back toting a bear ham and slabs of meat from over the ribs. Now he could pay his aunt and uncle back for all he'd eaten during the weeks he'd lived with them. He could leave in the spring. With warm weather he could go off and they'd not be bothered with him again.

He worked steadily, cutting up the meat. He made a sled of poles with traces of twisted elm bark. He loaded it with meat, as much as he could carry. The rest he wrapped in the bearskin. He tied this to a pole placed between two trees, high off the ground. A panther might get to it, but not the wolves. He and Sam could come back for it later.

He set out over the snow, pulling the load with the rough traces. He could hardly wait to get back to the cabin. He hoped they hadn't killed old Brit today. Wasn't it a lucky thing he hadn't run after Jared?

He thought a minute about that as he slid down a hill toward a thicket of pines. Had he been meant to stay with the Tadlocks all winter, to live with them on charity, in idleness, so that now he could save them when they were nearly out of food, and Uncle Adam sick?

Did folks always get a chance to pay back favors if they waited long enough? He remembered Henry Renfroe, who had helped Uncle Adam in the spring. He remembered how Jared had said he would have done without, rather than be beholden to a stranger. But Uncle Adam had paid Henry Renfroe back. He'd sent meal when the Renfroes were sick and all their meal was gone.

He dragged the heavy sled-load of meat up a hill and stood looking out over the snow-covered valley. He didn't see anything familiar, but he knew he was going in the right direction.

Jared never liked taking favors from other people. He hated being beholden. But suddenly Caje knew folks weren't really beholden to each other. You did what you could for other people, and when there was nothing you could do, sometimes you had to let others do for you. Folks had to get along with each other and sometimes it meant doing and sometimes it meant being done for.

A boy had to learn to do one as well as the other. Jared would spend all his days in the woods because he'd never

been able to let others do for him. He was always weighing and measuring, figuring how he'd have to pay back for every little thing done for him, never trusting anybody.

Uncle Adam wasn't like that. He'd taken help from Henry Renfroe when he'd needed help. But when he gave Henry meal, he hadn't reckoned it as paying Henry back. It was just his turn to be the helper. Uncle Adam and Aunt Jess wouldn't worry about taking from the Craigs, or from the men who were going to Salisbury, or from anybody. They knew they would do for anybody else in trouble, so they didn't mind taking when they had to.

As he started down to the hollow, Caje knew the Tadlocks had never expected any return for what they'd given him. They'd taken care of him because they could and because they wanted to. They would have given him anything, even if he'd never been able to do anything for them. When he went back to the cabin, he'd be going home.

The shadows were growing long. It had taken a good while to skin the bear and put the meat in the tree. He looked around anxiously. He'd never make it back before dark. Well, he'd journey as far as he could.

He tried to hurry, but he was tired and the meat was heavy. He came to a lot of rough drifted snow and had a hard time getting through. The cold blue light of evening settled over the hills, making strange shadows by every bush and tree.

He turned and looked back, watching the light fade from the winter sky. What was that running behind him in the dusk, those long gray shapes with gleaming eyes?

Wolves! Wolves were after him and the fresh meat!

132

The Wolves Close In

Caje began to pull the sled over the snow as fast as he could, but his legs were giving out. He kept glancing back at the big varmints. They were coming closer, silently, steadily. In ordinary times wolves weren't too brave. They weren't likely to give trouble. But these wolves were starving. The smell of fresh-killed bear had them half-mad already. They might keep their distance now, but a little more and they might leap at his throat and pull him to the snow.

Ahead of him a canebrake grew along the creek. He saw a sheltered place where the cane grew close and the great thick stalks made a sort of wall. He swerved in that direction, jerking the sled with all his might. He would have to make a fire, that was one sure way to keep the wolves at bay, now that darkness was on him.

He pulled the sled close to the cane and turned to look back at the wolves. Among the scattered trees he could see them, coming silently closer. With his tomahawk he quickly cut some stalks of the dried cane. Next he emptied the powder from his pan into his palm and plugged the touchhole. He placed a piece of tow cloth in the bottom of the pan and the powder over the top of this.

He glanced up. The wolves crouched not five feet away from him. He could see their fangs gleaming in the dim light. With his rifle close to the pile of cane he pulled the trigger. The flint struck the frizzle and made a spark in the pan. There was a flash as the powder caught. Quickly he grabbed the burning tow, rammed it into the dried cane, and began to blow gently. The flames caught.

He had an uneasy feeling that the wolves were creeping nearer, but he didn't dare turn away from the fire now. He only had one charge of powder left. He nursed the fire carefully, adding the dried cane to it a little at a time, until it caught well. There was a snarl and yelp and one of the wolves leaped at the sled-load of meat.

Caje jumped up with his tomahawk in his hand. He slashed down on the thick head once, twice, and the wolf lay still. There was a patter of feet on snow as the rest moved back. Behind him he heard the fire snapping and popping.

Desperately Caje looked around. He'd have to have wood. Cane burned too fast. There was a shagbark hickory about twenty feet away. A fallen oak lay beyond it.

Carefully he laid his plans. He drew the sled-load of meat as close to the fire as he could. He cut a lot of cane and heaped it on the fire. Then Caje grabbed the dead wolf and pulled it along the edge of the brake, away from the fallen oak. He

135

backed off and was glad to see the wolves leap upon the body, tearing at the thick fur.

"I reckon I'll be safe till they eat that 'un," Caje said half aloud as he hurried to the shagbark and stripped off great pieces of the bark. He fed part of this to the fire, then he went toward the fallen tree. He walked, though he wanted to run. But there was nothing that would set a wolf after you like running, Jared had always told him. So he tried not to hurry, even when one of the beasts turned away from the snarling, yelping pack around the dead wolf and followed him across the snow.

Caje turned quickly with raised tomahawk. "I'll bash your head, if'n you don't keep a keerful distance," he muttered aloud. The wolf drew back a step at the sound of the boy's voice. Caje was quick to see that and shouted, "Now git!" The wolf trotted back to the pack.

136

He made several trips to the fallen tree and got a good lot of wood. As he went, he sang, for the wolves fell back when he raised his voice. He sang about the blue bird nesting in a jay bird's eye, and the one about the old woman who fed her husband marrowbones to make him blind, and one of his mother's sad ones about lovers lost at sea. When at last he had gathered all the wood he wanted and sat down by the fire, he was really warm for the first time that day. After a little while by the fire, his head began to nod.

"I'll go to sleep, sure, a-setting here," he thought. He moved further away from the fire. He thought about cutting a piece of the bear meat and roasting it, but he decided against it. "Maybe if'n I stay hungry, it'll keep me awake," he told himself.

The wolves had finished the dead wolf now and some of them came to stare across the firelight at him. He stared back and by and by the gray faces blurred and he knew he was drifting

137

off to sleep. He moved further from the fire and rubbed snow on his face and hands.

Some of the wolves circled around toward him, edging closer.

"I'll sing," he said aloud. "It'll keep them varmints back a-ways and it'll keep me awake."

He sang one or two songs. He didn't rightly know all the words to them, but he did the best he could.

The wolves moved a little further back.

"I don't know no more songs, strangers," Caje went on good-naturedly. "I'll tell you the news from up yonder way. My pappy's done went off and left me. But he give me a good home afore he went. He did the very best he knowed how for me. It just took me a long time to find it out."

The night wore on. Two or three times Caje dropped off to sleep and woke to find the fire burned down low and the wolves coming nearer. He gathered more wood and finally he roasted some meat and ate it, for he didn't think he could get much hungrier and still live.

The wolves sat in a half circle, watching him. He forced his eyes open and sang his songs through again, though he was dizzy with weariness. He was never going to make it home to save his family. The night would never end. Soon the wolves would get him and the meat, and that would be an end of it.

It seemed years longer he sat there. His fire sputtered and sizzled. What was wrong with it? He got up once more to go for wood. It was raining! For a minute he could hardly believe it, he could only stand there with one hand out like a simpleton feeling the rain. It was raining! It had turned warm enough to rain.

But the fire! The rain would put the fire out and the wolves would have him then sure enough. He looked around wildly, wondering how to save himself. The wolves were gone. The night was nearly over, and the wolves were gone. The rain was too much for the varmints.

"I can go home now," he told himself aloud. He could follow this creek to the Tadlocks, he was pretty sure. He tightened the knots in his traces and set out over the snow.

The rain wet him to the skin in no time and he was half-frozen before he'd gone a hundred feet. But he didn't mind.

It was warm enough to rain. The hard winter was going to end after all. Spring was coming. He and the Tadlocks would live to plow the brown fields, to see the wide yellow blossoms on the poplar trees, to hear the redbird sing from the wild cherry tree.

The sun came up as he reached the foot of the hill. Sam was standing halfway down the hill in the snow, crimson with sunrise. "Sam!" Caje yelled.

Sam opened his mouth in astonishment. "Mammy!" he bawled finally. "It's Caje! He's come back. He's brung a heap of meat."

He began to run down the hill. His foot slipped and he went sliding down the drifts till he landed at Caje's feet. "I can't never get down this danged hill without falling," he said sorrowfully. And then Aunt Jess came running.

Caje slept by the hearth all morning. Once in a while he'd wake to hear the household sounds around him, and then he would go off to sleep again.

In the afternoon he woke, feeling rested and hungry. But still he lay on his pallet, watching the bright flames leap on the hearth. The cabin was full of the scent of cooking meat.

Wasn't it a good thing to have a warm cabin and a fire to come home to, Caje asked himself? Wasn't it fine to have a kettle of meat bubbling for supper, to have a pallet of quilts to lie on, and an old hound dog sleeping by your side? And wasn't it best to have folks around who were willing to look after you, come what may?

——*William O. Steele*

140

THINKING IT OVER

1. What part of this story seemed the most exciting to you?
2. Caje changed his mind about staying with the Tadlocks. Tell why Caje made the decision to
   - a. leave the Tadlocks forever and never come back.
   - b. go back to the Tadlocks, but leave when spring came.
   - c. stay on with the Tadlocks and help with the farm.
3. Think back to Whitey's adventure in "The New Spurs." Both he and Caje had problems in getting back home. Which boy do you think had the harder problem? Why?

THOUGHTS AT WORK

1. When Caje was in the wilderness, tell how he did the following:
   - a. kept warm. c. made a fire.
   - b. got food. d. kept awake.
2. Reread the seventh paragraph on page 138 and then list all Caje's troubles. Now tell about a bad day you have had. What happened to change it?
3. Tell the differences between how Caje's father and his Uncle Adam felt about "being beholden." Which one did Caje decide was right?
4. The characters in "Winter Danger" spoke in ways that may seem strange to you. Tell how you would say the lines below.
   - a. "I reckon I'll be safe till they eat that 'un."
   - b. "I'll bash your head, if'n you don't keep a keerful distance."
   - c. "I'll go to sleep, sure, a-setting here."
   - d. "It'll keep them varmints back a-ways. . . ."
   - e. "I'll tell you the news from up yonder way."
   - f. "I can't never get down this danged hill without falling."
5. In the beginning, Caje hated to be "beholden" to anybody. Think of a time when someone has given you something or has done something for you. How did you pay that person back?

The next two stories are related. The first story is an old Greek tale written almost 2,000 years ago. Perhaps it is true; perhaps it isn't. No one really knows. If you've never heard the story, you are in for a surprise! "Andy and the Lion," a modern story, was the first of several books James Daugherty both wrote and illustrated. Be ready to tell where he got the idea for his story.

Androcles and the Lion

Androcles,[1] a runaway slave, had fled to a forest for safety. He had not been there long when he saw a lion who was groaning with pain. He started to flee, but when he realized that the lion did not follow but only kept on groaning, Androcles turned and went to it. The lion, instead of rushing at him, put out a torn and bloody paw. Androcles, seeing the poor beast was in pain and wanting to help it, went up, took its paw, and examined it. Discovering a large thorn, the man pulled it out and thus relieved the pain. The grateful lion in return took Androcles to its cave and every day brought him food.

Sometime later both were captured and taken to Rome. Androcles was condemned to be killed by being thrown to a lion, which had not had food for several days. Androcles was led into the arena in the presence of the Emperor and his court. At the same time the lion was loosed. It came headlong toward its prey. But when it came near Androcles, instead of pouncing upon him, it jumped up and fawned upon him like a friendly dog. The Emperor, much surprised, ordered that Androcles be brought before him to tell his story.

The Emperor freed both the slave and the lion, for he thought such kindness and such gratitude were deserving of reward.

——*An Old Fable*

[1] Androcles (an'drə klēz)

Andy and the Lion

written and illustrated by James Daugherty

It was a bright day with just enough wind to float a flag. Andy started down to the library to get a book about lions. He took the book home and read and read. Andy read all through supper and he read all evening and just before bedtime his grandfather told him some tall stories about hunting lions in Africa. Every story ended with "and then I gave him both bar-r-r-e-l-l-s!" That night Andy dreamed all night long that he was in Africa hunting lions. When at last morning came Andy woke up. The sun was looking in at the window and Prince was tugging at the bed clothes. The lions had left but Andy kept thinking about them. Andy was still thinking lions after breakfast when his mother gave his hair a final brush and Andy started off to school.

Andy walked along swinging his books and whistling a tune. As he came to the turn in the road he noticed something sticking out from behind the big rock just at the bend. It looked very queer so Andy and Prince crept up cautiously to investigate. It moved! It was a lion! At this moment Andy thought he'd better be going and the lion thought so too. They ran and ran around the rock. Whichever way that Andy ran—there was the lion. Whichever way the lion ran—there was Andy. At last they both stopped for breath. The lion held out his paw to show Andy what was the matter. It was a big thorn stuck in his paw. But Andy had an idea. He told the lion to just be patient and they'd have that thorn out in no time. Fortunately Andy always carried his pliers in the back pocket of his overalls.

145

He took them out and got a tight grip. Then Andy braced one foot against the lion's paw and pulled with all his might until the thorn came out. The grateful lion licked Andy's face to show how pleased he was. But it was time to part. So they waved good-by. Andy went on to school and the lion went off about the business of being a lion.

In the spring the circus came to town. Of course Andy went. He wanted to see the famous lion act. Right in the middle of the act the biggest lion jumped out of the high steel cage and with a terrible roar dashed straight toward the people. They ran for their lives and in the scramble Andy found himself right in the lion's path. He thought his last moment had come. But then who should it be but Andy's own lion. They recognized each other and danced for joy. When the crowd came back ready to fight the lion and capture him, Andy stood in front of the lion and shouted to the angry people: "Do not hurt this lion. He's a friend of mine." Then the next day Andy led the lion and all the people in a grand parade down Main Street to City Hall. There the Mayor presented Andy with a medal for bravery. And the lion was very much pleased. And the next day Andy took the book back to the library.

———*James Daugherty*

THINKING IT OVER

1. Name as many things as you can that were the same in "Androcles and the Lion" and "Andy and the Lion." In what ways were the two stories different?
2. Is the *theme*, or lesson, taught in Mr. Daugherty's story the same as the *theme* of the Androcles story? Explain your answer by using examples from both stories.

THOUGHTS AT WORK

1. What surprised you in these stories? Do you think the events in both stories could have really happened? Why or why not?
2. Which author wrote his story to make you laugh? What made his story funny to you?
3. What do you think would have happened if Andy did not have the pliers with him?
4. Make up a modern-day fable that teaches a lesson. Your story can be funny or serious.

In Central Park, in New York City, there is a statue of a man sitting on a bench reading from a book. Maybe you have never seen the statue, but you have heard the man's name—Hans Christian Andersen. He is famous the world over for his stories. You may have read *The Emperor's New Clothes* or *The Steadfast Tin Soldier*. In this short biography of Hans Andersen, you will learn something about the man who wrote these tales. Perhaps you will understand why he became famous.

The Real "Ugly Duckling"

Once upon a time, more than a hundred years ago, there lived a boy named Hans Christian Andersen. He was the only child of a poor cobbler and his wife. The three lived in one room of a house in Odense[1] in Denmark. Here Hans Christian's father had his cobbler's bench where he worked making and repairing shoes. Because he was not a very good cobbler, only the poorest customers came to him, and not very many of them.

In their only room, near the cobbler's bench, there was a big bed with Hans Christian's small bed shoved under it during the daytime. And in a corner of the room was the kitchen where his mother did the very simple cooking for the family. There were white, starched curtains at the windows of this humble little house, and Anne-Marie, the mother, kept their single room clean and as neat as the crowded space allowed.

Hans Christian was a happy boy. His father and mother loved him dearly and did all they could for their son. His father made him a toy theater and his mother showed Hans Christian how to make clothing for his cardboard actors and actresses out of bright scraps left over from the dressmaking of the wealthy ladies whose washing Anne-Marie did now and then.

Also living in Odense was Hans Christian's grandmother. She, too, was very poor. But she knew hundreds of folk tales and would tell these tales of magic and adventure to her grandson whenever he came to see her.

[1] Odense (o′ᵮHen se)

Hans Christian loved these old tales. He made plays from them which he acted out with his toy actors in his toy theater. Slowly, the idea came to him that he would like to be an actor someday, himself. He dreamed of going to the great city of Copenhagen[2] and there winning riches and fame. So certain was he of his future, that he boasted of it to everyone. He would even prove his talent on the spot, reciting poetry and dancing for anyone who would stop to listen and watch.

Now his dreams might have been all right if Hans Christian had been talented. But, alas, a less likely actor could hardly be imagined than young Andersen.

To begin with, he was as homely a lad as ever was born into the world. He was tall for his age and clumsy. His legs seemed much too long for his body. His feet were overlarge, and so was his nose. Indeed, he looked somewhat like the storks which came to Denmark with every spring, and which were supposed to bring good luck with them. Whenever he danced, his audiences were overcome with laughter. There was no grace in his lanky, clumsy body and no gaiety in his long, sad face.

Still, the laughter seemed not to discourage Hans Christian. He knew very well that other boys did not recite poetry, nor did they entertain their friends with dances. He was the only one among the boys he knew who played by the hour with a toy theater. He simply was not like other boys in Odense. They could not

[2] Copenhagen (kō′pən hā′gən)

understand his interests, and his fine dreams of future glory seemed silly in anyone who showed so little promise. His mother knew that he was different too, but she had faith in him and was always gentle and loving.

When Hans Christian was seven years old, his father had marched away to war and Hans Christian and his mother shared the single room alone. It was during this period that his mother took him out of school because the boy often suffered fainting spells. Once in a great while, he managed to get to the theater and with every visit his desire to be an actor grew.

Later, when Hans Christian's father returned home, he was a broken man and soon after died. Now Anne-Marie had to support herself and her son. She did so by washing clothes for her neighbors. All day she stood in a cold river, beating the linens against a large rock. It was hard work and her health began to fail. To help out, young Hans Christian tried working in a cloth mill and then in a tobacco factory. But fainting spells forced him to leave both jobs.

Now it happened that Hans Christian could sing as well as recite poetry. He had a beautiful voice. At the tobacco factory, he was often asked to lighten the long hours for his fellow workers by standing on a bench and entertaining them with song. The stagestruck lad enjoyed this greatly and he sang with a will as often as he was asked. Because he sang so well, his audience did not laugh at him even though he looked so odd and seemed so different from themselves.

By the time Hans Christian was fourteen, his mind was made up. He determined to leave Odense and seek his fortune in the great city of Copenhagen. Like a lad in a fairy tale, he took leave of his mother, and with only a few coins in his pocket, he started out. His grandmother bade him a tearful farewell. He was never to see her again, but he never forgot the stories she had told him.

Arriving in Copenhagen, he went at once to the Royal Theater to get work as an actor. A man connected with the theater in Odense arranged for Hans Christian to meet a dancer at the Royal Theater. Hans Andersen was certain that when he met her, his future would be assured. His trust in people had always been as great as his trust in himself.

With the luck of a lad in a fairy tale, Hans Christian was shown into the living room of the celebrated Madame Schall.[3] She was completely astonished at the sight of her visitor. He greeted her wearing a shabby suit, high boots, and a top hat which fell down over his face. Removing the hat, Hans Christian at once began to tell Madame Schall all his hopes and dreams. Caught somehow by his very earnestness and his hopelessly funny appearance, the kind woman invited him to dance. At this, Hans Christian asked if he might take off his boots, and holding the hat as if he were beating time on it, he danced.

As Madame Schall watched the tall, thin, clumsy figure circling and leaping around her living room, it

[3] Madame Schall (mad′əm schôl)

153

suddenly occurred to her that the boy must be insane. She stopped his graceless antics at last and as gently and kindly as she could, informed him that he had no talent for dancing whatsoever. At this news, Hans Christian burst into tears. This so moved the dancer's heart that she promised to speak to the ballet-master at the Royal Theater about him. She added that Hans Christian could come and eat now and then at her house. Thus comforted, Hans Christian left rejoicing. Now he knew someone in the Royal Theater. His future was assured! But it wasn't, as he soon learned.

Other people in Copenhagen were kind too, and they gave Hans Christian good advice. Yet, they criticized him honestly and called him foolish to think that he could succeed in the theater. Although they meant it all for his own good, Hans Christian wept as he listened to their discouraging words. But his heart was not discouraged. The search for fame and fortune was going to be harder than he thought it would be, that was all. Hadn't he comforted his mother when he left home by saying, "First you suffer a great deal, then you become famous"?

Hans Christian did suffer a great deal. His suit became utterly ragged and his shoes were full of holes. Often he had nothing at all to eat, and only his dreams to warm him. But at last, just as in a fairy tale, luck smiled upon him.

Convinced at last that there was no hope of his ever becoming a dancer, Hans Christian decided to stake all on his singing voice. He knew he could sing. So, with his usual reckless confidence, he presented himself one evening at the home of a famous singing teacher named Siboni.[4] Great was the housekeeper's astonishment, when she answered his ring at the door, to find standing there a ragged youth, tall, lanky, and homely. She must have thought him a rather bold beggar, and she told him quickly that Siboni was at dinner with his guests. She was about to shut the door in his face when the boy began pouring out his sad story to her. He spoke with such earnestness that her heart was moved, as were so many hearts moved by the simple trust of this strange lad. She told him to wait and she would announce him to her master.

Going to the dining room, the housekeeper told Siboni about the boy waiting outside and repeated much of the story he had told her. Siboni and his three guests were interested. All of them were artists in one way or another. One was a poet, another a musician. Siboni, himself, was a famous singer. They were the kind of people Hans Christian had long dreamed of joining. Now his dream was about to come true. Siboni invited him in and asked him to sing. Next Hans Christian recited poetry. But his nervousness at being with this group of artists, whom he admired above anyone in the world, overcame him. When he reached an especially moving point in the poem, his eyes filled with tears. But instead of laughing at this deep feeling

[4] Siboni (si bō′nē)

155

as everyone else had always done, this audience applauded him. They too were men of deep feeling, and they could recognize another artist when they met him. It mattered not to them that this boy stood before them in rags. They recognized his gifts.

This performance gained Hans Christian a promise of singing lessons and food from the kind-hearted Siboni. It did seem as if Hans Christian's luck had changed.

Then, shortly after his fifteenth birthday, his voice changed. He could no longer sing. Now he decided that, since he couldn't sing and since he couldn't act, he would write plays for other actors. Immediately he thought of himself as a poet and was still sure that someday he would be great. In a very short time he turned out a play and presented it to the Royal Theater. It was immediately refused. He wrote another play and it too was refused. But fortune was again beginning to smile upon this determined youth. The plays had caught the attention of a very powerful citizen of Copenhagen — Jonas Collin.

Hans Christian Andersen had received almost no schooling during his sixteen years. The plays clearly showed this. Jonas Collin was worried that a boy of his age without any education might get into trouble. He cared nothing at all about Hans Christian's dream of becoming a great poet. But Jonas Collin knew that without an education he could not become a good and useful citizen. So he arranged to have Hans Christian sent to school.

The years that followed were hard ones. This tall, lanky youth of sixteen had to sit in the classroom with the very smallest children. For although he was able to read, he knew almost nothing of grammar or arithmetic or spelling. Only the friendship of the Collin family made it possible for Hans Christian to get through these long, hard years, when he worked and suffered insults not only from his schoolmates but from many of his teachers. Through it all he kept warm his hope of someday becoming a famous writer.

The day came at last when he finished his education and with the help of Jonas Collin he could spend all his time writing. His first book was a collection of poems. Next he wrote a novel. The book was well received, but no one remembers it now. For, while Hans Christian was waiting for his book to appear, he entertained himself by writing fairy tales. Remembering the stories his grandmother had told to him when he was only a little boy, Hans Christian, now thirty, began writing his own tales of magic and adventure.

He wrote them with such grace and charm that a book publisher immediately accepted them. The first fairy tale was called "The Tinder Box." This little book was followed by three more stories. Nothing like them had ever been published before. Sometimes borrowing from the stories he remembered, sometimes making up entirely new ones, Andersen wrote with such homely wisdom and humor, that the stories began to win readers not only in Denmark but in other countries.

Some people thought Andersen was wasting his time. But the children didn't think so! Nor did their parents. More and more tales began to appear and at last they were all gathered together in one book. Almost overnight, Andersen found himself famous. Everyone was reading his fairy tales, and they were being written in other languages. The King of Denmark invited him to dinner, and as time went by, Andersen became a close friend of this good man.

Indeed, he became the friend of all the outstanding writers in Europe. Wherever he went, people pointed him out. "There goes the author of 'The Little Mermaid'," they would say. "There goes Hans Christian Andersen. He wrote 'The Ugly Duckling'."

One day he was invited to be the guest of the city of Odense. He had returned to his childhood home a few times to see his mother before she died. But now he was coming as a guest of Odense. All the citizens wanted to do honor to this famous son of their city. And the night he arrived there, he found the whole city lighted in his honor. Every square was bright with lights, and along the streets candles had been set in the windows of all the houses. As he looked at the lights and listened to the songs sung in his honor, his heart overflowed with happiness. When he had been a poor boy, laughed at and made fun of on these same streets, he had never dreamed that he could one day be so happy. He had suffered but now he was famous.

Later, when he came to write the story of his life, he said that it had been like a fairy tale. And indeed it had. For the boy who had been born the son of a poor cobbler had become the friend of kings.

——*Doris Gates*

THINKING IT OVER

1. Hans Christian Andersen said that his life had been like a fairy tale. Do you agree? Why?
2. What events in the story show that Hans Christian believed in himself and trusted other people?
3. Why do you think Hans Christian was finally able to succeed in what he wanted to do?

THOUGHTS AT WORK

1. Name the people who had faith in Hans Christian and thought he would succeed. How did these people help him?
2. Make a list of the words or phrases found on pages 150 and 153 that you think best describe Hans Christian.
3. When Hans Christian left home, he told his mother, "First you suffer a great deal, then you become famous." In what ways did Hans Christian suffer before he became famous?
4. Describe someone you know who, like Hans Christian, is different from others. Have you ever made fun of someone who seemed different?
5. Why hadn't Hans Christian finished school when he was a child? Who helped him return to school?
6. Do you think Hans would have been able to write his fairy stories if he hadn't returned to school? Explain your answer.
7. Make a list of fairy tales written by Hans Christian Andersen. Read one tale from your list. Then tell what you liked about it.

I HAVE FELT LONELY

I have felt lonely, forgotten
or even left out, set apart
from the rest of the world.
I never wanted out. If anything I wanted in.

—Arthur Jackson, Age 15

OUTWITTED

He drew a circle that shut me out—
Heretic, rebel, a thing to flout.
But Love and I had the wit to win:
We drew a circle that took him in!

—Edwin Markham

161

THE UGLY DUCKLING

Have you ever called anyone an *ugly duckling*? After reading this story, one of Andersen's most famous tales, you will understand better what the expression means. In his stories Andersen liked to include wise sayings and lessons for his readers to think about. What did he want you to think about in this story? Can you guess where he got his idea for "The Ugly Duckling"?

It was glorious out in the country. It was summer. The cornfields were yellow, the oats were green, and the hay had been put in stacks in the green meadows. The stork went about on his long red legs and chattered Egyptian,[1] for this was the language he had learned from his good mother. All around the fields and meadows were great forests, and in the middle of these forests lay deep lakes. Yes, it was glorious out in the country.

In the midst of the sunshine there lay an old farm with deep canals about it. Near the water grew great burdocks, so high that little children could stand upright under the tallest of them. And here, where it was as wild as in the deepest wood, sat a duck upon her nest, waiting to hatch her ducklings. How long she had waited with seldom a visitor! The other ducks liked better to swim about in the canals than to sit down under a burdock and gossip with her.

At last one eggshell after another broke open and from all the eggs little heads stuck out.

"Peep! Peep!" they said. And they all came tumbling out as fast as they could, looking all round them under the green leaves. And the mother let them look as much as they chose, for green is good for the eyes.

"How wide the world is!" said all the young ones, for they certainly had much more room now than when they were in the eggs.

"Do you think this is all the world?" said the mother.

[1] Egyptian (i jip'shən)

"It stretches far across the other side of the garden, quite into the parson's field. But I have never been there yet. I hope you are all together," and she stood up. "No, I have not all. The largest egg still lies there. How long is this to last? I am really tired of it." And she sat down again.

"Well, how goes it?" asked an old duck who had come to pay her a visit.

"It lasts a long time with that one egg," said the duck who sat there. "It will not crack. Now, only look at the others. Are they not the prettiest little ducks one could possibly see? They are all like their father."

"Let me see the egg which will not hatch," said the old visitor. "You may be sure it is a turkey's egg. I was once cheated in that way, and had much anxiety and trouble with the young ones, for they are afraid of the water. I hate to tell you, but I couldn't get them to go in. I quacked and I clacked, but it was no use. Let me see the egg. Yes, that's a turkey's egg. Let it lie there while you teach the other children to swim."

"I think I will sit on it a little longer," said the duck. "I've sat so long now that I can sit a few days more."

At last the great egg broke. "Peep! Peep!" said the little one, as it crept forth. It was very large and very ugly. The duck looked at it.

"What a very large duckling," said she. "None of the others look like that. Can it really be a turkey chick? Well, we shall soon find out. It must go into the water, even if I have to push it in myself."

The next day was bright and beautiful. The sun shone on all the green trees as the mother duck went down to the canal with all her family. Splash! She jumped into the water. "Quack! Quack!" she said, and one duckling after another plunged in. The water closed over their heads, but they came up in an instant and swam expertly. Their legs went of themselves, and they were all in the water. The ugly gray duckling swam with them.

"No, it's not a turkey," said the mother duck. "See how well it uses its legs, and how straight it holds itself. It is my own child! On the whole, it's quite pretty if one looks at it rightly. Quack! Quack! Come with me, and I'll lead you out into the great world and present you in the duck yard. But keep close to me so that no one may tread on you, and watch out for the cats!"

And so they came into the duck yard. A terrible row was going on there, for two families were quarreling over an eel's head. And the cat got it after all.

"See how it goes in the world," said the mother duck, and she rubbed her bill into the ground, for she too wanted the eel's head. "Now, use your legs. Shake yourselves and don't turn in your toes. A well-brought-up duck turns its toes well out, just like father and mother—so! Now bend your necks and say, 'Quack!'"

And they did. But the other ducks round about looked at them and said angrily, "Look there. Now we're to have these ducklings hanging on, as if there were not enough of us already! And—ugh—how that duckling yonder looks. We won't stand that!" And one duck flew up at the ugly duckling and bit it in the neck.

"Let it alone," said the mother. "It does no harm to anyone."

"Yes, but it's too large and peculiar," said the duck who had bitten it, "and therefore it must be put down."

"Those are pretty children the mother has there," said an old duck with a rag around her leg. The rag meant that she was very special. "They're all pretty but the big one, and it was rather unlucky. I wish she could hatch it over again."

"That cannot be done, my lady," replied the mother duck. "The big duckling isn't pretty, but it has a really good disposition and swims as well as any other. Yes,

I may even say it swims better. I think it will grow up pretty and become smaller in time." Then she pinched the ugly duckling in the neck and smoothed its feathers. "Moreover it is a drake," she said, "and therefore his appearance is not so important. I think he will be very strong. He makes his way already."

"The other ducklings are graceful enough," said the old duck. "Make yourselves at home, and if you find an eel's head, you may bring it to me."

And now they were at home. But the poor duckling, which had crept last out of the egg and looked so ugly, was bitten and pushed and made fun of, as much by the ducks as by the chickens.

"He is too big," they all said. And the turkey cock, who had been born with spurs and therefore thought

himself an emperor, blew himself up like a ship in full sail and bore straight down upon the ugly duckling. Then he gobbled and grew quite red in the face. The poor duckling did not know where he should stand or walk. He was sad because he looked so ugly, the joke of the whole duck yard.

So it went on the first day. And afterwards it became worse and worse. The poor duckling was hunted about by every one. Even his brothers and sisters were quite angry with him and said, "If only the cat would catch you, you ugly creature." And the mother said, "If only you were far away." And the ducks bit him, and the chickens beat him, and the girl who had to feed the poultry kicked at him with her foot.

Then he ran and flew over the fence, and the little birds in the bushes flew up in fear.

"That is because I am so ugly," thought the duckling. And he shut his eyes and flew farther on. And so he came out into the great marsh where the wild ducks lived. Here he lay a long while, weary and sad.

Toward evening he left the marsh and wandering on, came to a miserable little hut. It was so dilapidated that it did not know on which side it should fall, and so it remained standing. A storm was coming up and the wind whistled around the duckling in such a way that the poor creature could hardly stand against it. And the wind blew harder and harder. Then the duckling noticed that one of the hinges of the door had given way, and the door hung slanting so that the duckling could slip through the crack into the room. And that is what he did.

Here lived a woman with her cat and her hen. The cat could arch his back and purr and give out sparks when his fur was stroked the wrong way. The hen had quite short legs, but she laid good eggs and the woman loved her as her own child.

In the morning the strange duckling was noticed at once. The cat began to purr and the hen to cluck.

"What's this?" said the woman looking all around. But she could not see well, and therefore she thought the duckling was a fat duck that had strayed. "This is a rare prize!" she said. "Now I shall have duck's eggs. I hope it is not a drake."

And so the duckling was admitted to the hut on trial for three weeks. But no eggs came. And the cat was master of the house and the hen was the lady. They always said, "We and the world," for they thought they were half the world, and by far the better half. The duckling thought one might have different opinions, but the hen would not allow it.

"Can you lay eggs?" she asked.

"No."

"Then will you hold your tongue?"

And the cat said, "Can you arch your back and purr and give out sparks?"

"No."

"Then you will please have no opinion of your own when sensible folks are speaking."

And the duckling sat in a corner and was very sad. Then one day the fresh air and the sunshine streamed in. The duckling was seized with a strange longing to swim on the water. He felt he had to speak of his longing to the hen.

"What are you thinking of?" cried the hen. "You have nothing to do. That's why you have these fancies. Lay eggs or purr and they will pass over."

"But it is so delightful to swim on the water," said the duckling. "It is so refreshing to let it close above one's head, and to dive down to the bottom."

"Yes, that must be a mighty pleasure, I am sure," said the hen. "I think you've gone crazy. Ask the cat about it. He's the cleverest animal I know. Ask him if he likes to swim on the water, or to dive down. I won't speak about myself!"

"You don't understand me," said the duckling.

"We don't understand you. Then pray who is to understand you? You surely don't pretend to be cleverer than the cat. I won't say anything of myself. Don't be a conceited child. And thank your Maker for all the kindness you have received. Did you not get into a warm room and have you not fallen into company from which you may learn something? But you are a chatterer, and it is not pleasant to associate with you. You may believe me, I speak for your own good. I tell you disagreeable things, and by that you may know I'm your true friend. Only take care that you learn to lay eggs, or to purr and give out sparks!"

"I think I will go out into the wide world," said the duckling.

"Yes, do go," replied the hen.

And so the duckling went away. It swam on the water and dived, but it was ignored by every creature because of its ugliness.

Now came the autumn. The leaves in the forest turned yellow and brown. The wind caught them so that they danced about. Up in the air it was very cold. The clouds hung low, heavy with hail and snowflakes. The poor little duckling did not have an easy time of it.

One evening—the sun was just setting in its beauty—there came a whole flock of great, handsome birds out of the reeds. They were dazzlingly white, with long necks. They were swans. They uttered a very peculiar cry, spread forth their glorious great wings, and flew away from that cold region to warmer lands, to fair open lakes. They mounted so high, so high that the duckling felt quite strange as he watched them. He turned round and round in the water like a wheel, stretched out his neck toward them, and uttered such a strange, loud cry that he frightened himself.

As soon as he could see the handsome creatures no

longer, he dived down to the very bottom of the pond, and when he came up again, he was quite beside himself. Oh, he could not forget those beautiful, happy birds. He knew not their name and he knew not where they were flying. But he loved them more than he had ever loved anyone. He was not at all envious of them. How could he think of wishing for such loveliness as they had? He would have been glad if only the farmyard ducks would have endured his company — the poor, ugly creature!

And the winter grew cold, very cold. The duckling was forced to swim about in the water to prevent the surface from freezing entirely. But it would be too sad to tell all the misery and care which the duckling had to endure in the hard winter. Soon spring had arrived. The duckling lay out on the marsh among the reeds for the sun began to get warm again and the larks to sing.

Then all at once the duckling could flap his wings. They beat the air more strongly than before and bore him swiftly away. Before he well knew how all this happened, he found himself in a great garden where the willow trees bent their long green branches down to the canal that wound through the region. Oh, here it was so beautiful, such a gladness of spring! Suddenly, from the thicket came three glorious white swans. They rustled their wings and swam lightly on the water. The duckling knew the splendid creatures and felt a sudden weight of sadness.

"I will fly away to them, to the royal birds. They will beat me because I, who am so ugly, dare to come near them. But it is all the same. Better to be killed by *them* than to be bitten by ducks, and beaten by fowls, and pushed about by the girl who takes care of the poultry yard, and to suffer hunger in winter!"

He flew out into the water and swam toward the beautiful swans. They looked at him and came sailing down upon him with outspread wings.

"Kill me!" said the poor creature. He bent his head down upon the water, expecting nothing but death. But what was this that he saw in the clear water? He beheld his own image. And, lo, he was no longer a clumsy, dark-gray bird, ugly and hateful to look at, but a — swan!

It matters nothing if one is born in a duck yard if one has only lain in a swan's egg.

The ugly duckling felt quite glad at all the misfortune he had suffered, now that he realized his happiness in all the splendor that surrounded him. And the great swans swam round him and stroked him with their bills.

Into the garden came little children who threw bread and corn into the water. The youngest cried, "There is a new swan!" And the other children shouted with joy, "Yes, a new one has arrived." They clapped their hands and danced about, and ran to their father and mother. Bread and cake were thrown into the water and they all said, "The new swan is the most beautiful of all, so young and handsome!" And the old swans bowed their heads before him.

Then he felt quite ashamed and hid his head under his wings, for he did not know what to do. He was so happy and yet not at all proud. He thought how he had been persecuted and hated. And now he heard the children saying that he was the most beautiful of all birds. Even the willow tree bent its branches straight down into the water before him. The sun shone warm and mild. Then his wings rustled, he lifted his slender neck and cried rejoicingly from the depths of his heart, "I never dreamed of so much happiness when I was the Ugly Duckling."

——*Hans Christian Andersen*

THINKING IT OVER

1. Why were Hans Christian and the ugly duckling unhappy? How did they both find happiness?

2. Where do you think Hans Christian got his idea for this story? Who really was the ugly duckling?

3. When people believe in themselves and what they are doing, they have confidence. Why didn't the ugly duckling have confidence in himself? When did he find confidence?

THOUGHTS AT WORK

1. Tell how the ducks and chickens in the duck yard treated the ugly duckling. Why did they treat him in this way?

2. Think of a time when someone made fun of you. How did you feel? What did you do about it?

3. To help us understand how humans behave, Andersen made the animals talk and act like people. Tell in what ways the following animals talked and acted like people:
     a. the ugly duckling
     b. the ugly duckling's brothers and sisters
     c. the old duck with a rag around her leg
     d. the hen who lived in the little hut

4. Just like a human mother, the mother duck defended her duckling. Find examples of this on pages 165–167.

5. What to you was the happiest part of this fairy tale? What was the saddest part?

6. "What you are inside is more important than how you look or where you come from." Why do you think this saying is true of the ugly duckling? Think of an example to show what this saying means to you.

7. Use your imagination and think of how the ugly duckling's egg might have gotten into the duck's nest.

THREE SHORT STORIES

All of the selections so far in Unit II have been written by adults. The next three short stories will show you that children too can write about their experiences. If you read carefully, you can learn something about these young authors as they tell their stories. How do their stories make you feel? Where do you think they live? Are they like people you know?

The Lost Key

Joyce lived in California in a large city. She liked people and it was very nice and hot in California. Every day before school, her father would go over to her cousin's house and leave her little sister. Then Joyce would pick her sister up after school.

One day she stayed after school and played tetherball with another girl. She told the girl to hold her door key. The girl held the key and forgot and took it home with her. Joyce did not know where the little girl lived. She looked everywhere but could not find the girl with her door key. She and her sister had to wait outdoors very, very late until someone came home from work.

——G. W., Age 9

GOING FISHING

Jobie and his brother were going fishing. His brother brought the tackle. Jobie's uncle has a motor boat. They went to the beach. He started the motor and they were off. On the way, Jobie fell out of the boat and he almost drowned. His big brother jumped into the water and pulled him into the boat. He had some extra clothes in the boat. Jobie changed into dry clothes. His brother caught two fish. His uncle caught three fish and Jobie caught one fish. On the way home they went to Burger King and bought five whopper burgers.

——D. J. R., Age 10

THE NIGHT AT THE DRUGSTORE

In January when we had that snow storm, about nine o'clock, my grandmother did not feel well. So my brother and I had to go to the drugstore to get some medicine for her.

When we got outside, it was snowing lightly. We walked five blocks to the drugstore. When we got into the store, a man with a black jacket and blue cap that covered his face stuck a gun in my brother's back and said to us, "This is a hold-up." There were six of them, four were dressed in brown jackets and dark green caps that covered their faces.

The one who stuck the gun in my brother's back told us to go to the back of the store. When we got there, the owner was on the floor. The stick-up men took all his money and then some things from the store. After that, they locked him, my brother and me in the bathroom. The owner told us we would have to wait for someone to come to the store and open the door. About fifteen minutes later a man did come.

Then the owner called the police, and I called my mother. My aunt answered the phone. I told her that the drugstore had been held up. Then she told my mother, and she said that they were coming to get us.

The police came and they asked us questions, and then my mother and aunt took us home. When we got home, they asked us what had happened, and were we afraid? We told them yes.

This is a real story.

—Calvin D., Age 14

178

THINKING IT OVER

1. After reading the stories, what could you tell about each of the authors? Where do you think they lived?
2. Which story did you like the best? What did you especially like about the story?
3. Pretend that one of the three stories happened to you. How would you have acted?

THOUGHTS AT WORK

1. If you could talk with the three authors, what questions would you ask them about their stories?
2. If you could choose different titles for these three stories, what titles would you give them? Explain your choices.
3. What do you know about city life? How did these stories help you to understand a little more about people and life in a large city?
4. Name the problem in each story and tell how it was solved.
5. Were some parts in the stories not completely explained? What were they? How would you explain them?
6. You have now read stories that other children have written. Write a story of your own about something that happened to you.

Cowboys were proud of their abilities and perhaps a little distrustful of newcomers who didn't understand and appreciate the rugged ways of life in the Old West. Many of the stories which grew out of the cowboys' experiences were set to music and sung around the campfires. This ballad tells of a trick some cowboys played on a newcomer they thought was a greenhorn.

THE ZEBRA DUN

We were camped on the plains at the head of the Cimmaron,
When along came a stranger who stopped to argue some.
He looked so very foolish, we began to look around;
We thought he was a greenhorn just escaped from town.

Such an educated fellow, his thoughts just came in herds;
He astonished all those cowboys with his jaw-breaking words.
He just kept on talking till he made the boys all sick
And they began to think to see how they could play a trick.

He said he'd lost his job out on the Santa Fe,
Was bound across the plains now to strike the Seven D.
We asked him how it happened; he said, "Trouble with the boss,"
And asked if he could borrow a fat saddle horse.

This tickled all the boys to death, they laughed up their sleeves:
"We will lend you a fine horse, fresh and fat as you please."
Shorty grabbed a lariat and roped the Zebra Dun
And gave him to the stranger while we waited for the fun.

Old Dunny was an outlaw that had grown so awfully wild
That he could paw the moon down, he could jump for a mile;
But Dunny stood there still, just as if he didn't know,
Until we had him saddled and all readied to go.

When the stranger hit the saddle, old Dunny quit the earth
And traveled right straight upward for all that he was worth,
Pitching, squealing, screaming, and throwing wall-eyed fits,
His hind feet perpendicular, his front feet in the bits.

We could see the tops of mountains under Dunny's every jump,
But the stranger seemed to grow there, just like a camel's hump;
The stranger sat upon him and curled his black moustache
Like a summer boarder waiting for the hash.

He thumped him on the shoulders, and he spurred him when
    he whirled;
He showed all those cowpunchers who was top man in this
    world;
And when he had dismounted and stood there on the ground,
We knew he was a cowboy and not a gent from town.

The boss was standing close by, watching all the show;
He walked up to the stranger and said he needn't go:
"If you can use a lasso like you rode the Zebra Dun,
You're the man I've been looking for since the year One."

He spent the season with us, and the cowboys all agreed
There was nothing that he couldn't do, save stopping a
    stampede.
So there's one thing and a sure thing I've learned since I have
    been born,
Every educated fellow's not a plumb greenhorn.

——*An American Ballad*

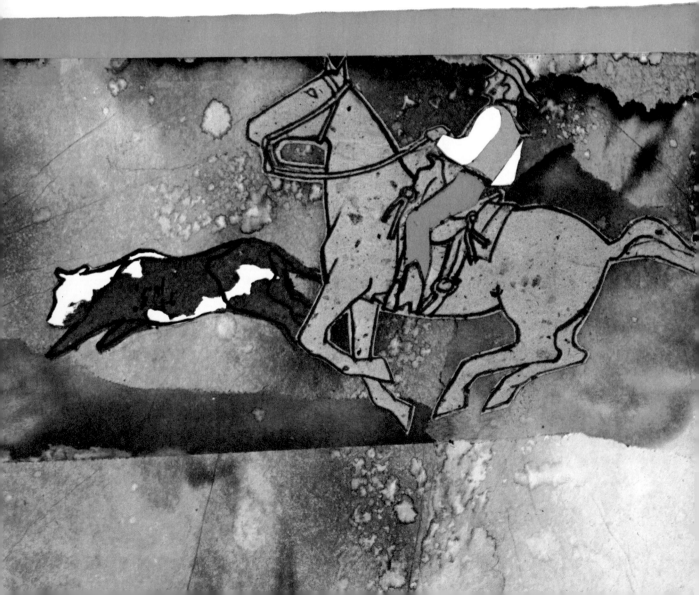

✦❧BIBLIOGRAPHY❧✦

Meeting with a Stranger, by Duane Bradley.
  Should a young Ethiopian sheepherder change his ways and learn from the pink-faced American, or remain loyal to his tribal customs?

The White Bird, by Clyde Bulla.
  A captured bird helps a lonely pioneer boy understand friendship and loyalty.

Cinders, by Katherine Gibson.
  When the good fairy forgets to turn Cinderella's coachman back into a mouse at midnight, a new story begins.

Visit to a Chief's Son; An American Boy's Adventure with an African Tribe, by Robert Halmi.
  With his stepfather on hand to photograph their experiences, Kevin and his new African friend discover and laugh about their differences.

Half-Breed, by Evelyn Sibley Lampman.
  Should he be "Pale-eyes" and live with his Indian mother, or be Hardy Hollingshead and live with his white father? This was the choice a boy had to make in this story based on a real situation.

Ben and Me, By Robert Lawson.
  Important events in the life of Ben Franklin are told from a mouse's point of view.

Captured by the Abnakis, by Clem Philbrook.
  Two pioneer boys, captured by Indians, lived to tell this true story which took place in 1695.

Fables from Aesop, retold by James Reeves.
  Famous short tales, mostly about animals, with wise lessons and observations about the way humans behave.

Old Tales of the Sea

Powerful, dangerous, and mysterious, the sea has always captured man's imagination. Since earliest times he has told stories about the sea. The old tales of this unit, about imaginary people and make-believe happenings, were told and retold for hundreds of years before they were written down. You will see why these stories are still remembered and enjoyed.

The Battle
That
Tilted the Sea

This folk tale takes place in the South Pacific on an island called Raiatea (rä yä tā'ä). The island is protected from the rough open sea by a natural wall, or reef, made from the shells of millions and millions of tiny coral sea animals. Through openings, or channels, in the reef the sea flows into a lagoon which surrounds the island. The calm water of the lagoon is a perfect place for fishing and swimming — usually. The people of Raiatea had a real problem. You decide whether their solution is real or not.

Once, because two boys of Opoa[1] went fishing in a holy place, the island of Raiatea was destroyed by a flood. Several hundreds of years later the waters withdrew, and men lived there again.

The chief of the island at this time was a man named Covered-with-Scars, and he had a ten-year-old son called Hiro.[2]

Hiro was a very wise and cunning boy. He knew many things that most boys don't bother to learn about. For instance, he knew where the bush turkeys buried delicious eggs on the sandy beaches. He knew where the best breadfruit grew. He knew the best pools in which to catch grouper, parrot fish, and bonito. And he knew all about the great sea monsters that guarded the openings in the coral reefs around the islands. In fact, Hiro knew so much that his father, Covered-with-Scars, often asked his advice about important matters.

One day Covered-with-Scars said to Hiro, "My son, I am very troubled."

"What about, Father?" asked Hiro.

"Too many sharks are getting past the guardian of our reef into the lagoon," said Hiro's father. "Ten of my people have been eaten by them in the past week alone. If this keeps up, we won't have anybody left alive on the island. What do you suppose is the matter?"

Hiro thought for a minute, then said, "The giant octopus that guards our reef must have gone to sleep again, Father. That's my opinion."

[1] Opoa (ä pō′ə)   [2] Hiro (hir′ō)

Covered-with-Scars nodded. "That's what I think too," he said.

"Shall I go and wake him up?" asked Hiro.

"It won't do any good, I'm afraid," said Hiro's father. "He'll stay awake for a few days and then fall asleep again, letting the sharks come into the lagoon as they please. No, Hiro. We need a better answer to our shark problem than that lazy old octopus."

"He may be lazy," Hiro defended the octopus stoutly, "but he's a fine shark fighter. When he's awake, no shark can get past him, Father. He's not like the giant turtle that guards the Tahaa[3] reef, or the giant eel that stands in the passage to Bora Bora.[4] They stay awake all the time, it's true, but they can't fight sharks as well as our lazy octopus."

"Be that as it may," said Covered-with-Scars, "something must be done to protect our people from the sharks. Have you any ideas, Hiro?"

"Give me a little time," said Hiro. "Perhaps I can think of something."

"Take all the time you need, my son," said Hiro's father. "But be sure you think up a cunning plan— one better than waking up that sleepy old octopus."

So Hiro went off and thought a long time about how he could protect the people of the island from the sharks. And he finally thought of a possible way to do it. But he wasn't sure it would work, and he said nothing to his father about his plan.

[3] Tahaa (tä hä'ä)   [4] Bora Bora (bôr'ä bôr'ä)

196

Instead, he swam far out in the lagoon the next morning, all by himself. He floated around out there until he saw a big shark that had come in through the reef opening past the sleeping octopus. The shark saw Hiro at the same time and came swimming up to take Hiro in one bite for his breakfast. But just as he opened his mouth wide to snap off Hiro's leg, Hiro cried out in a loud voice, "Wait, shark! Do not eat me! I have a message for your master, the King of the Sharks!"

"That doesn't sound very likely," said the shark, shutting his mouth so his sharp teeth wouldn't show.

"All I want," said Hiro, "is a chance to talk to your king."

"Get on my back and I'll take you to him," said the shark. "And if you've lied to me about having a message for him, I'll eat you up then."

So Hiro mounted the shark's rough back and held onto his big dorsal fin tightly. He was carried as swift as an arrow through the reef opening into the great ocean. There—deep, deep down under the waves—the King of the Sharks lay on the sea bottom, covered with barnacles, sand, and seaweed.

"This boy on my back says he has a message for you, Master," said the shark on which Hiro was riding.

The King of the Sharks moved his tremendous body slightly so that the barnacles and seaweed began to slip off his skin. "What is your message, boy?" asked the King of the Sharks.

"I thought you'd want to know," replied Hiro, "that the giant turtle who guards the reef opening at Tahaa tells everybody that you're getting old and weak. He says you can no longer conquer even the weakest reef guardian of the islands. The turtle of Tahaa challenges you to a battle, Your Majesty."

At once the King of the Sharks became very angry. He swished his huge tail, shook the barnacles off his belly, and gnashed his many rows of teeth together like underwater thunder. He roared angrily, "We'll see about that upstart turtle!" And he set off with the speed of lightning to the reef opening at Tahaa, where

the giant turtle guarded the entrance. Hiro, on the other shark, followed him to see the excitement.

When the huge turtle saw the King of the Sharks approaching, he called out very fiercely, "Halt, Shark! You cannot go past me into the lagoon, even though you are the King of the Sharks himself! I am the guardian here, and you shall not pass!"

"See if you can stop me, you foolish turtle!" roared the Shark King. He swam at the turtle. And almost before Hiro knew what was happening, the Shark King opened his enormous jaws very wide and swallowed the turtle down, shell and all. "Old and weak, am I?" laughed the King of the Sharks. "What do you think now?" He turned around and saw Hiro and said, "There, boy. That ought to teach him to challenge his betters, don't you think?"

Cunningly Hiro said, "He wasn't the only reef guardian that thinks you're old and weak, Your Majesty. The giant eel who guards the reef opening at Bora Bora thinks so too. He challenges you to battle also."

"He does, does he?" And the King of the Sharks set out instantly for Bora Bora, seething with anger once more. "I'll show him that the King of the Sharks is still the most powerful creature in the world!" Hiro and the shark that carried him followed again, anxious to see the outcome of this battle.

No sooner did the Shark King come in sight of the Bora Bora reef than the giant eel who guarded the passage rose up to his full height. Standing upon his tail, with his needle-pointed teeth bared, he said, "Hold on, Shark! I am the guardian here. You shall not go past me into the lagoon, even though you are the King of the Sharks!"

"Get out of my way, eel," shouted the Shark King, "or I'll treat you as I treated the turtle of Tahaa!"

"How is that?" asked the eel.

"Like this," replied the Shark King. And he opened his mighty jaws and swallowed down the giant eel as easily as though he were a tiny sardine.

"Now, boy," said the Shark King to Hiro, "do you believe I am the most powerful creature in the sea?"

"I certainly do, Your Majesty," said Hiro. "But that

giant octopus who guards the reef at Raiatea doesn't agree with me. He's a lazy old fellow, and seldom on the job. But he thinks he can whip you in battle any time you care to try him."

"There's no better time than now!" cried the King of the Sharks. He snapped his teeth together furiously and made such a racket that the noise hurt Hiro's ears. "Come on. We shall teach your octopus at Raiatea a lesson he'll never forget!" And he swam rapidly off to Raiatea. Hiro followed, still clinging to his shark's back.

When they approached the reef opening at Raiatea, Hiro shouted at the Shark King, "Wait, Your Majesty! You want to fight him fair, I'm sure. And perhaps he's asleep. So why not be sure he's awake and ready to fight his best? Call out to him that you are coming!"

Immediately, the Shark King called out in a voice that could be heard for a hundred miles, "Octopus of Raiatea! I, the King of the Sharks, am coming to fight you! Wake up, you lazy fighter, and prepare to meet your death!" The Shark King was all blown up with pride and self-confidence after defeating the turtle and the eel so easily.

Well, the octopus of Raiatea woke up. He yawned and stretched and replied in a sleepy voice, "I was having a lovely nap. But now you've spoiled everything by waking me up. So come on and fight me, if you must, although I'd much rather go back to sleep. I am the guardian here, and you shan't get past me, shark!"

Then, to prepare for the battle, the octopus reached four of his long strong legs downward beneath the sea and clasped them around a large rock buried in the sea bottom to anchor himself. Then he stretched his other four legs across the opening in the coral reef and waited for the Shark King's charge.

It came at once. Like an angry black shadow flitting through the depths, the Shark King swam at the octopus. Jaws snapping, he shot headlong against the four legs of the octopus that were barring the reef entrance. Instantly, those huge snaky legs wrapped themselves around the Shark King's body like bands of iron. Then the octopus let go his hold on the rock under the sea. He brought his other four legs up and wrapped them around the Shark's thrashing body. Only the Shark's

202

gnashing jaws were free of the octopus' legs. And although the Shark twisted his mighty head this way and that, trying to bite off those crushing legs, he couldn't quite reach them with his teeth.

Meanwhile, the octopus slowly began to draw his legs tighter and tighter around the King of the Sharks, squeezing, squeezing, squeezing the great fish until he gasped and groaned. Madly the Shark threw himself about, trying to escape the grip of the octopus. But those strong legs only squeezed tighter and tighter.

The terrible battle between these two sea monsters went on and on for six hours. Each struggled with every muscle and nerve and trick to defeat the other. Their fight caused a mighty turmoil in the sea from the surface of the waves clear down to the deepest deeps. The battle was so fierce that it caused the whole ocean floor to tilt slightly. Mountainous tidal waves formed and went crashing into the land all over the world.

At last the Shark King whispered, "That's enough, octopus. I give in! You're squeezing me to death. I confess myself beaten. Now let me go. I was only joking about killing you anyhow. So let me go, what do you say?"

"Oh, no!" replied the octopus, squeezing harder than ever. "I shall kill you, King of the Sharks, for spoiling my nice nap!"

"Please let me go, good octopus," begged the Shark.

The octopus paid no attention. He went on squeezing. Then, when the Shark King was nearly dead, Hiro left his place on the small shark's back and went over to the octopus. "I am one of your people of Raiatea, dear guardian," he said. "While you have slept, many sharks have gone past you through the reef and eaten a lot of people from the island. So why not spare the life of this King of the Sharks now? Then you'll be able to sleep as much as you like from now on — and keep your people safe from sharks as well."

"How is that?" asked the octopus. "I admit I am very sleepy much of the time, and I don't keep a very good watch on the reef opening. But I don't quite see how sparing this monster's life will help things in any way."

Hiro said, "Make him promise you that he will never trouble any man, woman, or child of Raiatea ever again. Make him solemnly promise that all his shark people will leave us alone forever—whether we are swimming, fishing, bathing, or sailing. If he promises that, we won't need a reef guardian any more. You can sleep comfortably for the rest of your life, if you care to."

The octopus loosened his strangling legs slightly from around the King of the Sharks so that the fish could talk. "You heard what this boy said just now, didn't you?" the octopus asked the Shark King sternly. "Will you promise all that if I spare your life?"

"Yes! Yes! Gladly!" cried the Shark King, drawing a deep breath. "I and my people will never trouble the people of this island again. I swear it. Only spare my life!"

So the octopus unwrapped his legs and let the King of the Sharks go free. And Hiro, knowing that now he was safe, climbed on the Shark King's back. He asked to be taken home to his father's house so he could spread the word of the Shark King's promise. The giant octopus, relieved of his duties as reef guardian, yawned widely and went back to sleep.

That is why the people of Raiatea have no fear of sharks to this day.

Retold by James Holding

THINKING IT OVER

1. Old tales that explain why things happen are often called "why" stories. Why, according to this story, do the sharks of the deep sea stay out of the lagoon?
2. Hiro tricked the Shark King into doing just what he wanted. What did Hiro know about the Shark King that made him think his trick would work?
3. Think of another title for this story and tell why you think your title is a good one.

THOUGHTS AT WORK

1. How did this "why" story explain tidal waves?
2. How did you know that this story couldn't really happen?
3. Why do you think Hiro didn't fight the Shark King himself?
4. Why didn't Hiro let the octopus kill the Shark King?
5. Name the reef guardians. How many battles took place? Think of other folk tales in which the same number is used.
6. Can you think of other folk tales in which a small hero outwits a large enemy?
7. Storytellers often add new ideas of their own as they retell a story. If you were retelling this story, what ideas would *you* want to add?

Long Trip

The sea is a wilderness of waves,
A desert of water.
We dip and dive,
Rise and roll,
Hide and are hidden
On the sea.
   Day, night,
   Night, day,
The sea is a desert of waves,
A wilderness of water.

——*Langston Hughes*

207

As you read this Japanese folk tale, be prepared to go below the sea to a strange world where everyday cares are left behind. Can you tell why this folk tale has long been a favorite in Japan and why its fame has spread throughout the world?

Urashima Taro and the Princess of the Sea

Long, long ago, in a small village of Japan, there lived a fine young man named Urashima Taro.[1] He lived with his mother and father in a thatched-roof house which overlooked the sea. Each morning he was up before the sun, and went out to sea in his little fishing boat. On days when his luck was good, he would bring back large baskets full of fish which he sold in the village market.

One day, as he was carrying home his load of fish, he saw a group of shouting children. They were gathered around something on the beach and were crying, "Hit him! Poke him!" Taro ran over to see what was the matter, and there on the sand he saw a big brown tortoise. The children were poking it with a long stick and throwing stones at its hard shell.

"Here, here," called Taro. "That's no way to treat him! Why don't you leave him alone, and let him go back to the sea?"

"But we found him," said one of the children. "He belongs to us!"

"Yes, yes, he is ours," cried all the children.

Now, because Urashima Taro was a fair and kindly young man, he said to them, "Suppose I give each of you something in return for the tortoise?" Then he took ten shiny coins out of a small bag of money and gave one to each child. "Now, isn't that a fair bargain?" he asked. "A coin for each of you, and the tortoise for me."

"Yes, yes. Thank you!" called the children, and away they ran to the village candy shop.

Taro watched the old tortoise crawl away slowly toward the sea and called, "You'd better stay at home in the sea from

[1] Urashima Taro (ü rä'shə mə   tä rō)

now on, old fellow!" Then, smiling happily because he had been able to save the tortoise, he turned to go home. There his mother and father were waiting for him with bowls of steaming rice and soup.

Several days passed, and Taro soon forgot all about the tortoise whom he had saved. One day he was sitting in his boat feeling very sad because he could catch no fish. Suddenly he heard a voice from the sea calling, "Urashima-san! Urashima-san!"

"Now who could be calling me here in the middle of the sea?" thought Urashima Taro. He looked high and low, but could see no one. Suddenly, from the crest of a big wave, out popped the head of the old tortoise.

"I came to thank you for saving me the other day," said the tortoise.

"Well, I'm glad you got away safely," said Taro.

"This time I would like to do something for you, Urashima-san," said the tortoise. "How would you like to visit the princess who lives in the Palace of the Sea?"

"The princess of the sea!" shouted Taro. "I have heard often of her beauty, and everyone says her palace is more lovely than any place on earth! But how can I go to the bottom of the sea, and how can I enter her palace?"

"Just leave everything to me," said the old tortoise. "Hop on my back and I will see that you get there safely. I will also take you into the palace, for I am one of the palace guards."

So Urashima Taro jumped onto the smooth round back of the tortoise, and away they went. Swish, swish . . . the waves seemed to part and make a path for them as the tortoise swam on. Soon Taro felt himself going down . . . down . . . down . . . into the sea, but he wasn't getting wet at all. He heard the waves lapping gently about his ears. "That's strange," thought Taro. "This is just like a dream—a nice happy dream."

Before long, they were at the bottom of the big blue sea. Taro could see bright-colored fish playing hide-and-seek among the long strands of swaying seaweed. He could see clams and other shellfish shyly peeking out at him from their shells. Soon Taro saw something big and shiny looming in the hazy blue water.

"Is that the palace?" he asked anxiously. "It looks very beautiful."

"Oh, no," answered the tortoise. "That is just the outer gate."

They came to a stop and Taro could see that the gateway was guarded by a fish in armor of silver. "Welcome home," the guard called to the tortoise, as he opened the gate for them to enter.

"See whom I have brought back with me," the tortoise answered happily. The guard in the armor of silver turned to Urashima Taro and bowed most politely. Taro just had time to return the bow when he looked up and saw another gate. This one was even larger than the first, and was made of silver stones and pillars of coral. A row of fish in armor of gold was guarding the second gate.

"Now, Urashima-san, if you will get off and wait here, I will tell the princess that you have come," said the tortoise, and he disappeared into the palace beyond the gate. Taro had never seen such a beautiful sight in all his life. The silver stones in the gate sparkled and glittered as though they were smiling at him. Taro had to blink hard.

Soon the tortoise was back at his side telling him that the princess was waiting to see him. He led Taro through the gate of coral and silver, and up a path of golden stones to the palace. There in front of the palace stood the beautiful princess of the sea with her ladies-in-waiting.

"Welcome to the Palace of the Sea, Urashima Taro," she said, and her voice sounded like the tinkling of little silver bells. "Won't you come with me?" she asked.

Taro opened his mouth to answer, but not a sound would come forth. He could only look at the beautiful princess and the sparkling emeralds and diamonds and rubies which glittered on the walls of the palace. The princess understood how Taro felt, so she just smiled kindly and led him down a hallway paved with smooth, white pearls. Soon they came to a large room, and in the center of the room was an enormous table and an enormous chair. Taro thought they might have been made for a great king.

"Sit down, Urashima-san," said the princess, and as he sat in the enormous chair, the ladies-in-waiting appeared from all sides. They placed on the table plate after plate of all the delicious things that Taro could think of. "Eat well, my friend," said the princess, "and while you dine, my maids will sing and dance for you." Soon there was music and singing and dancing.

213

The room was filled with laughing voices. Taro felt like a king now! He thought surely this was all a dream, and that it would end soon. But no, after he had dined, the princess took him all through the beautiful palace. At the very last, she brought him to a room that looked as though it were made of ice and snow. There were creamy pearls and sparkling diamonds everywhere.

"Now, how would you like to see all the seasons of the year?" whispered the princess.

"Oh, I would like that very much," answered Taro, and as he spoke, the east door of the room opened slowly and quietly. Taro could scarcely believe the sight before his eyes. He saw big clouds of pale pink cherry blossoms and tall green willow trees swaying in the breeze. He could hear bluebirds singing, and saw them fly happily into the sky.

"Ah, that is spring," murmured Taro. "What a lovely sunny day!" But before he could say more, the princess led him further on. As she opened the door to the south, Taro could see white lotus blossoms floating on a still green pond. It was a warm summer day, and he could hear crickets chirping lazily, somewhere in the distance. She opened the door to the west and he saw a hillside of maple trees. Their leaves of crimson and yellow were whirling and dancing down among golden chrysanthemums. He had seen such trees each fall in his own little village. When the princess opened the door to the north, Taro felt a blast of cold air. He shivered, and looked up to see snowflakes tumbling down from gray skies. They were putting white caps on all the fence posts and treetops.

"Now you have seen all the seasons of the year," said the princess.

"They were beautiful!" sighed Taro happily. "I have never seen such wonderful sights in all my life! I wish I could stay here always!"

Taro was having such a very good time that he forgot all about his home in the village. He feasted and danced and sang with his friends in the Palace of the Sea, and before he knew it, three long years had gone by. But to Taro they seemed to be just three short days.

At last Taro said to the princess, "Alas, I have been here much too long. I must go home to see my mother and father so they will not worry about me."

"But you will come back?" asked the princess.

"Oh, yes, yes. I will come back," answered Taro.

"Before you go I have something for you," said the princess, and she gave Taro a small jewel box studded with many precious stones.

"Oh, it is beautiful, Princess," said Taro. "How can I thank you for all you have done for me?"

But the princess went on, "There is just one thing about that box," she said. "You must never, never open it if you ever wish to return to the Palace of the Sea. Can you remember that, Urashima Taro?"

"I will never open it, no matter what happens," promised Taro. Then he said good-bye to all his friends in the palace. Once again he climbed on the back of the old tortoise and they sailed toward his village on the seacoast. The princess and her ladies-in-waiting stood at the coral gate and waved to Taro till he could no longer see them. The tortoise swam on and on, and one by one all the little bright-colored fish that had been

216

following them began to turn back. Before long, Taro could
see the seacoast where he used to go fishing, and soon they
were back on the very beach where Taro had once saved the
tortoise. Taro hopped off onto the smooth white sand. "Good-
bye, old friend," he said. "You have been very good to me.
Thank you for taking me to the most beautiful place I have
ever seen."

"Farewell, Urashima-san," said the old tortoise. "I hope we
may meet again some day." Then he turned and crawled slowly
back into the sea.

Now that he was in his own village once more, Taro was
most anxious to see his parents. He ran along the path which
led to their house with his jewel box tucked securely under
his arm. He looked up eagerly at each person whom he passed.

He wanted to shout a greeting to them, but each face seemed strange and new. "How odd!" thought Taro. "I feel as though I were in some other village than my own. I don't seem to know anyone. Well, I'll soon see Mother and Father," he said, and hurried on. When he reached the spot where the house should have been, there was no house to be seen. There was just an empty lot full of tall green weeds. Taro couldn't believe his eyes. "Why, what has happened to my home? Where are my parents?" he cried. He looked up and down the dusty path and soon saw an old, old woman coming toward him. "I'll ask her what has happened to my home," thought Taro.

"Old woman, please, can you help me?" asked Taro.

The old woman straightened her bent back and cocked her gray head, "Eh, what did you say?" she asked.

"Can you tell me what happened to Urashima Taro's home? It used to be right here," said Taro.

"Never heard of him," said the old woman, shaking her head.

"But you must have," Taro replied. "He lived right here, on this very spot where you are standing."

"Now let me see," she sighed. "Urashima Taro. Yes, it seems I have heard of him. Oh, I remember now. There is a story that he went out to sea in his fishing boat one day and never came back again. I suppose he was drowned at sea. Well, anyway, that was over three hundred years ago. My great-great-grand-father used to tell me about Urashima Taro when I was just a little girl."

"Three hundred years!" exclaimed Taro. His eyes were like saucers now. "But I don't understand."

"Well, I don't understand what you want with a man who lived three hundred years ago," muttered the old woman, and she trudged on down the road.

"So three years in the Palace of the Sea has really been three hundred years here in my village," thought Taro. "No wonder all my friends are gone. No wonder I can't find my mother or father!" Taro had never felt so lonely or so sad as he did then. "What can I do? What can I do?" he murmured to himself.

Suddenly he remembered the little jewel box which the princess had given him. "Perhaps there is something in there that can help me," he thought, and forgetting the promise he had made to the princess, he quickly opened the box. Suddenly, there arose from it a cloud of white smoke which wrapped itself around Taro so that he could see nothing. When it disappeared,

Urashima Taro peered into the empty box, but he could scarcely see. He looked at his hands and they were the hands of an old, old man. His face was wrinkled; his hair was as white as snow. In that short moment Urashima Taro had become three hundred years older. He remembered the promise he had made to the princess, but now it was too late and he knew that he could never visit the Palace of the Sea again. But who knows, perhaps one day the old tortoise came back to the beach once more to help his friend.

Retold by Yoshiko Uchida

THINKING IT OVER

1. How did the tortoise thank Taro for his kindness? In your opinion, had the tortoise done a favor for him? Explain your answer.
2. Someone has said, "You always pay for what you get." What did Taro get? What price did he pay?
3. What did you think of the ending of this story? How would you have changed it?

THOUGHTS AT WORK

1. Why do you suppose the author began the story with children mistreating a tortoise? Did these children act like children you know? If so, how?
2. Japanese people have a great love of beauty. Name the beautiful things described in this story.
3. Use your imagination and give some reasons why Taro suddenly grew old when he opened the box.
4. Why did Taro stay so long at the Palace of the Sea? Why did he finally leave?
5. How was time in the Palace of the Sea different from time in Taro's village? When did Taro discover there was a difference?
6. Taro broke his promise and opened the box the princess had given him. Think of another story in which someone broke a promise and then was sorry for it.
7. Find and reread your favorite description. Then draw a picture of what the words make you see and feel.

THOR'S FISHING

This myth was first told over a thousand years ago by sailors of the Northland called Vikings. They worshiped gods who had supernatural powers but looked like humans. The Vikings' favorite god was red-bearded Thor, the god of lightning and thunder. He often did battle with terrible giants and monsters. If you think carefully as you read, you will discover what qualities the Vikings admired most in their gods and heroes.

The Vikings who lived in the northern part of Europe during ancient times told wonderful stories of their gods. One of their favorite gods was Thor, whose mighty hammer struck lightning through the heavens. Even the giants of Jotunnheim,[1] who were old enemies of the gods, even these feared Thor.

Now once when Thor had journeyed as far as Jotunnheim, night fell before he could return to the home of the gods. So Thor approached the dwelling of a giant named Hymir[2] and asked for shelter.

Hymir eyed Thor with a frown of hatred and distrust, for he knew well this was one of the gods. However, he thought best to be civil, now that Thor was actually before him. So with gruff politeness he asked him in to supper.

Thor was a brave fellow at table as well as in battle, and at sight of the good things before him, his eyes sparkled. Three roast oxen were on the giant's table, and Thor fell to with a will and finished two of them himself. Hymir stared in amazement.

"Truly, friend, you have a goodly appetite," he said. "You have eaten all the meat I have in my larder. If you dine with me tomorrow, I must insist that you catch your own dinner of fish. I can't be expected to supply food for such an appetite!"

Now this was not hospitable of Hymir, but Thor did not mind.

"I like well to fish, good Hymir," he laughed. "When

[1] Jotunnheim (yō′tün hām)   [2] Hymir (hē′mir)

you go forth in your boat in the morning, I will go with you and see what I can find for my dinner at the bottom of the sea."

When the morning came, the giant made ready for the fishing, and Thor rose early to go with him.

"Ho, Hymir!" exclaimed Thor. "Have you bait enough for us both?"

Hymir answered gruffly, "You must dig your own bait when you go fishing with me. I have no time to waste on you."

Then Thor looked about to see what he could use for bait. Presently he saw a herd of Hymir's oxen feeding in the meadow.

"Aha! Just the thing!" he cried.

Seizing one of the biggest oxen of all, he trotted down to the shore with it under his arm. When Hymir saw this, he was very angry. He pushed the boat off from shore and began to row away as fast as he could, so that Thor might not have a chance to come aboard. But Thor made one long step and planted himself snugly in the stern of the boat.

"No, no, brother Hymir," he said, laughing. "You invited me to go fishing, and a-fishing I will go. For I have my bait, and my hope is high that great luck I shall see this day."

So he took an oar and rowed mightily in the stern, while Hymir, the giant, rowed mightily at the prow. No boat ever skipped over the water so fast as this one did.

Far and fast they rowed, until they came to a spot where Hymir cried, "Hold! Let us anchor here and fish. This is the place where I have best luck."

"And what sort of little fish do you catch here, O Hymir?" asked Thor.

"Whales!" answered the giant proudly. "I fish for nothing smaller than whales."

"Pooh!" cried Thor. "Who would fish for such small fry! Whales, indeed. Let us row out farther where we can find something really worth catching. There must be creatures around bigger than whales." And he began to pull even faster than before.

"Stop! Stop!" roared the giant. "You do not know

what you are doing. These are the regions of the dreadful Midgard[3] Serpent, and it is not safe to fish in these waters."

"Oho! The Midgard Serpent!" said Thor, delighted. "That is the very fish I am after. Let us drop in our lines here."

Now you must know that the Midgard Serpent was so huge that he encircled the earth. He lived deep in the ocean and when he stirred, great waves were sent rolling across its surface. It was this very monster which Thor intended to catch.

Thor baited his great hook with the whole head of the ox which he had brought. He cast his line, as big around as a man's arm, over the side of the boat. Hymir also cast his line for he did not wish Thor to think him a coward. But his hand trembled as he waited for a bite. He glanced down into the blue depths with eyes rounded as big as dinner plates through fear of the dreadful creature who lived down below those waves.

"Look! You have a bite!" cried Thor so suddenly that Hymir was startled and nearly tumbled out of the boat. Hand over hand he pulled in his line, and lo, he had caught two whales—two great flopping whales—on his one hook! That was a catch indeed.

Hymir smiled proudly, forgetting his fear as he said, "How is that, my friend? Let us see you beat this catch in your morning's fishing."

[3] Midgard (mid'gärd)

Lo! Just at that moment Thor also had a bite — such a bite! The boat rocked to and fro, and seemed ready to roll itself over every minute. Then the waves began to roll high and to be lashed into foam for yards and yards about the boat, as if some huge creature were struggling hard below the water.

"I have him!" shouted Thor. "I have the old serpent. Pull, pull, monster! But you shall not escape me now!"

Sure enough, the Midgard Serpent had Thor's hook fixed in his jaws. Struggle as he might, there was no freeing himself from the line. The harder he pulled, the stronger grew Thor. In his godly might, Thor grew so huge and so forceful that his legs went straight through the bottom of the boat and his feet stood on the bottom of the ocean. With the ocean bottom

as a brace for his strength, Thor pulled and pulled, and at last up came the head of the Midgard Serpent, up to the side of the boat. The creature burst out of the water mountain high, dreadful to behold. His monstrous red eyes were rolling fiercely and his nostrils spouted fire. From his terrible sharp teeth dropped poison which sizzled as it fell into the sea. Angrily they glared at each other, Thor and the serpent, while the water streamed into the boat, and the giant turned pale with fear at the danger facing him on all sides.

Thor seized his hammer, preparing to smite the creature's head. But even as he swung the great hammer high for the deadly blow, Hymir cut the fishline with his knife. Down into the depths of the ocean sank the Midgard Serpent amid a whirlpool of foaming water. But the hammer had sped from Thor's iron fingers. It crushed the serpent's head as he sank downward to his den on the sandy bottom. It crushed, but did not kill him, thanks to the giant's trickery. Dreadful was the turmoil the serpent caused beneath the waves. It burst the rocks and made the caverns of the ocean shiver into bits. It wrecked the coral groves and tore loose the draperies of seaweed. The fishes darted about in every direction, and the sea monsters wildly sought new places to hide themselves when they found their homes destroyed.

The sea itself was stirred to its lowest depths, and the waves ran trembling into one another's arms. The earth, too, shrank and shivered. Hymir, cowering low in the boat, was glad of one thing. The terrible Midgard Serpent had vanished out of sight. And that was the last ever seen of him, though he still lived, wounded and sore from the shock of Thor's hammer.

Now it was time to return home. Silently and sulkily the giant swam back to land. Thor waded ashore, bearing the boat upon his shoulders, filled as it was with water and weighted with the great whales which Hymir had caught. He brought his burden to the giant's hall.

Here Hymir met Thor crossly enough, for he was ashamed of the whole morning's work, in which Thor had appeared so much more of a hero than he.

Retold by Abbie Farwell Brown

THINKING IT OVER

1. Why do you suppose Hymir cut Thor's line when it held the Midgard Serpent?
2. From what you have learned about Thor and Hymir, what do you think the ancient Vikings admired in a person? What things did they *not* admire?
3. When the Vikings told this story, what parts do you think they liked best? Explain your answer.

THOUGHTS AT WORK

1. Why did Hymir pretend to be polite to Thor? What did Hymir do that showed his real feelings about Thor?
2. The Viking gods often did things that humans couldn't do. What did Thor do that only a god could do?
3. Reread the paragraph on page 229 that describes the Midgard Serpent. Use this description to draw a picture of this monster.
4. List all the things that happened because Thor threw his hammer at the Midgard Serpent.
5. In "The Battle That Tilted the Sea," Hiro defeated the Shark King by using his quick wits. How did Thor get the best of Hymir?
6. Authors often use words in unusual ways to make their descriptions more interesting. Find some of these words in the sentences below and tell why they are interesting.
    a. The waves ran trembling into each other's arms.
    b. The earth shrank and shivered.
    c. The sun watched the children at play.
7. What caused the great waves in this story? What caused them in "The Battle That Tilted the Sea"? Try to find out what *really* causes waves.

This old Norwegian folk tale, rewritten as a play, explains a mystery that puzzled people long ago. According to this play, why is the sea salt?

Characters:
Storyteller
Rich Brother
Poor Brother
Old Beggar
Poor Brother's Wife
1st Visitor
2nd Visitor
3rd Visitor
4th Visitor
5th Visitor

6th Visitor
Sea Captain
Members of his Crew

(The curtain is down. Storyteller strolls to center stage from left. He carries a guitar. At center stage he makes a deep bow to the audience over his guitar which he holds in place.)

STORYTELLER:

There were two brothers as
   you shall hear,
And one was rich and one
   was poor.
The poor one stands at the
   rich one's door,
A-begging of food and nothing more.

(Storyteller returns to the left
side of the stage and sits
cross-legged on the floor as
the curtain rises. . . .)

SCENE I

TIME: *Long ago*

PLACE: *A wood with the ter-*
race of a house just visible
at right of stage. (The Rich
Brother and the Poor Brother
are talking. The Rich Brother,
richly dressed, stands on his
terrace, his back to his front
door. The Poor Brother is in
rags and stands facing his
brother, but in such a way
that the audience can see his
face, which wears a pleading
expression.)

RICH BROTHER: This is the
   fourth time you've come
   begging, and I say I have
   had enough. Begone and
   don't bother me again!

POOR BROTHER: But, Broth-
   er, I beseech you. My wife
   are I are without a morsel
   to eat. Help me this *one*
   time and I will bother you
   no more.

RICH BROTHER: (*Hesitates,*
   scowls, then throws up his
   hands.) Very well then. But
   this is the last time. (*He*
   enters the house and reap-
   pears with two loaves of
   bread and a side of bacon.)
   Here, take this and begone.
   (*He goes quickly back into*
   the house.)

(*Poor Brother turns from the*
terrace and walks down the
path through the wood. From

stage left, an old beggar enters and meets him on the path.)

OLD BEGGAR: In the name of charity, give a poor old starving man a morsel to eat.

POOR BROTHER: I have just been a-begging myself and yet I am not so poor that I can't help someone who is worse off than I. At least I have food and you have none. Here, take this. *(He hands over the two loaves and is about to cut the side of bacon in half when the beggar stops him.)*

OLD BEGGAR: Oh enough, enough! Do not cut the bacon. Keep it for now and your generosity will be rewarded.

POOR BROTHER: And how will that be? Surely you are hardly in a position to reward me.

OLD BEGGAR: I will tell you something. (*He draws close to Poor Brother as if to share a secret.)* Not far from here is the entrance to the underground home of the dwarfs. Go there with the bacon. They love bacon and I happen to know they have none, so they will want yours. But don't give it to them until they agree to give you in return a little hand mill, which they keep hidden behind the door. When you have it, meet me here and I will tell you how to use it.

POOR BROTHER: Thank you, good man. Now tell me how to find the entrance to the dwarfs' home.

OLD BEGGAR: *(Turning to point down stage left, while Poor Brother bends to follow the direction in which he is pointing.)* You follow that path until you come to a large stone and then . . .

CURTAIN FALLS

(Storyteller strolls to center stage as before.)

STORYTELLER: The Poor Brother found the home of the dwarfs where they live down among the roots of these very trees. *(Gesturing.)* They wanted the bacon, just as the old man said they would, and they offered many fine things in exchange for it. But the Poor Brother wouldn't trade unless they gave him the mill. So at last they did.

(Storyteller returns to the left side of the stage and sits cross-legged on the floor as the curtain rises. . . .)

SCENE II

TIME: *A little later*

PLACE: *The path in the wood. (Poor Brother hurries toward the Old Beggar, who has been waiting for him. Poor Brother is carrying the mill.)*

OLD BEGGAR: Good, good! I see you have it.

POOR BROTHER: *(Grinning happily.)* That I have, and I am eager to know how it works, for surely this is a magic mill.

OLD BEGGAR: It is a magic mill. You have only to ask it for whatever you want and it will grind out your wish. It will keep on grinding until you say, "Good little mill, I thank you for enough." *(He shakes his finger under Poor Brother's nose.)* Now don't forget those words, "Good little mill, I thank you for enough."

POOR BROTHER: You can be sure I won't. And thank you, kind sir. This is my lucky day! *(He turns and hurries along the way he has come as the . . .)*

CURTAIN FALLS

235

(Storyteller strolls to center stage as before.)

STORYTELLER: The Poor Brother ran home to his wife. He could hardly wait to show her the wonderful mill. Besides, he himself was eager to see what it could do for, don't forget, he was very, very hungry.

(Storyteller returns to the left side of the stage and sits cross-legged on the floor as the curtain rises. . . .)

SCENE III

TIME: *A little later*

PLACE: *Inside the Poor Brother's cottage. There is a window without any curtain over it, a bare table with a drawer in it, and some rough, straight chairs. There is a door at right. All has an air of poverty and want. (Poor Brother's wife is sitting in front of an empty, cold fireplace.)*

POOR BROTHER: *(Rushing in.)* Look, Wife. Just see what I have here. This is our lucky day!

WIFE: *(Looking around, but not leaving the chair.)* I see nothing but a little hand mill. What has taken you so long? I am cold and I am hungry. Where is the food you went to get?

POOR BROTHER: *(Placing the mill on the table.)* It is all here. This is a magic mill. It will grind whatever you want. Speak, Wife, what would you like to eat?

WIFE: *(Getting slowly out of her chair and approaching the table.)* Sausages. I'd like some sausages and some good white bread.

POOR BROTHER: *(Leaning over the mill.)* Grind sausages and white bread!

(There is a grinding noise. There should be a drawer in the table which the Poor Brother now opens. The drawer should be facing away

237

from the audience. From the drawer the Poor Brother draws a long string of sausages, pretending it comes from the mill. Next he lifts out some loaves of white bread.)

POOR BROTHER: Look at this, Wife. (He holds up the string of sausages as the grinding noise continues.) And just look at this. (He shows her the loaves of white bread.) Didn't I say this was our lucky day?

WIFE: (Overjoyed.) Husband, husband, you are right! This is our lucky day! What a fine husband you are.

POOR BROTHER: (Loudly over the grinding noise.) Good little mill, thank you for enough. (The grinding noise stops.)

(Poor Brother and Wife look at one another with joy, then they join hands and dance around the table as the . . .)

CURTAIN FALLS

(Storyteller strolls to center stage as before.)

STORYTELLER: Now that they knew how to get all the food they wanted, the Poor Brother and his wife planned a feast for all the poor people of the town. When the Rich Brother heard about this, he hurried over to the Poor Brother's house to find out where he had gotten the money to pay for so much food.

(Storyteller returns to the left side of the stage and sits cross-legged on the floor as the curtain rises. . . .)

SCENE IV

TIME: A little later

PLACE: Inside the Poor Brother's cottage as before. Now there is a white cloth on the table. (Three couples besides Poor Brother and his wife are standing around the table helping themselves to the feast spread there.)

1ST VISITOR: *(Popping berries in his mouth.)* What wonderful strawberries!

2ND VISITOR: *(Smacking his lips.)* Taste this roast beef.

3RD VISITOR: *(Smelling and then eating the cheese.)* I never ate such delicious cheese.

4TH VISITOR: *(Wiping her mouth.)* Nor I such wonderful cake.

5TH VISITOR: *(Reaching across the table greedily.)* I must have one of those jelly tarts.

6TH VISITOR: *(Grabbing up the plate.)* No you don't. There are just enough for me.

WIFE: *(Hurrying over.)* Let her have them. The mill will grind as many more as we want.

1ST VISITOR: Will it grind *anything* you want? Even money?

5TH VISITOR: Of course, silly. Didn't you hear them say it is a magic mill?

1ST VISITOR: *(Taking Poor Brother by the arm.)* Ask it to grind money, enough money for us all.

POOR BROTHER: A fine idea. (*He starts toward the shelf where the mill is sitting, when there comes a loud knock on the door.*)

WIFE: (*Opening door.*) Why, Brother! What brings you to our humble house? Come in, come in. You are welcome!

RICH BROTHER: (*Entering and approaching the table, too astonished to answer her greeting. Visitors step back as he draws near.*) What is this? What is this? How did you come by all this wonderful food? I gave you only bacon and bread.

POOR BROTHER: *(Approaching with the mill in his hands.)* By means of this, Brother. This is a magic mill. It will grind anything we wish.

RICH BROTHER: *(Reaching for the mill.)* Then I must have it. You must let me borrow it. I promise to bring it back. Yes, yes. I must have it! (*He seizes the mill and starts out the door.*) I promise to bring it back. (*He runs out.*)

POOR BROTHER: *(Running after him.)* Stop, stop! There is something you must know. Come back! (*He stops in doorway and shakes his head.*) He must think I want to take the mill from him. See how fast he is running.

WIFE: Let him go. We can get the mill later if he does not bring it back.

POOR BROTHER: *(Turning to her.)* You don't understand. He doesn't know how to make the mill stop.

(*Everyone stares from one to another, shaking their heads, as the . . .*)

CURTAIN FALLS

(*Storyteller strolls to center stage as before.*)

STORYTELLER: (*Striking some chords and chanting.*)

The Rich Brother took the mill on the run

For he thought that now he'd have some fun.

But he couldn't make it stop with pleading or swearing,

So he's up to his neck in soup and herring.

(*Storyteller returns to the left side of the stage and sits cross-legged on the floor as the curtain rises. . . .*)

SCENE V

TIME: A few minutes later

PLACE: Inside Poor Brother's cottage as before. (The Villagers have gone and Poor Brother and Wife are seated at the table licking their fingers and looking well-fed, when the door bursts open and Rich Brother rushes in. He is wet and bedraggled and highly excited.)

RICH BROTHER: Come, come quickly! It's the mill; it's your *miserable* mill. How I wish I had never heard of it! You played a trick on me, that's what you did. Now, come and untrick me!

POOR BROTHER: *(Rising from his chair.)* What happened? What did you ask it to grind?

RICH BROTHER: Soup, you fool. Seeing all the good food here made me hungry. So as soon as I got home, I asked the mill to grind soup and serve up herring. Now my house is awash in soup, my garden is flooded, and there are herring all over the house.

WIFE: *(Starts laughing as Rich Brother talks, then throws her apron over her face and rocks back and forth in a fit of merriment.)*

(Rich Brother and Poor Brother run out of the house as the . . .)

CURTAIN FALLS

(Storyteller strolls to center stage as before.)

STORYTELLER: The next one to hear about the magic mill was a sea captain who traveled back and forth across the ocean bringing shiploads of salt to his countrymen. He thought it would be a good thing to borrow the mill and have it grind salt. Then he wouldn't have to go a-sailing for a good long time.

(Storyteller returns to the left side of the stage and sits cross-legged on the floor as the curtain rises. . . .)

SCENE VI

TIME: *Some weeks later*

PLACE: *Inside Poor Brother's cottage. But what a change! There is a white, fluffy curtain at the window. There is a picture above the hearth and a fire glowing within it. (In a comfortable rocker sits the Wife wearing a fine gown and a lace cap on her head. Her back is to Poor Brother and the Sea Captain who are sitting on a sofa, legs crossed and at ease.)*

SEA CAPTAIN: As I was saying, if you would let me borrow the mill, I could fill my ship with salt here and sail home instead of having to go to a very distant port each trip.

POOR BROTHER: You'd be sure to bring the mill back to me.

SEA CAPTAIN: Of course I would. I'm an honest man.

POOR BROTHER: Very well, then. You may borrow the mill. *(He goes across the room to where the mill sits on its shelf.)* Here you are, only there is one thing you must remember . . .

SEA CAPTAIN: *(Grabbing the mill out of Poor Brother's hands and not waiting for him to finish his sentence.)* Don't you worry, I'll remember to bring it back. I'll remember. *(He rushes out of the room as if he were afraid Poor Brother might change his mind as the . . .)*

CURTAIN FALLS

(Storyteller strolls to center stage as before.)

STORYTELLER: But the Sea Captain wasn't an honest man. No sooner did he have the mill aboard his ship, than he ordered his crew to weigh anchor and set sail for home. And as soon as the ship was under way, he ordered the mill to grind salt. It began to grind and soon all the sacks were full and then the hold began to

243

fill. But the Sea Captain couldn't make the mill stop grinding.

(*Storyteller returns to the left side of the stage and sits cross-legged on the floor as the curtain rises. . . .*)

SCENE VII

TIME: *A few minutes later*

PLACE: The deck of a sailing ship. (Sailors appear at right as the Sea Captain comes running onto center stage from left.)

SEA CAPTAIN: Man the boats! Man the boats! The ship is filling with salt. It will sink; it *is* sinking. We shall all be drowned! (*They all go running off right as the . . .*)

CURTAIN FALLS

(*Storyteller strolls to center stage as before.*)
STORYTELLER:
 The ship *did* sink to the
  bottom of the sea
 And the mill kept grinding
  as busy as could be.
 It has kept on grinding with
  never a halt,
 And that is the reason why
  the sea is salt.
(*Storyteller plays a few chords on the guitar, then bows deeply and exits.*)

the End

Norwegian Folk Tale Retold

244

THINKING IT OVER

1. Which characters were greedy? In what ways were they punished for being greedy?
2. How does the play explain why the sea is salt? Try to find the scientific answer to this question.
3. Who was your favorite character? Why did you like him?

THOUGHTS AT WORK

1. Do you think Rich Brother and Poor Brother were selfish? Do you think either of them was generous? Why?
2. The play doesn't tell, but why do you think Rich Brother was rich and Poor Brother was poor?
3. There is a saying, "A fool and his money are soon parted." Put mill in the place of money and tell how this saying proved to be true in the play.
4. Before presenting the play, you should answer these questions:
    a. How many characters take part? How can you change the number of characters to fit your group?
    b. Where does each scene take place?
    c. What scenery, costumes, and "props" will you need?
    d. How could you present the play without a curtain?
5. To add more action to the play, pantomime some of the parts. Reread what the storyteller says before Scene II, Scene V, and Scene VII. Then decide how you could act these parts without speaking.
6. An actor should use his face and voice to show how a character feels. Say each line below and show with your face and voice how the character felt when he said the following:
    a. "Begone and don't bother me again!"
    b. "Help me this one time and I will bother you no more."
    c. "Come, come quickly!"
    d. "What has taken you so long?"

Jason and the Argonauts

Jason is one of several great heroes whom the ancient Greeks admired. These heroes were mortals and not gods, but they dared to face dangers and undertake impossible tasks that frightened ordinary men. As you read this story about Jason and the Argonauts (är′gə nôts), you will discover why the Greeks admired them.

Who were the Argonauts? Before we can answer that question, we must go to another story which happened a bit earlier than the story about Jason and the Argonauts.

THE STORY OF THE GOLDEN FLEECE

It seems that once upon a time there were two children, a brother and sister. Their names were Phrixus[1] and Helle[2] and they were the children of a Greek king.

Their own mother had died and their father had taken a second wife who had borne him a son. This woman had a wicked heart. She hated Phrixus because she considered him a threat to her own son's right to the throne when the king should die. Therefore, she plotted to have Phrixus killed.

One year there was a failure of the wheat crop. It was a terrible time. Everywhere people were starving and praying for an end to their suffering. Ino,[3] the wicked queen, used the crop failure as a way to get rid of Phrixus. She bribed a soothsayer to say that the wheat would not grow again unless Phrixus was killed and offered up to the gods.

The king would not agree to this terrible plan. But his starving people at last forced him to allow the awful deed, for the king too believed in soothsayers.

So Phrixus was led to an altar where a priest, knife in hand, awaited him. A large crowd filled the temple where the altar stood. Among them was Helle who walked, sorrowing, beside her brother.

But just as the priest was about to kill the boy, a wonderful ram covered with golden fleece appeared as if from nowhere. Down he came, and when he rose

[1] Phrixus (frix′səs)   [2] Helle (hel′ā)   [3] Ino (ē′nō)

again, Phrixus and Helle were both clinging to his gleaming back. Before the eyes of the astonished crowd, he flew with the children out of the temple and away toward the east. But just when the ram reached the strait which separates Europe from Asia Minor, Helle lost her hold and fell to the sea. She was drowned, and the strait was called the Hellespont[4] in her honor.

Phrixus and the golden ram continued on until they came to the land of Colchis.[5] To celebrate his escape, Phrixus killed the ram and offered it up on an altar to Zeus[6] to thank the god for having saved him. The ram's golden fleece was hung in a sacred grove where it was guarded day and night by a fire-breathing dragon. The fame of the fleece spread throughout all the world.

Now to the story of Jason and the Argonauts.

THE SEARCH BEGINS

Jason too was the son of a king and the rightful heir to his father's throne. But his wicked uncle, Pelias,[7] had seized the throne. Jason was only a lad at the time, and had been sent into hiding. Thus he escaped his cruel uncle who wanted him killed.

The years went by and Jason grew to manhood. When he learned how his uncle had cheated him of his throne, he decided to return to his kingdom and claim it for himself.

[4] Hellespont (hel'is pont)   [5] Colchis (kol'kis)   [6] Zeus (züs)
[7] Pelias (pē'lē əs)

248

It had been foretold by another soothsayer that Pelias would lose his throne to a stranger who came into the kingdom wearing only one sandal. So Pelias was never able to rest easy in the kingdom he had stolen. Every stranger who came through the city gates was watched to make sure he was either barefooted or properly shod.

Now it happened that as Jason neared the kingdom he intended to claim for himself, he had to wade across a stream. It was a rather large stream and swift, and the stones on the bottom were slippery. Halfway across, he stumbled and one of his sandals was twisted from his foot against a rock. Jason continued on his way, one foot shod, and one foot bare.

He came to the great gate of the city and entered. Following a crowd, he came at last to the market place where many people had gathered. They seemed to be eyeing Jason in great excitement, and he wondered why this was.

Meanwhile, messengers had raced to tell King Pelias that a stranger had entered his city wearing one sandal. Quickly Pelias started for the market place. He soon discovered Jason, who was standing apart from the crowd. The king eyed the handsome youth, noting with dread his one bare foot. However, he hid his fear from the young stranger and spoke pleasantly to him.

"Where have you come from, stranger, and what is your purpose here?"

Jason, who had easily recognized the king, now walked bravely forward. "I have come to claim what is mine by right," he said. "My name is Jason and this kingdom belongs to me. Yet I do not wish to take it by the sword. Keep whatever wealth you have and give over to me the throne."

The clever Pelias readily agreed, speaking in the same pleasant voice to smother his fear and hatred.

"It shall be as you wish, Jason. But first you must fulfill a duty. Phrixus, whom the golden ram fled away with, was my nephew. Now he is dead and I wish to have the Golden Fleece. If you will bring it here to me, I will step down from the throne and give over to you the kingdom without a fight."

Pelias knew full well that no one could take the Golden Fleece while the dragon guarded it. His life would be lost if he tried.

But Jason felt his manhood challenged and eagerly agreed to take the risk. It was an adventure for a hero and would prove his right to be a king.

He went at once to Argus,[8] the shipbuilder, and from him ordered a ship with fifty oars, twenty-five on each side. Then he sent out a call to all the heroes in Greece to come and share the adventure with him. They came. Among them were the Sons of the North-wind, who had mighty wings growing out of their shoulder blades.

When all the company was gathered together, they climbed aboard the ship, which had been named *Argo* after its builder. The heroes seized their oars and with a great shout began rowing out to sea.

Adventure rode with these Argonauts, as they were called, and many were the dangers they dared and overcame before they reached the land of the Golden Fleece. One of the strangest of their adventures began when they visited a famous hero named Phineus.[9]

[8] Argus (är'gəs)   [9] Phineus (fin'ē əs)

251

AN ADVENTURE WITH THE ARGONAUTS

A great misfortune had come upon Phineus because he had angered one of the gods. Now, in his old age he had become blind. But worse than this, evil and foul-feathered birds visited him whenever he sat down to eat. These birds were called Harpies. No sooner was the food placed in front of Phineus, than the Harpies flew down from out the sky, seized what they could, and spoiled all the rest. A terrible odor followed after them, enough to sicken anyone who smelled it. Because of the Harpies, poor old Phineus was slowly starving to death.

In his misery he had only one hope. It had been foretold many years before that he would eat untroubled by the Harpies when the Sons of the Northwind should visit his country along with certain Greek heroes. So matters stood when at last one day the Argonauts rowed the *Argo* into the harbor of the island where Phineus dwelt.

As soon as the old man learned that the Greeks had arrived, he left his house and stumbled toward the harbor, a great hope swelling in his breast. When at last he had reached the place where the *Argo* was tied, he collapsed from hunger and weakness. The Argonauts marveled as they looked with pity on his shrunken form and helpless state.

"Oh, noble Greeks," he cried in a weak and faltering voice, "if you are truly the heroes that were foretold to me, then the Sons of the Northwind must be among you."

The two winged brothers stepped forward and put their hands on the old man's shoulders. "What do you seek of us?" they asked him.

"Only that you will take pity on me and rid me of the Harpies so that I may eat and gain strength again," said Phineus. "In exchange for this, I will tell you of the kingdoms before you and of the dangers you will meet there. For well I know, that if you have come thus far upon your travels from the land of Greece, you will explore farther."

Then Jason, leader of the Argonauts, stood forth. "We are on our way to Colchis in search of the Golden Fleece and welcome whatever advice you can give us."

"Let us prepare a feast that we may lure the Harpies here," said the Sons of the Northwind. "Thus we may rid Phineus of these terrible birds forever."

A feast was prepared at once, but no sooner was meat placed in front of Phineus, than the terrible Harpies came raging out of the clouds overhead. They descended upon the feasting table and started to snatch the food off his plate. Before they could lay their filthy claws upon it, the Sons of the Northwind leaped into the air with mighty wings spread and swords drawn. With a shriek, the Harpies turned and tried to fly away from the pursuing brothers. The Sons of the Northwind were almost upon them when suddenly, Iris,[10] the messenger of Zeus, appeared beside the brothers.

"Sons of the Northwind," she addressed them, "halt your flight. The harpies cannot be killed by the sword. Because you have been brave enough to pursue them, the prophecy will come true. I swear to you by the River Styx,[11] — and no god can go back on that oath — I swear that the Harpies will never bother Phineus again. Return to the feasting." So she spoke and flew back to high Olympus,[12] the home of the gods. And the Sons of the Northwind returned to their feasting.

Now Phineus could enjoy the feast and it went on

[10] Iris (ī′ris)   [11] Styx (stiks)   [12] Olympus (ō lim′ pəs)

far into the night. At last when the starving old man could hold no more, he turned his blind face to Jason.

"In order to reach Colchis," he began, "you must row between the Clashing Rocks. These are two floating islands which the sea current pushes together, then pulls apart, over and over again. You must pass between them to continue on your journey, but if you will do as I tell you, you can escape shipwreck and death. If a dove can fly between the Clashing Rocks, then you can risk it. If you do not want to be ground to splinters, you must row as swiftly as the dove flies. I will give you a dove for the test, and you must follow her unswervingly, if she flies between the Clashing Rocks. It is your only hope. And if you succeed in this, no further sea dangers will threaten you."

The next day Phineus placed a dove in Jason's grateful hands. Then the Argonauts took leave of the old man and started once more upon their dangerous journey.

For several days they sailed along smoothly, then suddenly a terrible sound fell upon their ears. It seemed as if two worlds had crashed together, and a dreadful chill struck into the hearts of the Argonauts. They were sure this must be the roar of the Clashing Rocks.

Jason rose from his place in the *Argo,* the dove held in his hands. The frightened helmsman stood at the tiller, watching tensely. Ahead, the Argonauts could see the churning water and the two islands striking together, then drifting apart and coming together to

strike again. Jason set the bird free, and the men watched it with eager faces. For Phineus had said that they might risk the passage if the dove flew safely through.

Swiftly the dove left Jason's hand and approached to where the Clashing Rocks loomed above the surface of the sea. But already the Rocks were starting to draw near to one another. The water swirled and foamed in the narrowing strait. All about was noise of air and water. Suddenly the cliffs of the two islands met, just catching the tail feathers of the dove as it sped through. Yet it had passed between the Rocks without harm. So now the Argonauts must follow.

Again, the Rocks fell apart, opening a current of ocean between them. The *Argo* was drawn into that current. On both sides, the moving cliffs loomed above the ship, and now once more were drawing toward each other. The men bent to their oars until they thought their hearts would burst with the effort of their rowing.

256

And just as those looming cliffs seemed about to crush them, the *Argo* sped forward and cleared the danger with only a slight scraping of the stern.

Now the Argonauts were beyond the Clashing Rocks with a calm sea before them. The men rested on their oars, their shoulders sagging, their chests heaving. But weary and shaken as they were, their hearts were light. For Phineus had told them that once they had passed between the Clashing Rocks, no further sea dangers would lie before them.

The Argonauts finally reached Colchis where hung the Golden Fleece. There Jason, after many adventures and dangers, at last escaped with the treasure. He later won back his kingdom, too, and made the prophecy come true about the man with one sandal.

Greek Hero Tale Retold

THINKING IT OVER

1. The stories about Jason are called "hero" tales. They tell of the impossible tasks he accepted to prove his courage. What were Jason's tasks in this story?
2. Why did Pelias *say* he wanted Jason to bring him the Golden Fleece? What do you think his real reason was?
3. How do you think the story of Phrixus might have ended if there had been no ram with golden fleece?

THOUGHTS AT WORK

1. What prophecy did the soothsayer make that helped Ino, the wicked queen, carry out her plot against Phrixus?
2. Why were the people so excited and the king so frightened when Jason entered the city wearing only one sandal?
3. Why did the king call Jason "a stranger"?
4. At Colchis the Golden Fleece was guarded by a dragon. Make up an adventure telling how you think Jason overcame the dragon and brought back the Golden Fleece.
5. Do you think the advice Phineus gave the Argonauts was as valuable as the help they had given him? Explain your answer.
6. Say the underlined phrases below in your own words.
    a. If you do not want to be ground to splinters, row swiftly.
    b. When a terrible sound fell upon their ears, a dreadful chill struck into the hearts of the Argonauts.
    c. "What do you seek of us?" the two winged brothers asked Phineus.
    d. "You must follow the dove unswervingly," said Phineus.
    e. The Argonauts bent to their oars until they thought their hearts would burst with the effort of their rowing.
7. Jason's Argonauts were famous heroes. Why were they called Argonauts? What group of modern-day heroes has a similar name? How are they like the Argonauts?

258

❧ BIBLIOGRAPHY ❧

The Seven Voyages of Sinbad the Sailor, from the Arabian Nights.
A wealthy Baghdad merchant tells wondrous tales about his bad
luck and good fortune in foreign lands.

Ingri and Edgar Parin d'Aulaire's Book of Greek Myths, retold by
Ingri and Edgar Parin d'Aulaire.
The stories of mighty Zeus, Pandora, Hercules, and King Midas
are included in this colorfully illustrated collection of Greek
myths and hero tales.

Sea Monsters, by Walter Buehr.
Explanations about the mysterious sea creatures, real and imaginary, that have been seen by seafarers through the ages.

Wonder Tales of Sea and Ships, by Frances Carpenter.
The sea is wonderful and exciting in these twenty-six folk tales
and myths from all over the world.

The Wave, by Margaret Hodges.
This ancient Japanese folk tale tells of a wise old farmer who
sacrifices much to warn his village about a great danger.

Thunder of the Gods, by Dorothy Hosford.
In this collection of Norse legends, you will discover how the
Norsemen believed the world began and how Thor got his hammer.

Sea-Spell and Moor-Magic: Tales of the Western Isles, by Sorche
Nic Leodhas
These ten tales, from the misty islands off Scotland, are full of
magic spells, fairies, giants, and folk humor.

A Book of Mermaids, by Ruth Manning-Sanders.
You will discover in these sixteen stories of half-human, half-fish
creatures, that not all mermaids are beautiful and some are even
called *mermen*.

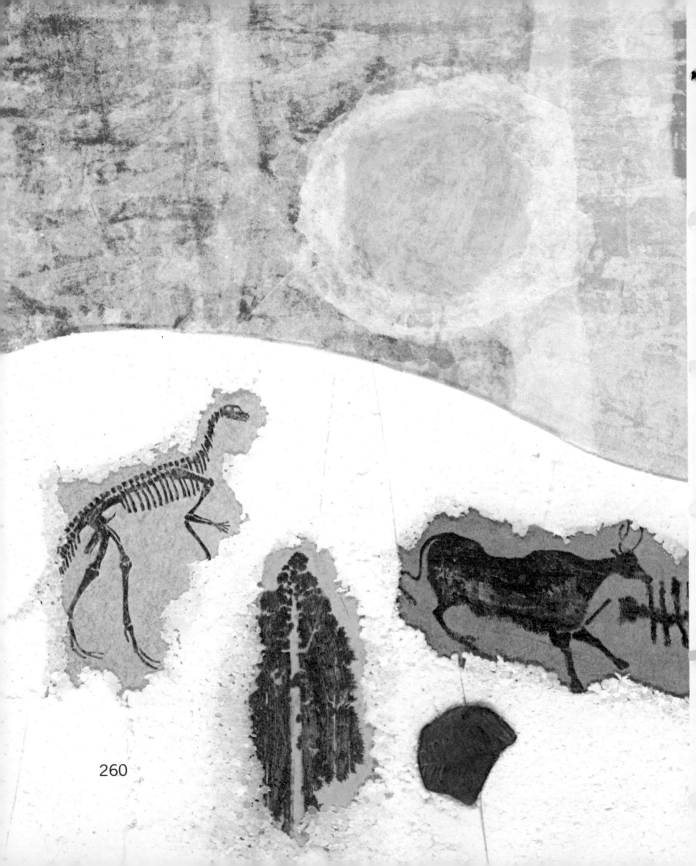

when the world was young

Around 200 million years ago, dinosaurs roamed the earth and the climate was warm and moist. Shallow seas and lowland swamps covered the land. Then very slowly the climate and surface of the land changed. The dinosaurs died out.

Then many millions of years passed. Huge sheets of ice formed and melted many times. Man and the ancestors of many animals we know today appeared on earth.

In this unit you will find many of the selections are like mystery stories. They tell how scientist-detectives have pieced together clues to tell the story of what life was like when the world was young.

Introducing Dinosaurs

You may already know a good deal about dinosaurs, but you will find new information in this selection. Think over what you now know about the "terrible lizards" and the world they lived in. What does "Introducing Dinosaurs" tell you that you didn't know about dinosaurs?

Dinosaurs were the strangest animals that ever existed on this earth. They were the sort of creatures you might think of as living on another planet or the kind you dream of in a bad nightmare. The word dinosaur means "terrible lizard." It is a good description. Dinosaurs were reptiles, cold-blooded animals related to crocodiles, snakes, and lizards. At one time they ruled the entire world.

Some were of huge size, heavier than a dozen elephants. Those had long snakelike necks, small heads, and twenty-foot

TRACHODON

tails. They waded along the edges of lakes and rivers, half sunk in mud and water, feeding on soft plants.

Others walked on powerful hind legs and stood as tall as a palm tree. Their small arms ended in clutching hands and curved claws longer than those of the biggest bear. Their mouths were more than a yard deep, bristling with great dagger-like teeth. They killed other dinosaurs and tore the flesh off their bodies, gulping it in hundred-pound chunks.

Some were huge potbellied reptiles thirty feet long. They walked upright, balanced by heavy tails. Their faces were drawn out and flattened into wide, horny beaks like a duck's bill. Two thousand small teeth filled their mouths. They loved to wallow in lakeshore mud, chewing plants and herbs. But they were good swimmers too. When a hungry flesh-eater leaped

263

TYRANNOSAURUS

BRONTOSAURUS

out of the forest, they dashed for deep water where he couldn't follow.

Other dinosaurs were short-legged and square-bodied, as big as an army tank. Long horns projected forward like two machine guns from a bony shield over an ugly, hooked beak. They lumbered through the jungle, and all other animals fled in terror.

Another fantastic reptile carried a line of triangular plates down the middle of its back. On the tip of the ten-foot tail were four huge spikes, three feet long. At the same time there lived a dinosaur completely protected by a heavy shell. Its thick tail ended in a huge mass of bone. He could swing it like a war club and give a crushing blow.

Some dinosaurs were slender and swift, skipping over the plains faster than a race horse. And some were very small, no larger than rabbits. They hid among the rocks or in the thickest forest for protection.

264

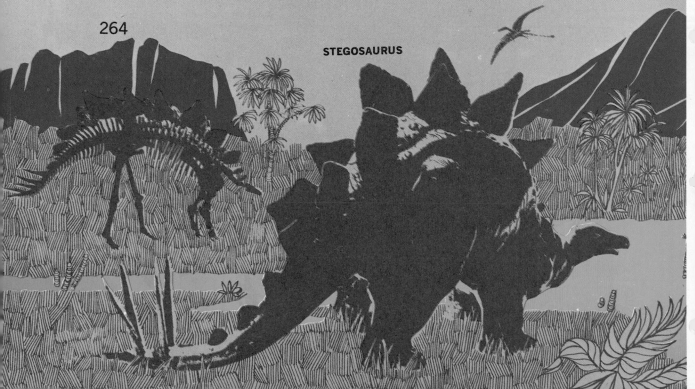

STEGOSAURUS

What I tell you about these unbelievable creatures is true. They really did live. We know they did because we find their bones buried in the earth. These bones have been fossilized, or turned to stone.

Also we find their footprints in stone. It is just as if you had stepped in soft mud, and the tracks your feet made had become solid rock. In the same way the impressions of plants and trees and insects have been preserved in stone. So we know what the country was like when the dinosaurs lived, in the Age of Reptiles.

People ask if there are any dinosaurs living today. The answer is no. They all died out at the end of the Age of Reptiles. Why they disappeared we don't know. We only know they did. When you see pictures in the "funnies" of dinosaurs with men, that is all imagination. No human being ever saw a dinosaur alive. They had become extinct 60 million years before man came upon the earth.

TRICERATOPS

CAMPTOSAURUS

ORNITHOLESTES

The Age of Reptiles lasted 140 million years. During that great length of time dinosaurs ruled the land. In the air strange goblin-like reptiles sailed through the gloomy skies. Some of them had long faces, peaked heads, and twenty-foot wings. They make one think of fairy-tale witches flying on broomsticks.

The oceans were full of other reptiles. There were great sea serpents with wide flat bodies, long slender necks, and small heads filled with sharp teeth. There were also giant lizards, forty feet long, and others that looked like fish. Truly the land, the sea, and the air were frightening in the Age of Reptiles.

But the earth back in that far, dim past was not as it is today. The climate was different. In most places it was tropical or subtropical like southern California or southern Florida. The climate was the same almost everywhere. There were no cold winters. If there had been, the reptiles could not have flourished the way they did. They didn't like cold weather. In those days the weather was warm and damp the year round. Thick jungles, low lands, and swamps stretched across most of the world.

In the Age of Reptiles the great mountain ranges had not yet been born. The Himalayas,[1] now the highest mountain range in the world, did not exist. There were no Rocky Mountains. Instead, the low-lying country of western America and

[1] Himalayas (him′ə lā′əz)

FOSSILS

ICHTHYOSAURUS

of central Europe held great inland seas. What is now the state of Kansas was covered with water, also Wyoming and Montana. The land lifted at times and sank and rose again. One hundred forty million years is a long time, and many changes took place.

Our geography books would not have been of much use then. The continents were not as they are today. There were land bridges which do not exist at the present time. North America and Asia doubtless had a wide land bridge across the Bering Strait.[2] North and South America were more broadly united than today. Possibly North America and Europe were joined across Greenland and Iceland. Asia and Australia were joined by land in what is now the East Indies.

This is the way scientists think the world geography looked during much of the Age of Reptiles. You can see, therefore, that animals could have traveled from one continent to another. They were not cut off by the climate, mountains, and oceans that exist today.

That is why dinosaur bones are found over much of the world. They have been discovered in North and South America from Canada to Patagonia,[3] in different parts of Europe, in Africa and Asia, and even in Australia.

[2] Bering Strait (bir'ing strat)
[3] Patagonia (pat'ə gō'nē ə)

——*Roy Chapman Andrews*

267

ELASMOSAURUS

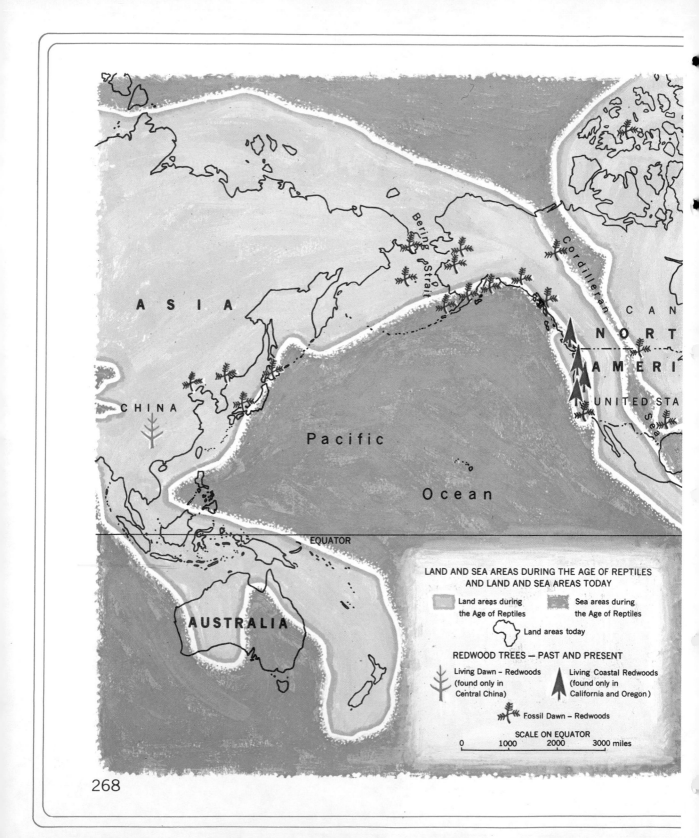

ASIA

Bering Strait

Cordilleran

CAN

NORT

AMERI

CHINA

UNITED STA

Pacific

Ocean

EQUATOR

AUSTRALIA

LAND AND SEA AREAS DURING THE AGE OF REPTILES
AND LAND AND SEA AREAS TODAY

Land areas during
the Age of Reptiles

Sea areas during
the Age of Reptiles

Land areas today

REDWOOD TREES — PAST AND PRESENT

Living Dawn – Redwoods
(found only in
Central China)

Living Coastal Redwoods
(found only in
California and Oregon)

Fossil Dawn – Redwoods

SCALE ON EQUATOR

0   1000   2000   3000 miles

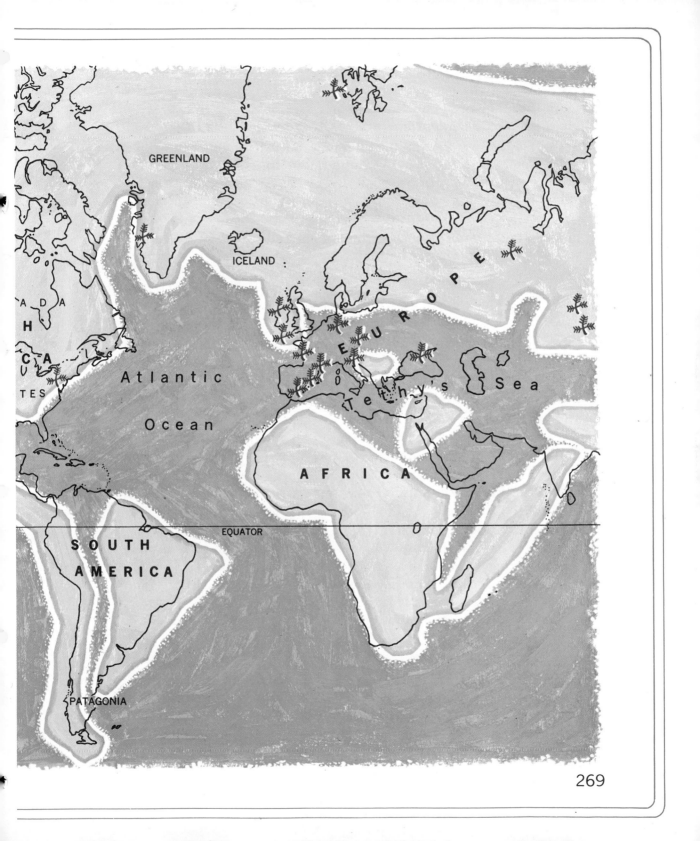

GREENLAND

ICELAND

H

C A D A

E U R O P E

C A

T E S

Atlantic

Ocean

Tethy's Sea

AFRICA

EQUATOR

SOUTH
AMERICA

PATAGONIA

THINKING IT OVER

1. Find four reasons why the author could say, "Dinosaurs were the strangest animals that ever existed on this earth."
2. Reread each paragraph listed below. Match each one with a reptile picture in the story. Write the name of each reptile.
   - a. page 262, paragraph 2
   - b. page 263, paragraph 1
   - c. page 263, paragraph 2
   - d. page 264, paragraph 1
   - e. page 266, paragraph 1
   - f. page 266, paragraph 2
3. In the Age of Reptiles the earth was not as it is today. Tell three ways in which it was different.

THOUGHTS AT WORK

1. Dinosaurs died out long before man lived on earth. Name two ways scientists have found out about them.
2. Scientists aren't sure why the dinosaurs died out after 140 million years. Can you think of some possible reasons?
3. The author compared dinosaurs to other animals and objects we know, such as elephants. Reread the first three pages and find as many comparisons as you can.
4. At the top of your paper write this sentence: The Trachodon was a strange-looking animal. Then reread paragraph 2 on page 263 and list four facts that explain the sentence.
5. The map on pages 268 and 269 shows how the world looked during the Age of Reptiles and how it looks today. Use this map to answer the following questions:
   - a. Across what body of water was there a land bridge?
   - b. What sea once covered the Rocky Mountains?
   - c. Which two continents did Greenland and Iceland join?
   - d. Were Asia and Australia once joined together?
6. Would you consider running a race with a dinosaur? Why or why not?
7. Write a report telling about a dinosaur and where it lived. Use reference books for your information.

The Brontosaurus

The Brontosaurus
Had a brain
No bigger than
A crisp;

The Dodo
Had a stammer
And the Mammoth
Had a lisp;

The Auk
Was just too Aukward—
Now they're none of them
Alive.

Each one,
(Like Man),
Had shown himself
Unfitted to survive.

This story
Points a moral:
Now it's
We
Who wear the pants;

The extinction
Of these species
Holds a lesson
For us
ANTS.

—*Michael Flanders*

271

The Story of the
Dawn Red-Wood Trees

No man ever saw the dinosaurs alive. Yet, you will be reading two newspaper accounts of a journey that took two scientists back 100 million years to the time of the Age of Reptiles. Impossible? No, but as you will see, the trip was exciting and sometimes dangerous.

One hundred million years ago, when dinosaurs were kings of the animal world, dawn-redwoods were kings of the forest. The dinosaurs are now extinct, and scientists had always believed that the dawn-redwoods had died out also. Then why did Dr. Ralph W. Chaney, of the University of California, look for these ancient ancestors of our own California and Oregon redwoods?

The story began in 1947. The first clues that the trees might have survived came when a Chinese forester brought out some needles and cones. He had taken them from trees growing in a little-known part of China.

272

To find out what the puzzling specimens were, the forester sent them to two Chinese scientists. The scientists knew that the redwoods found in the United States had very ancient ancestors. The fossil remains of these ancient trees had been found in Europe long ago. Both scientists agreed that the living specimens looked amazingly like the fossils.

They decided to send some of the specimens to America —to Dr. Ralph Chaney, one of the world's greatest experts on prehistoric plants. He too agreed with the scientists from China. The specimens looked exactly like the fossils of the dawn-redwoods.

"If this is proved true," Dr. Chaney exclaimed, "it will be the greatest botanical discovery of the century."

Proof seemed necessary. No trained scientist had seen the trees. The whole thing might be a mistake, or some kind of joke.

In minutes, Dr. Chaney was studying maps as well as airline schedules, preparing for a trip to China. To report on the expedition, the *San Francisco Chronicle* asked their science reporter Dr. Milton Silverman to go with Dr. Chaney. In a few days, they were on their way, beginning a trip that was to cover thousands of miles and last for months.

Science Makes a Spectacular Discovery

Story of a Tree Whose Family Lived with the Dinosaurs

By Milton Silverman
Science Writer, The Chronicle

MO-TAO-CHI (Szechwan Province), March 15 (Delayed) – A race of ancestral redwood trees which flourished 100 million years ago is surviving here in a far-off valley deep in the heart of China.

These trees are known as the dawn-redwoods – themselves between five and six centuries old.

Their race is older than the human race, as old as the giant dinosaurs.

They are the ancient ancestors of the modern redwoods now growing in California and Oregon.

With the prehistoric animals, dawn-redwoods had supposedly become extinct about 20 million years ago, leaving behind only the fossil traces of their needles and cones.

Three of these "living fossils," however, were seen alive here today by Dr. Ralph Chaney, one of the world's greatest experts on prehistoric plants. He is the first modern scientist to see them.

He proved that they were alive – an amazing story of survival – after traveling more than 10,000 miles by airplane from San Francisco to Chungking (chŭng′ king′) and then by river boat down the Yangtze (yang′ tsē′) River to the river port of Wan-Hsien (wän-shen).

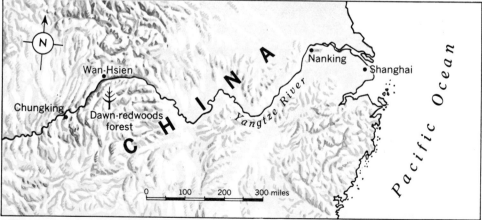

The route: by air from Shanghai to Nanking to Chungking, then by sampan down the Yangtze River to Wan-Hsien, then over the mountains to the valley.

The Journey into the Interior

There were no roads leading to the valley where the trees were reported to be. There was only a winding trail that led up and down and around an endless line of steep canyons.

We began with seven coolies to carry our baggage – heavy winter clothes, sleeping bags, medical supplies, scientific equipment, Army K-rations, and a few cans of food for an emergency – and a dozen men to carry us in sedan chairs.

These sedan chairs proved to be a pain, and not in the neck.

They were useful only on rare trail stretches, where walking was just as easy as riding. In traveling the slippery, dangerous, and often steep mountain trails, walking was quicker and much more comfortable for American-built backbones.

Traveling from dawn to dark, we made 15 miles the first day, climbing

after another.

Bandits Reported

At night we reached a village where we learned that bandits were working in the area. The police were all out chasing them.

We stayed in a cold, dark, dirty inn, first spraying the place with DDT.

The next morning we discovered that while police were searching the hills, the bandits had come into the town to hide and had passed about 100 feet from us.

On the second day we hired for protection a few soldiers – ragged, straw-sandaled youths equipped with old guns – each of them cost us about 18 cents a day.

Dr. Chaney in a sedan chair carried by coolies through a village street.

Arrival at a Village

Late in the afternoon on our third day we arrived at an old village of about 1,000 people. The last visitors they had seen had passed through more than a year before.

Accordingly, we were greeted by the villagers as an event. Adults lined the single, narrow, main alley. Crowds of older children raced along beside and ahead of us, and small babies were lifted to their fathers' shoulders to see the sight.

When we went out to see the dawn-redwoods, nearly everyone in town went with us. The soldiers who were with us were not able to keep all the townspeople back while Dr. Chaney made his measurements and took his photographs.

During the performance, untold numbers of chickens and pigs were walked on, one of our soldiers slammed his own shins with his gun, and four children and one adult slipped into the not altogether clean water of a nearby rice paddy.

The people hadn't had such a good time, the Magistrate told us later, since the village tax collectors had fallen into their own cesspool.

Many meals were eaten in inns like this one which were open to the street. Coolies stand by our baggage.

A small temple built at the base of a 100 foot-dawn-redwood tree.

Examining the Trees

There is no doubt that members of the dawn-redwood race have really survived. We have seen them, touched them, photographed them, measured them, and examined their green buds. We have even climbed them.

All three of the dawn-redwoods seen today are growing close together on a rice-paddy bank. Two are small, slender trees. The third, worshiped by villagers as the home of a "tree god", is more than 10 feet wide and nearly 100 feet high.

"But three trees are not very many," Dr. Chaney declared, very disappointed. He had also hoped to see them growing in their natural environment.

To tell the age of the tree, Dr. Silverman uses a borer to take out a core.

The Trip Continues

Accordingly, we headed farther south seeking reported "many dawn-redwoods" near a village called Shui-Hsa-Pa (shü e-shä-bä) not shown on even the best Chinese and American maps.

With the party is a young Chinese

year, and who believes he can guide us there.

Unfortunately, he traveled to the area last year by a different and much longer route. We are taking what should be a more direct shortcut— which he believes to be just what Americans would do.

Like most shortcuts, this one had its drawbacks. It began as a rock-paved trail, wandered across a gentle sloping valley, and then started up a range of mountains whose heads are all hidden in clouds.

Thereupon, the trail turned into a steep, winding path which vanished upward in fog and mist, and a freezing, driving rain turned the ground into red, slippery mud.

At a height of 5,700 feet—more than a mile above sea level—the path leveled off through a long, windy pass and then pitched downward into a valley and across to a village.

Journey's End

The local magistrate, who arranged to have us sleep in a Buddhist temple, was somewhat surprised at our arrival.

"That one is a very bad route," he said. "Many people are killed trying to cross that way. If you slip, you fall many hundreds of feet. Very dangerous. I suppose you know there are many bandits and wild boar and even tigers on those mountains."

We hadn't known.

A rocky, winding trail led through a valley with steep terraced slopes.

277

Ancient Redwoods Found in Chinese Valley

By Milton Silverman
Science Writer, The Chronicle

SHUI-HSA-PA (Hupeh Province), March 17 (Delayed)—We have found a lost world—a world that existed more than a million centuries ago. It is a mysteriously protected bit of the earth as it appeared during the Age of Reptiles, when enormous dinosaurs and flying lizards were lords of all the earth.

Here, on this red sandy soil, once lived the horn-headed dinosaur and the frightening flesh-eating Tyrannosaurus. Here are the trees—ancient oak, sassafras, birch, sweet gum, and laurel—which sheltered the Brontosaurus, the enormous plant-eater.

Here is where the Pterodactyl, the great flying reptile with its 27-foot wing spread, came flying over the hills to find its prey.

And here, by the hundreds, are the dawn-redwoods—the ancient race of trees which were kings of the forest a hundred million years ago, just as the dinosaurs were kings of the animal world.

There are no dinosaurs here today, except as fossil remains in the rocks. But the trees are alive. Somehow or other, their race has managed to survive.

Dr. Chaney, left, and Dr. Silverman hold a cross-section of a dawn-redwood.

Lost Valley Found

This is the Valley of Dawn-Redwoods, lying almost out of reach in the Mountains of Seven Hump, deep in the heart of China.

It is certainly not a land of make-believe. It really exists.

It was reached today by Ralph W. Chaney at the end of a five-day trip over muddy, slippery mountain trails from Wan-Hsien, a river port on the Yangtze River.

"We have come a hundred miles by trail and a hundred million years in history," Dr. Chaney said. "Now, for the first time, we can see with our own eyes how the world really looked in the Age of Reptiles."

278

THINKING IT OVER

1. What made the dawn-redwoods so important that Dr. Chaney traveled 10,000 miles and faced many dangers to see them?

2. What things did you learn from the maps and pictures that you couldn't learn from reading the newspaper articles?

3. The first article on pages 274–277 is divided into seven parts. Each has a subtitle. Write three of these subtitles and beneath each one write three important facts you found in that part.

THOUGHTS AT WORK

1. What dangers and hardships did Dr. Chaney and his expedition face on the trip?

2. Name four ways Dr. Chaney and Dr. Silverman examined the first three dawn-redwood trees. Why do you suppose the two scientists examined them so carefully?

3. Pretend you were one of the children in the first small village where Dr. Chaney stopped. Describe what happened and tell how you felt when everyone went to examine the trees.

4. What did Dr. Chaney mean when he said, "We have come a hundred miles by trail and a hundred million years in history"?

5. The phrases below tell how Dr. Chaney traveled from California to the home of the dawn-redwoods. Read all the phrases, then write them in the correct order. The map on page 274 will help.
    a. On foot, following trails through canyons to a small village
    b. By plane from San Francisco across the Pacific Ocean to Shanghai
    c. By boat down the Yangtze River to Wan-Hsien, and then along the trail leading across the mountains
    d. On foot going south, taking a shortcut to the valley
    e. By plane to Nanking
    f. By plane to Chungking

THE ICE AGE

This selection, which is about a time millions of years after the dinosaurs died out, is divided into three parts. The first part tells how great sheets of ice slowly changed the earth. The second part explains how scientists have learned something about the Ice Age. And the third part gives you information about the men and animals who lived during the Ice Age.

Each of these parts is jam-packed with information. A single sentence tells the alert reader a great deal. Reading a science selection is a cautious, go-slow affair. Read carefully.

THE SECRETS OF THE WINTRY PAST

Slowly—inch by inch, foot by foot—the ice crept forward. From the far north great sheets of ice spread out, swallowing the land. From the high mountains rivers of ice reached down and filled the valleys.

All things gave way before the ice.

Ice ground up rock. It carved the sides of mountains. It dug great hollows in the earth. It scooped up dirt, gravel, stones, and boulders. Whole forests fell, trees snapping like toothpicks before the flow of ice.

281

There was snow, driven by howling winds. There was rain that fell and froze. The ice grew thousands of feet thick. And growing, it pushed farther south. Year after year it flowed on, covering meadows, lakes, and hills.

The ice was felt far away, for winds sweeping across it carried the cold of winter to the land ahead. All living things fled before the cold — or died.

And this went on for thousands of years.

Sometimes the ice would melt at the edges and shrink back. Then the forward flow would start again. Creeping, grinding, carving, scraping, the ice of ever-winter would swallow the land.

Finally the great tongues of ice, the great sheets of ice, drew back for good, leaving behind their floods of melt-water.

In time, life came back to the land, for the ice was gone. It had drawn back to the far north, back to the mountain heights.

The land, of course, was changed. There were new lakes and rivers born of melting ice. Ice had carved out hills and valleys. There was land scraped bare of soil. There was land made rich by soil the ice had dropped.

On this ice-free land, plants grew and spread. Animals came to live on it. And men followed the animals.

Thousands of years went by. Men made the land theirs. They grazed herds, planted crops, and built cities where once sheets of ice had glittered in the sun. And no one guessed the wintry secrets of the past.

THE SECRETS ARE UNLOCKED

The earth holds many secrets of its past. For thousands of years the Ice Age, the time of ever-winter, was one of those secrets. Only two hundred years ago men still did not dream that thick sheets of ice had once covered a third of the earth's land.

In the places where men lived, there was no year-round ice. In winter snow might fall and water freeze. But the spring sun melted the snow and ice and called the land to life, making it green with plants. This same thing happened year after year.

In some parts of the world there were glaciers, big masses of ice that did not melt away in summer. But glaciers were found only in the far, cold places—in polar lands and in the high mountains. There the glaciers were, and there they stayed.

The only people who had ever known about the ice were those who lived during the Ice Age. Some saw the ice. Some fled the floods when the glaciers began to shrink and melt. But these were early people who could not write, and they left no record of the ice or floods. What they had seen and known became forgotten. Men who lived later did not learn of it.

And so it happened that two hundred years ago the Ice Age was still a secret. No one knew that it had taken place. Yet the story of the Ice Age had been written. It had been written, not by people, but by the ice itself. Where the ice had been, it left its marks upon the land. By learning to read these marks, scientists discovered the Ice Age.

There were, for example, many puzzling boulders. These boulders were puzzling because they did not match any kind of rock in the place where they were found. It was clear that something must have carried them miles from the place where they had formed.

Scientists had wondered about these boulders for years. Most scientists thought that a great and sudden flood must have carried and dropped the boulders. Then, in the early 1800's, a new idea was put forward. Perhaps, some scientists said, glaciers had carried the boulders. Perhaps these glaciers once reached down from the mountains, scooping up rocks and carrying them along. When the glaciers melted and shrank, they dropped the rocks and left them behind.

Was this new idea true? To find out, daring Swiss scientists climbed the Alps. They camped on glaciers and studied them. And they made several discoveries. One was that glaciers move. In time, ice from the upper end of a glacier flows to the lower end, where it melts. Moving, the ice leaves its marks on rocky, mountain walls. It polishes some rock smooth. It makes deep scratches in other rocks.

284

The marks of modern glaciers were found in the Alps. The same kinds of marks were found in many other places where there are no glaciers today. That was how scientists started to read the secret of the Ice Age, as written in the earth. That was how they learned of a time when sheets of ice and rivers of ice flowed over lands that are now green and free of ice.

Since that time of discovery, scientists have learned much more. They now know that the earth has had several ice ages. The older ones took place hundreds of millions of years ago. Their marks are very faint, but they can still be read. The last ice age is the one we call the Ice Age.

No one yet knows when the Ice Age began, but some scientists think it started some ten or twenty million years ago. It did not come suddenly upon the earth as a huge snowstorm. Instead, it began as a slow cooling of the air. As time passed, the air grew cooler and cooler, and the oceans also cooled. In faraway places, more snow fell in winter than the summer sun could melt. Year after year the snows fell and piled up. The weight of new snows packed the old snow into ice. The ice grew thicker and thicker.

With their great weight of ice and snow, the glaciers began to flow. Rivers of ice crept down from the mountains. Sheets of ice spread out over polar lands. Only an ocean could stop the ice, for glaciers are land ice and do not form over water. Where glaciers met an ocean, their tongues broke off and floated away as icebergs. But on land the glaciers flowed on and on, over mountains, hills, and plains. New snows fell on this ice and made it even thicker. The ice flowed on, covering large parts of Asia, Europe, and North America. In North America the ice reached as far south as where St. Louis is today.

Then something happened, and the glaciers stopped growing. They melted and shrank back, back to the far places of the earth. After a time they began to grow again. Once more ice covered once-green lands. And this happened four times during the Ice Age. Four times the great glaciers reached down. Four times they melted and shrank back. The last started to draw back about 19,000 years ago. By 6,000 years ago most of the land was once more free of ice. The land was beginning to look very much as it does today.

In the past 150 years scientists have learned much about the Ice Age, but there are some secrets they have not yet discovered. What caused the cooling and made the glaciers grow? What stopped them from growing and made them shrink? Why did they grow and shrink four times? Has the Ice Age ended, or will the glaciers grow a fifth time? Many scientists have ideas about these questions, but no one can answer them for sure.

Over the years scientists have also asked many questions about life in the Ice Age. They have wondered about the animals that lived during the Ice Age. Why did some kinds die out, while others did not? Why did some kinds live through the Ice Age but die out at its end? And what about early man? Did he keep away from the ice? Or did he find a way to live near the wall of ice and hunt the cold-loving animals? Some of the answers to these questions have been found, as you will see in the next part of the story. But you will also discover that many mysteries still remain about "Life in the Ice Age."

LIFE IN THE ICE AGE

There was a time when elephants crashed through the forests of North America, when camels lived upon the land along with horses, deer, and mammoths. Huge herds of bison, or buffalo, roamed the plains. Saber-toothed tigers sprang from hiding at passing horses or deer. Giant, shaggy-coated ground sloths uprooted trees and ate their leaves. The land was alive with wolves, lions, wild pigs, bears, and dozens of other kinds of animal.

Then the ice came. By the end of the Ice Age, three-fourths of all these animals had disappeared from North America. Some are still found in other lands, but some are long gone from the earth.

The Ice Age made itself felt in many ways.

To begin with, there was the ice, creeping forward, covering the land, and making whole forests fall. Where the ice lay thick upon the land for thousands of years, there could be no life at all.

Then there was the cold that moved ahead of the ice, carried by winds that swept the glaciers. Because of the cold, plants of the north kept spreading south, while southern plants spread farther south. At times when the ice melted and drew back, the plants spread slowly north again.

The shifting of plant life was important because plants are the basic form of food on earth. Many animals eat plants. Other animals eat the animals that eat plants. And men eat both plants and animals.

So when plant life moved, animal life also moved. In the last part of the Ice Age, whole groups of people moved too. These people were herders and hunters. Where the animals went, the people followed. And the animals followed the plants.

Of these animals, some kinds survived the Ice Age. Some kinds survived in one place and died out in another. Still other kinds died out everywhere.

The saber-toothed tiger was one of the animals that died out everywhere. A big, fierce killer, the saber-tooth ruled wherever he lived. No other animal was his match. Yet the ice wiped him out, while animals that served the saber-tooth as food survived.

The giant ground sloth also died out. These sloths were cousins of the small sloths that live today in

South America. Clumsy and slow-moving, they were bigger than grizzly bears. Their skin was covered with little pieces of bone and with thick hair, which protected them from meat-eating enemies. There is reason to think that early men tamed the sloths which were harmless plant-eaters. The men survived, but the sloths did not.

The end of the mammoths is even more puzzling. Mammoths were huge animals of the elephant family. As cold spread over the land, some mammoths grew thick, shaggy fur. They became cold-loving animals that hugged the northern borders of the land. When the Ice Age ended, mammoths changed again. They survived the floods and the warmer times. Then they died out. Perhaps they were killed off by early hunters, who killed herds of animals by driving them over cliffs. Perhaps something else happened. No one knows.

To many people the greatest mystery of all has to do with horses. During the Ice Age, big herds of horses grazed the plains of North America, Europe, and Asia. In Europe and Asia horses survived both the Ice Age and its end. In America they did not. Yet American bison grazed the same plains as the horses, and the bison survived. No one knows what happened to the horses. But there were no more horses in the Americas until, long after, explorers and settlers brought them in from Europe.

There are also great gaps in what we know about the people who lived during the Ice Age. So far we do not know whether people came to North America during the Ice Age or only as it was ending. We do know, though, that 20,000 years ago there were people living in Europe. These people were cave dwellers, and they were skilled hunters and herders. They could not write, but they drew pictures on the walls of their caves, and they made carvings. Their paintings, like their carvings, tell a story of animals. To these people, animals were both food and clothing.

On the walls of the caves, long-dead animals parade. There are woolly rhinoceroses. There are mammoths and bison and horses. There are lions, bears, hyenas, and saber-toothed tigers.

A whole Ice Age village has been uncovered in Czechoslovakia.[1] Here Ice Age hunters camped. They made shelters and warmed themselves with fires. Piles

[1] Czechoslovakia (chek′ ə slō vä′ kē ə)

of bones show that they hunted mammoths, rhinoceroses, lions, horses, arctic foxes, and reindeer. They killed small animals with spears. They trapped big animals by digging deep pits and covering these over. When a mammoth or a rhinoceros fell into the pit, the hunters killed it with huge stones.

Most Ice Age people lived well south of the glaciers. Some hunted near the edge of the glaciers. Perhaps some even lived near the edge of the ice. Certainly, they *could* have.

They had fire, which they would have needed for warmth. They would have found animals, which they needed for food. From the same animals they could have gotten warm furs for robes and clothing. With their tools of bone and hard stone, the people could have made clothing like that worn today by Eskimos.

Fire, food, clothing. The people would have needed one more thing—shelter. There were some caves, but not enough. Still, the people had the skills and tools to make tents. They could have felled and trimmed poles. They could have skinned animals, dressed the skins, and laced the skins around tent poles. There are tribes in cold parts of the world that use such tents today.

Did these people live near the edge of the glaciers? Did they see the ice move forward or shrink back? We do not know, but we are still learning. Perhaps the surprising thing is that we know so much.

——*Patricia Lauber*

THINKING IT OVER

1. What were the titles of the three sections in "The Ice Age"? Which section did you find the most interesting? Why?

2. Choose one of the mysteries that still remain about the Ice Age. Think of some answers that might solve it.

3. Skim the first section of "The Ice Age," and find the words and phrases that describe what the ice did as it slowly crept forward. Which word did you like the best? Why?

THOUGHTS AT WORK

1. Write the sentence: The Ice Age made itself felt in many ways. Reread page 282 and list four facts that explain this statement.

2. Look on page 284 and find two of the marks that the glaciers left upon the land.

3. Skim page 294 and find the things the Ice Age people would have needed to live near the edge of the glaciers. Do you think you could ever live near a glacier? Explain your answer.

4. Write these two headings: Age of Reptiles, The Ice Age. Then write the following words beneath the correct heading:

terrible lizard	glaciers	Brontosaurus
bison	mammoth	Pterodactyl
ground sloth	rhinoceros	horse
Tyrannosaurus	saber-toothed tiger	man

5. Are we living in the Ice Age today? Explain your answer, then check what you have said by reading paragraph 2 on page 287.

6. The people who lived thousands of years ago could not write. How did they leave their story? Why is it important?

7. Scientists have known about the Ice Age for only about 200 years. What was happening in our country around 200 years ago?

FOUR BOYS AND THE
FRENCH CAVE OF LASCAUX

Most of us hope that someday, someway, we might make a great scientific discovery. This story tells about four boys who made such a discovery accidentally. Someone has said, "Chance favors the alert mind." What does this saying mean? How does it apply to this selection?

Four boys discovered the wonderful prehistoric cave paintings of Lascaux[1] in central France. Their story began one morning in September, 1940, during the Second World War, in the town of Montignac.[2]

Montignac is on the Vézère[3] River. Limestone cliffs rise up all about it. Among these cliffs are several caves which, by 1940, scientists had already explored. Like almost everybody in this area, the boys knew about those caves. They had visited the nearest ones with their teacher. They had listened carefully when he told them how to recognize ancient bones and stone tools. They hoped to be lucky enough themselves to find some new clues to prehistoric cave men.

On the morning their story begins, however, the boys weren't thinking about prehistoric times. France had been conquered by Nazi Germany just three months

[1] Lascaux (las kō')   [2] Montignac (môn'tē nyak')
[3] Vézère (vā zâr')

before, and the usually cheerful town of Montignac had become a sad place. When the boys wanted to escape it for a few hours, they wandered among the forested cliffs along the river. That's why they set off for the cliffs on the morning of September 12, with a little dog named Robot[4] who belonged to one of them.

Suddenly, while the boys were climbing the hill called Lascaux, one of them noticed that Robot was no longer at their heels. Marcel,[5] the dog's owner, whistled for him and called out his name. But the frisky dog didn't come bounding back to his place.

[4] Robot (rō bō′) [5] Marcel (mär sel′)

Marcel's friend, Jacques,[6] and the other boys called Robot too. Still he didn't appear or answer them with his bark. Finally they decided he must have been hurt, and they turned back anxiously to look for him.

Every few seconds they stopped to whistle and shout, and to listen for some kind of answer. At last they heard excited barking. But it sounded so faint and so far away that they couldn't imagine where the dog was.

They called again. Again the bark replied. This time they realized that the sound came from under their feet, from somewhere underground. A moment later they found a small hole, not much larger than a rabbit burrow. They realized that Robot had somehow fallen down it and couldn't get out.

Swiftly the boys fell to work to enlarge the opening. They cut away the roots of shrubs with their knives and dug out small stones, calling to Robot all the while to promise him that he would soon be free. But the little dog didn't appear even when the hole had been doubled in size. His barking didn't seem to come any closer.

"I'll have to go down and get him," Marcel said.

So the boys made the hole bigger still, until Marcel could squeeze himself into it.

"Don't worry, Robot," he called. "I'm coming!"

Marcel pushed himself into the opening head first, and worked his way for several yards along a steeply

[6] Jacques (jäk)

sloping tunnel. When he thought he had reached the bottom and tried to get to his feet, he lost his balance and found himself rolling helplessly downward. His journey came to an end with a jarring thud.

The other boys heard the rattle of stones and the crash of their friend's landing. "Are you all right?" Jacques shouted.

Marcel shook himself. He felt bruised, but otherwise he was not hurt. And Robot was leaping about him, licking happily at his hands and face.

"I'm all right and so is Robot," he called upward. "But it will be a hard climb to get out again."

"What's down there?" the other boys wanted to know.

Marcel flicked the switch on the small flashlight that had been in his pocket. "A cave, I think," he said. And then he added excitedly, as he swung the beam around, "Yes—a cave! Come on down! But be careful or you'll fall the last part of the way."

One after another the other boys slid down, clutching at roots and rocks as they tried to slow their fall. Finally they all stood together on the bottom, brushing themselves free of dirt while Robot barked his welcome.

"Look!" Marcel told them, pointing his flashlight. "Over there!"

Only a few feet away an enormous animal loomed out of the surrounding darkness, bright red against a paler background. Then they saw another animal, and still another.

For a moment the boys were startled until they realized that the beasts were figures painted on the wall of the cave in striking black and bright yellow and red.

"They're like the pictures at the Font-de-Gaume[7] Cave!" one boy whispered in awe. "Only there are so many more of them!"

"Let's explore!"

With Marcel in the lead, they moved forward slowly into the center of a great hall-like cavern almost a

[7] Font-de-Gaume (fōn'dgōm')

hundred feet long. The pictures were all around them, on both long walls and even stretching up onto the curved ceiling.

There were prancing wild horses with tossing manes. There were prehistoric bulls—four of them, three times larger than life, sprawled across the ceiling. There were bison and long-antlered deer. One row of deer heads looked exactly like a group of animals swimming across a stream—across the Vézère River itself, perhaps—with only their heads showing above the water.

It was late when the boys reluctantly scrambled back up the steep slope, taking Robot along with them. By then they knew that they had made a discovery so important that they would have to show it to other people, their teacher first of all. But they had already promised each other that they would keep their exciting find a secret until they had a chance to explore it completely themselves. Cautiously they made their plans.

The next morning the boys left Montignac one by one, so that no one would become curious as to the group's purpose. Each boy carried a flashlight in his pocket. They met at the entrance to the cave and again Marcel led the way down the sloping tunnel to the cavern thirty feet below the surface.

That day they explored not only the big hall at the foot of the slope, but the two passages leading out of it at its far end. One passage ran straight forward. The other ran to the right, and divided into two smaller branches after a short distance.

The walls of both the passages were painted too. Altogether there were so many pictures, some painted on top of others, that the boys couldn't begin to count them all. There were pictures of single animals, some bigger than life, like the bulls on the ceiling of the hall, others scarcely larger than a man's hand. There were groups of animals shown together. There were animals that seemed to be standing still, and others that seemed to be leaping or falling or racing. Here and there were crisscrossed lines that looked as if they might be pictures of animal traps, and long straight lines that looked like spears.

The strangest picture of all was right at the bottom of a deep pit at the end of one of the passages. It was strange because there was a man in it, drawn in single lines like a stick figure drawn by a small child. He seemed to be hurt, for he was toppling backward. On one side of him was a wounded bison with wildly staring eyes looking right at the boys as they crouched at the bottom of the pit. Perched on a stick on the other side of the man was a bird, crudely drawn, but looking very much alive, as if he were watching over the death of the beast and the man.

The next day and the day after that, the boys returned to their cave. At each visit they found something they hadn't noticed before, and grew more excited than ever about their own secret prehistoric art museum. But they knew they couldn't keep their secret forever. On the fifth day they told their teacher what they had found. At first the man thought they must be joking. Even when he was convinced that the boys had actually discovered a prehistoric painted cave, he couldn't believe that it was as important a find as they insisted it was. But finally he agreed to go and look at it himself.

The teacher didn't speak at all when he first stared around the big painted hall. He just gasped in amazement. Then he said, "We must waste no time. We must send at once for Abbé Henri Breuil."[8]

The boys knew that name. They knew that the French priest Abbé Breuil had been chosen to copy the famous paintings at Altamira.[9] They had heard the story of how, as a young man, he had lain on his back for weeks, under the low Altamira ceiling, in order to set down every line and every shade of those paintings. The copies he had made of them, printed in a book, had shown the whole world the glories of that Spanish cave.

Since that time Abbe Breuil had become France's —perhaps the world's—greatest expert on prehistoric art. If Abbe Breuil decided that the paintings the boys had discovered were worth copying, too, then the cave

[8] Abbé Henri Breuil (ä bā′ än rē′ brû′y′) [9] Altamira (äl tä mē′rä)

on Lascaux hill would also become famous throughout the world.

Abbé Breuil came at once. Not even the difficulties of travel in wartime France could prevent his coming. And after his first words, the boys knew that the town of Montignac would never seem such a sad place again. They knew that from then on there would always be something exciting happening on the Lascaux hill.

For Abbé Breuil, and the other experts who soon joined him in Montignac, agreed that the cave was one of the greatest art treasures in France. They said it must be opened to the public so that all the world could admire the paintings. But the experts also agreed that the priceless paintings might be destroyed if the cave were opened to the public without being carefully prepared.

These men knew that the paintings had survived for thousands of years only because the air in the sealed-up cave had remained at the same degree of temperature and moisture all that time. If the cave were opened and outside air poured through it, those conditions would change and the pictures might soon begin to grow dim and peel off the walls.

So they sent for engineers to plan a special air-conditioning system to protect the prehistoric art. Other engineers made plans to enlarge the cave's entrance and cover it with heavy airtight doors. Still other experts designed a lighting system that would show the paintings to their best advantage. Until 1945, when the war ended and France became free once again, very little actual work could be done. Even after the war it took time to build the special air-conditioning and ventilating machinery that was needed.

Finally, in 1948, everything was finished. The famous Lascaux cave was opened to public view, and people began to arrive at Montignac from all over the world. Two young guides were waiting to show these visitors through the Hall of the Bulls, as the big cavern had been named.

The guides had been carefully trained for their job, and could tell the visitors many things about the Lascaux paintings. They could point out, first of all, how cleverly the artists had used the roughness of the rock. By drawing the outline of a bull around a bulge in the wall—instead of drawing it on a smooth, flat place—a prehistoric artist had made a picture that seemed to have thickness as well as height and width. The bulging rock made the animal look real and alive.

The guides could also explain that the cavemen probably made their paints by mixing certain materials with animal fat. Charcoal from a fire, the guides said, gave the artists their black paint, and powdered minerals gave them their red and yellow colors.

The guides could explain the painting methods the artists used too. The earliest cave men simply dipped their fingers in paint and used their fingertips for drawing lines on the stone. Later artists probably used brushes made out of feathers. Some of the prehistoric painters also used a method something like our modern spray painting. They spread fat on the wall, and then blew powdered color at it through a hollow reed. The color stuck to the greasy surface and formed a layer of paint that had a light, misty look.

The guides told the visitors that no one knew for certain why prehistoric men had made hundreds of pictures deep inside Lascaux and certain other caves. But most experts agreed, the guides said, that the pictures were made because the cave men believed in magic. When a cave man went into a dark corner of a cave and drew a bison with a black line like a spear piercing its body, he was—the experts believed—trying to work a magic spell that would make him a successful hunter.

The guides could tell the visitors all these things because they had learned them from experts like Abbé Breuil. But when the young men described the discovery of Lascaux, they were telling a story they knew better than any of the experts did.

The two guides who were on hand in 1948 to show the wonders of the Lascaux cave were Marcel Ravidat[10] and Jacques Marsal.[11] Eight years before, on an autumn day in 1940, they had been two of the four teen-aged boys who had followed little Robot down a hole and found, deep in the earth, the greatest collection of prehistoric cave paintings yet known to the world.

[10] Ravidat (rä vi dä′)   [11] Marsal (mär säl′)

——*Sam and Beryl Epstein*

THINKING IT OVER

1. Pretend you were deep in the cave when Marcel flashed his light on the walls. Tell what you saw and how you felt.

2. What facts did the author have to know to write this true story? Why did you feel you were there when the events took place?

3. According to most experts, why did prehistoric man draw pictures in caves? Can you add other possible reasons?

THOUGHTS AT WORK

1. The author gave both facts and opinions about the cave paintings. Decide whether each statement below is *fact* or *opinion*.
   a. The pictures were all around the boys on both long walls.
   b. One row of deer heads looked as if it were swimming.
   c. The bird perched on a stick was crudely drawn.
   d. Some pictures were painted on top of others.
   e. The crisscrossed lines might be pictures of animal traps.
   f. The long straight lines looked like spears.

2. The science experts could tell how the paintings were probably made, but who could tell best how they were discovered? Why?

3. How did the boys keep their secret about the cave? Why do you think they finally told their teacher?

4. If the boys hadn't taken their dog along, do you think the cave would ever have been discovered? Why or why not?

5. Why did the cave paintings survive for thousands of years?

6. Read paragraph 4 that begins on page 305 and find four ways the engineers made the cave ready for the public to visit. What title would you give to this paragraph?

7. On page 304 find the flashback telling about events that happened before this story took place. What helpful information does it give about Abbé Breuil?

The cave boy in this selection couldn't watch adventure stories on television and he didn't need to. He made his own adventure! The author of this story tells in an indirect way much about cavemen. What do you learn about how they hunted, how they lived, and what they thought?

THE GREAT HUNT

A hunting party is following a trail down from its cave home to the floor of the valley below. At the head of the line of men is Marek, the shaman or priest, of this tribe. Right behind him is his young son, Marek-son.

By late morning, the hunting party has reached the other side of the valley and is approaching a pass leading into a land of plains and hills, a grazing land. Here game can be found in good times.

The sun, which had burned palely through the overcast at dawn, is now partly hidden by shreds of cloud. A wet, raw wind has risen and bites into the faces of the men.

As the weather worsens, Marek studies the sky anxiously. He knows that the sudden storms of spring can be most dangerous.

And now, halfway through the rugged pass, the storm breaks upon the hunters.

Hurriedly they seek shelter, climbing up the steep walls of the ravine. They are seeking places high enough to be safe from the flash flood that experience has taught will come hurtling upon them.

A loud rumble of thunder echoes in the ravine. Lightning flickers against the low clouds. Gusts of wet, icy wind lash against the hunters huddled behind the rocks.

The clouds burst and a wall of water roars down the narrow pass. Timbers, boulders, and trapped animals are carried along in the fury of its passage. It is well that the cave dwellers have chosen high shelter from the storm.

Now, as suddenly as it came, the storm is over. Marek has left his place of safety. The others clamber down from the rocks. Only a trickle of water runs along the floor of the ravine.

Cautiously Marek leads the party ahead. Suddenly, just in time, he stops them. With a roar, a huge boulder hanging out from the cliff comes crashing down almost upon them. Swiftly the hunters draw back, but only for a moment. When the small rocks and mud have stopped falling in the wake of the boulder, they move forward.

Marek-son climbs to the top of the ravine's cliff and examines the landslide. He looks all about him, back the way the party has come and ahead where he can see the flatlands. He hopes bison will be grazing there. Far off, across the plains, he can see a cluster of black specks steadily growing smaller. He strains his keen eyes to make them out.

Something has frightened the game. The storm? The approach of the hunters? It is true that the bison and horses become more difficult to stalk as they are more often hunted. But this is the first time in Marek-son's experience that the vast prairie has been bare of game from horizon to horizon.

This, he knows, must mean failure for the hunters and for his father. His eyes narrow as he carefully searches out the answer.

There is something strange out in the middle distance. There is something especially strange about one huge form that seems to lean against a tangled grove. Forgetting the hunters still below him on the floor of the ravine, Marek-son sets out swiftly to investigate this strangeness. Descending to the flatlands, the boy loses sight of the object, but his sure sense of direction makes him head confidently for one grove of trees.

As he nears it, his sense of smell, sharp as an animal's, adds to his excitement. There is a strong, musky odor that grows stronger as he approaches the grove.

Marek-son knows he must approach any game with caution. All animals are alert, and easily angered, and can be dangerous. His nose tells him that this is no animal of his experience, and his natural caution causes him to stalk the grove even more cautiously than usual.

Even so, as he enters the grove, he nearly bumps into a living mountain of flesh. He can't believe that a thing so huge can be alive. He knows instantly that if he makes a mistake, it will mean his death.

Now a sudden excitement shakes the hairy creature that towers into the branches of the trees around him. The beast bellows with anger as it becomes aware of Marekson's presence in the grove. Its huge head lowers itself almost within reach of the young hunter. Something snakelike reaches toward him.

Long tusks root wildly in the earth.

The son of the shaman has been trained to stand firm against fear. Swiftly, he darts into the underbrush where he is safe for a moment. The beast is too huge for him to attack. The whole party of hunters would be hard put to kill such a monster. Yet there must be a way.

Suddenly the boy remembers the painting he has seen in the magic cave over which his father rules. This is the great mammoth! Marek-son recalls clearly, too, the spear in the leg of the animal in the cave painting. This beast is as huge as ten bison. If it can be killed, there will be rich food for all the tribe. If he can only wound the beast in the way of the cave painting, perhaps the men, when they come up, can somehow manage to kill it.

Marek-son weighs his spear in his hand. If he were to hurl it here among the trees, he would surely do little harm to such a huge beast. Yet he does not dare to leave the grove that protects him.

If he could only strike the mammoth in the lower leg! He works his way behind the animal. Evidently its sight is poor, for it continues to beat the underbrush the hunter has just left. Marek-son comes so close to his target that he can see the bugs crawling in its long, matted hair.

With all his strength, the boy stabs his spear deep into the heavy leg, just above the hoof. Almost with the same movement, he hurls himself back into the cover of the underbrush. But at that very instant he feels a violent blow across his back. For the moment that Marek-son remains conscious, it seems to him that he is part of the landslide back in the ravine. He feels as if he is being hurled down a long boulder-strewn slope.

The hunters approaching from the ravine have come close enough to the grove so that they hear the squeals and bellows of the big beast, as it fights to get at the one who has hurt it. They quicken their steps to a run and, reaching the grove, immediately attack the mammoth. All afternoon they fight it, some hurling their lances, then watching their chance to rush in and grab their weapons out of the beast's flesh as it whirls to strike at yet another attacker. Now the sky is darkening. But the mammoth, standing at bay near the edge of the plain, seems as powerful as ever.

As the day ends, the hunters are growing desperate. They know they may lose this prize if night falls before they have slain it. Their attacks become more reckless, and the great beast fights back with his murderous trunk.

Marek has remained in the grove with his son who is becoming conscious again. Marek-son moves restlessly in pain. Marek has cleaned the boy's wounds and covered the red streak across his back with a comforting herb.

The shaman, like the hunters, is worried about the approach of night. It is his responsibility to bring the hunt to a successful end. Even more than the hunters, he is aware that the dark is full of danger and that it can mean escape for the beast.

He bends over his son. The boy's eyes, still dull with shock and pain, meet his father's. Suddenly Marek-son remembers something, something very important. Painfully, he speaks his tribe's word for "landslide."

The landslide! The falling boulder had left a pit gaping at the edge of the cliffside.

Marek understands his son's meaning and his face brightens. Placing a spear beside the boy for protection against prowling animals, he leaves quickly, for he must return to the hunt.

As he comes again to where the hunters are still fighting the mammoth, the men shout with joy as they recognize their shaman. Most of them are without weapons now and can only hurl rocks at the great beast.

Quickly Marek tells the hunters of his plan. He sends half the party on ahead. Next he makes a small fire with flint and leaves, while the others make torches out of fallen branches and prairie grasses.

Waving their flaming torches overhead, the hunters

316

frighten the terrified mammoth with fire. It bellows wildly in great terror, for of all the weapons of man, fire is the one most feared by all his prey.

Night comes quickly now. Moving clumsily in the dark, the monster climbs the rise toward the top of the ravine, hurried on by the torches burning on all sides of it. Reaching the top, it turns to face the hunters. They cannot approach it from below, but Marek seizes a flaring branch and hurls it into the woolly face of the beast.

Squealing horribly, its hair burning, the mammoth steps back.

The hunters who have gone ahead have lined a path with fires along which the others drive the beast with their torches. At the end of the path the pit has been hidden with brush. On the edge of the pit, the mammoth stands for a long moment, its feet seeking firm ground. But the stony earth crumbles away beneath its great weight. With a loud bellow, it slides into the hole. There is an earthshaking thud and a howl of victory from the hunters.

The great mammoth is captured!

The sun has risen and set three times over the valley of the cave dwellers and it is evening again. There has been a long line of carriers, the women and children of the cave, bearing back the great supply of meat that the mammoth provides. Afterward there has been a funeral ceremony for two hunters killed in the hunt. There have been both joy and sadness in these three days.

The torches light the magic room where Marek-son lies. His spear, brought from the scene of battle, has been placed beside him. Marek has taken care of him during these long days and nights. Now the shaman raises a torch to light the ceiling above his son. The boy's eyes widen, and for the first time his interest seems caught. In his eyes a gleam of health and interest tells the father that his boy will recover.

It is something above the young hunter that holds his attention. There on the ceiling of the magic cave, painted onto the ancient drawing of the mammoth, is a figure stabbing a spear into the mammoth. In that figure Marek-son recognizes with growing pride his part in the hunt. The painting tells him all he needs to know about the outcome of the great hunt of his people — the cave dwellers of thirty thousand years ago.

——*Richard M. Powers*

THINKING IT OVER

1. What part of the hunt did you think most exciting? Tell about it as if you were there at the time.
2. What two important things did the cave painting tell Marek-son? How was each of them important to the great hunt?
3. Tell at least three facts you learned about cave dwellers. Which one was the most interesting to you? Why?

THOUGHTS AT WORK

1. Tell two important ways Marek-son helped in the great hunt.
2. Pretend you are Marek, the shaman, and explain to the hunters your plan for killing the mammoth.
3. Why was the landslide important to Marek's plan for capturing the mammoth?
4. You can answer this question more easily if you recall what you learned about the Lascaux cave paintings. Why do you think the word *magic* was used to describe the cave where Marek-son saw the painting of the mammoth?
5. What does each phrase below describe?
   a. a wall of water
   b. a strong, musky odor
   c. burned palely through the overcast at dawn
   d. a living mountain of flesh
   e. as he is being hurled down a long boulder-strewn slope
   f. an earthshaking thud
6. Find on page 318 the sentence, "The sun has risen and set three times . . ." What does it tell you?
7. Could this story be about the people who made the drawings in the cave at Lascaux? Give reasons for your opinions.
8. Reread paragraph 1 on page 314. Explain whether you think Marek-son "stood firm against fear" when he discovered the mammoth.

THE MAMMOTH

MAMMOTH, whom we've saved for last,
    Is often known as "Woolly."
If you could only pat his side,
    You'd understand this fully.

His ancestors were Asia-born
    But wandered to Alaska,
Then southward down through Canada
    To places like Nebraska,

Ohio, Indiana—yes,
   In fact about all over.
The Mammoth was a restless beast,
   We might well call him Rover.

He roved through groves and meadowlands,
   This beast so big and strong,
And if he had no suitcase—well,
   He had his trunk along.

In Ice Age times his thick brown coat
   And undershirt of gray
Were envied by his less-dressed friends
   Who shivered night and day.

They also wished they had that hump
   Of fat upon his back.
When food was scarce, he just absorbed
   An in-between-meals snack.

And oh, those handsome gleaming tusks
   With tips that upward twirled.
I wonder, were they natural
   Or did he have them curled?

—Richard Armour

321

Here is a true story of an important discovery. A thoughtful boy found something many of us would have missed. The scientists who studied the boy's discovery were like detectives in many ways. What does this selection tell you about how scientists—any scientists—study clues to solve a mystery?

THE SHASTA BISON

One winter day in 1933, Burnett Day was helping his father "work the sheep" near the base of Mount Shasta in California. The sheep were warm in their thick wool coats, but Burnett was cold. He wanted to get home. As he followed the sheep up the trail, he tossed pebbles at the tails of the ones who fell behind. It helped hurry them a little.

Burnett stooped over to pick up an odd-shaped pebble from the bank along the trail. It stuck fast. He tugged at it a moment and then looked more closely. This bank was mostly loose sand with some gravel in it. Anything as small as a pebble should come out easily, but this object seemed to be rooted deeply. He scraped a bit of sand from around it and found that it looked like a cow's horn. He tugged again with no better result. Curious, he dug and tugged until he was sure it was actually a horn. Yet, it looked like a rock. How could a thing like this happen? This was no place to bury a cow! It must be something else — but what?

Burnett skipped after the sheep and hurried them along home, so he could ask his father to come and see the horn-shaped rock. Back on the sheep trail they both scraped more sand away. "This is no ordinary cow's horn," exclaimed Mr. Day. "If it belonged to a cow at all, it must have been Babe, the Blue Ox. We

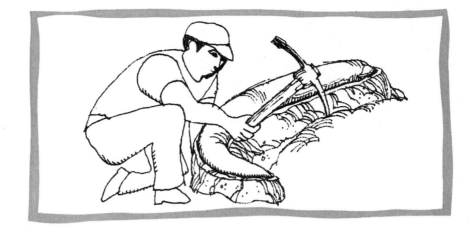

shouldn't fool with it because it might be something important. We'll pull the sand up around it so no one will notice it's been dug out, and then I'll see what I can find out about it."

Over the phone, a paleontologist at the University of California said it sounded like something that should be checked. So, the next day, lanky Dr. V. L. Vander-Hoof[1] arrived on the spot with a collection of shovels, trowels, brushes, shellac, and most important, years of experience in identifying fossil bones. Ever so carefully, the Days and Dr. VanderHoof cleared the sand and gravel away from the horn. Close to the fossil they used trowels and brushes instead of shovels so they would not damage the bone. As each new bit of

[1] VanderHoof (van'dėr hüf')

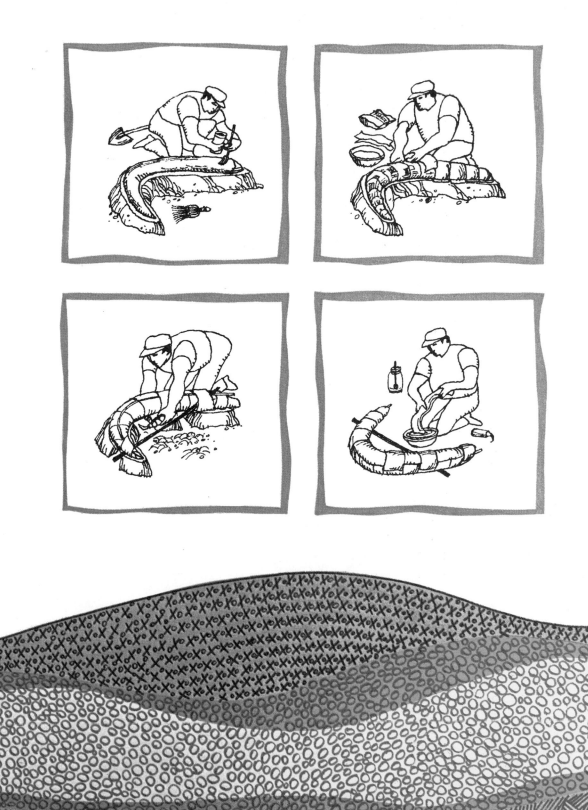

bone was cleared from the sand, they brushed shellac onto it. Sometimes bones that have been buried a long time fall apart when air reaches them. Shellac protects them until they can be taken to the laboratory.

A few hours later eighteen inches of horn had been uncovered and a small crowd had gathered to watch. People wondered how a Texas longhorn had wandered into California. By the time the base of the horn was uncovered, they had stopped talking about cattle— even about Babe. The horn was three and a half feet long and seven inches in diameter!

"If you think that's big," said Van (no one called him Dr. VanderHoof any more), "you should have seen it in its original shape. This is only the core that we're digging up."

Horns of cows and bison are in two parts. The *core*

in the center is hard and bony. The *sheath*, or covering around it, is more like the material in fingernails. It decays more quickly than the core and is not often preserved as a fossil.

The core was all that had been seen by most of the onlookers. Van, himself, saw more. He noticed that a layer of sand around the core was a little different in color from the rest. It also held together a little better. To Van this was clear evidence of the horn sheath, and he was filling his notebook with its description and measurements. By using plenty of shellac, he could even save parts of the sheath. Horn cores about the same size had been found before, but Van was sure that the sheaths were still unknown. Even if nothing was here but this one horn, it was still a find, because the sheath measurements would add a new bit to human knowledge.

Digging was hard work, but excitement was high. What was this huge animal? Was it all there, or just the horn? It took two days to find out. The skull was complete with both horn cores. Only a few small bits were missing. Several cubic yards of sand and gravel were moved in the hope of finding the complete skeleton but it wasn't there. Perhaps the rest of the bones had been scattered by meat-eating animals. Perhaps they had been washed away by the same storms that had covered the heavy skull with sand and gravel. Anyway, the enormous skull had been well worth the effort of digging.

Before the skull was completely uncovered, Van was fairly sure it was a bison, and a big one. But he waited until he had seen the teeth. He knew when he saw them that the animal had been a plant-eater. This was to be expected because horned animals are always plant-eaters. But the details of the tooth pattern showed that it was not like a horse, a deer, an elephant, or any other animal except a bull or a bison. A bull's horns start out in one direction from the skull, while a bison's start out in another. These horns went the way the bison's do. Besides, the forehead was broad and arched. All of the evidence pointed toward the bison. The only question was which bison.

Whenever an important fossil is found, a paleontologist studies it. He learns everything about it that he thinks is worth knowing. Then he writes a complete account of everything he has learned. He takes pictures and makes drawings so that all of the details are on record. Generally, his museum or university publishes his description of the fossil and sends copies to all other scientific centers where the information might be useful.

Pieces of a few other skulls of this kind of giant bison had been found in other places. Part of Dr. VanderHoof's job, then, was to compare his fossil with the descriptions and pictures of all the others. The teeth of the Shasta bison were exactly like the pictures of all the fossils given the name of *Bison latifrons*.[2]

[2] latifrons (lä ti′frōns)

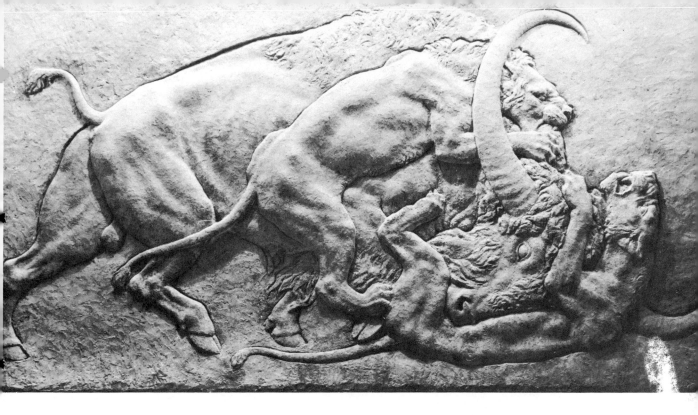

Measurements of the skull and the horn cores agreed closely. In fact, no difference of importance was found. So this skull was given the same name, *Bison latifrons.* *Latifrons* is made up of Latin words meaning "broad front." Look at the picture of the *Bison latifrons* and you'll agree that it is well named.

When it was discovered in 1933, the Shasta bison skull was more complete than any *Bison latifrons* found before that time. It was the only one that showed the shape of the entire horns. How easily that interesting information could have been lost! It would have been lost if less skill had been used in uncovering the horns.

Before Dr. VanderHoof was satisfied, he wanted to know the fossil still better—to see what it had looked like in the flesh. A large order, perhaps, but such things can be done.

Dr. VanderHoof asked for the help of a paleo-sculptor, a man who makes life-size models from fossil remains. The paleo-sculptor was William G. Huff. He and Dr. VanderHoof pooled their knowledge and skill to rebuild the Shasta bison head in the shape it had had in life.

The first step was to make a plaster cast of the skull and horn cores. A plaster cast is just like the original

fossil, but it is made of plaster of Paris. The making of a cast is a simple job unless the object is very large or its shape is complicated. First, the object is covered with plaster of Paris. When this has hardened, it is carefully cut away from the object into several sections. These are coated with paraffin on the inside surfaces and put back together to form a shell. The hollow inside the shell is the exact shape of the original object. Then the hollow is filled with more plaster of Paris, which is allowed to harden. The paraffin keeps the new plaster from sticking to the shell. The shell is taken apart again and removed, revealing a cast that is exactly the size and shape of the original object.

A plaster cast of the bison skull was not easy to make because the skull was so big. It was done in several sections that were later fitted together very carefully. The result was a cast just like the original skull. It could be used as a base for plaster muscles and coat.

With Dr. VanderHoof's measurements as a guide, Mr. Huff added to the plaster cast until the cores of the horns were covered to the same size and shape as those of the living animal. He put more plaster over the cast of the bony skull, building it up to look like the modern bison. Where bone ridges showed that certain cheek muscles must have been big, he built them up with more plaster. The final step was the fur coat. Fur is seldom preserved as fossil material. As fossils go, this one was not very old, so it was thought that it looked much like the modern bison. Modern bison have wavy fur, and there is no evidence that *Bison latifrons* was different. Modern bison have wavy beards, so *Bison latifrons* probably had a wavy beard. Mr. Huff provided the wavy coat and beard by molding and shaping the plaster with several tools. Vertebrae found with some of the other skulls of the giant bison showed that it, like the modern relative, had a high shoulder hump. Now the Shasta bison was as complete as the fossil evidence would allow.

A little tug at a horn tip in the gravel led to a remarkable fossil head with a horn spread of seven feet. If the horns had been straight, the distance from tip to tip would have been almost twice as great. The body, to carry such a head in the normal bison position, would have had to be about eight feet high at the shoulders. The modern five-foot bison would look like a calf next to this giant. The Shasta bison proved to be one of the largest bison ever found.

The life-size model of the Shasta bison head was finished in time to be displayed at the Golden Gate Exposition in 1939 and 1940. Thousands of people saw it there and learned a little more about the animal world of two hundred thousand years ago—all because a boy tossed stones at some sheep and because a scientist and a sculptor worked patiently together.

—*William W. Fox and Samuel P. Welles*

THINKING IT OVER

1. The life-size model of the Shasta bison head would never have been exhibited if four people had not worked together. Who were they and what did each one do?

2. Why was it important for the Days to get help from a paleontologist? What might have happened to the Shasta bison if they had not called Dr. VanderHoof for help?

3. Fossils of other bison had been discovered before Burnett Day found the Shasta bison. Why was his discovery so important?

THOUGHTS AT WORK

1. Why was the bison fossil called the Shasta bison? Look at the drawing on page 332 and think of another name.

2. Tell how Dr. VanderHoof uncovered the Shasta bison's skull and horns. What tools did he use?

3. What does a paleontologist do to prepare a report about an important fossil discovery? If you need help, reread page 328.

4. Below are six steps the paleo-sculptor followed in making the plaster cast of the horns and skull. Put them in order.
   a. The plaster sections are coated with paraffin on the inside surfaces, and put back together to form a shell.
   b. The skull and core of the horn are covered with plaster.
   c. The plaster shell is taken apart and removed.
   d. When the plaster hardens, it is cut away from the fossil into sections.
   e. There is a plaster cast of the exact size and shape of the original skull and horn.
   f. The hollow sections are filled with plaster and allowed to harden.

5. Reread the paragraphs listed below. Write one sentence for each paragraph telling what it is about.
   a. paragraph 3, pages 328–329   b. paragraph 1, page 332

6. Only the skull and the horn cores of the Shasta bison were uncovered. What do you suppose happened to the rest of the bison?

333

THey LeD THe Way

You may think that important discoveries about life when the world was young were made only by trained scientists. But this is not always so. Important discoveries have been made by all sorts of people—miners, cowboys, women, students, and scientists. Who knows, you might be next.

Roy Chapman Andrews, an American naturalist exploring in the Gobi Desert in Mongolia, found the first dinosaur eggs in 1923, buried in rock for 135 million years.

In March, 1823, Mrs. Gideon Mantell, wife of a fossil hunter, discovered the first dinosaur remains near Lewes, Sussex, England. She saw in a rock some pointed objects which turned out to be the huge teeth of a giant reptile similar to an iguana.

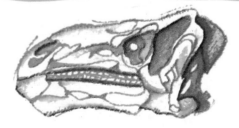

Canadian miners digging in 36 feet of frozen muck in 1954 unearthed seeds believed to be 10,000 years old. Six seeds were planted and grew into lupine plants, thus becoming the world's oldest living things!

334

In 1925, a black cowboy, George McJunkin, found flint spearheads and bones of extinct bison in a washout in Folsom, New Mexico. This discovery led scientists to believe that man lived in America 10,000 to 15,000 years ago.

A twenty-year old college student, Paul Truex, spotted three jellyfish fossils, believed to be 425 million years old, off a highway in Pennsylvania.

Dr. Louis Leakey, a paleontologist working in East Africa in 1960, found a jawbone over 1,800,000 years old. It is believed to be from one of the early ancestors of modern man.

the day we die

The day we die
Then the wind comes
To wipe us out,
The traces of our feet.
The wind creates dust
Which covers
The traces that were
Where we had walked,
For otherwise
It would be
As if we were
Still alive.
That is why it is the wind
That comes
To wipe out
The traces of our feet.

——*Bushman (Africa)*

336

❧ BIBLIOGRAPHY ❧

Odd Old Mammals: Animals After the Dinosaurs, by Richard Armour.
A long funny poem packed with facts about ancient mammals,
from the pygmy hippopotamus to the woolly mammoth.

The Caves of the Great Hunters, by Hans Baumann.
Abbé Breuil talks about the Lascaux Cave with the four boys who
discovered it and tells them about another cave in Altamira,
Spain.

Discovering Dinosaurs, by Glenn O. Blough.
Information on what dinosaurs looked like, and how paleontolo-
gists find fossils.

Life Story, by Virginia Lee Burton.
The story of our universe, from the birth of the sun to the present
minute, told as if it were a play divided into acts and scenes.

How to Know Dinosaurs, by Carla Greene.
The dinosaurs, grouped according to when they lived, are described and compared, and some of the possible reasons for their
disappearance are discussed.

Beasts of the Tar Pits: Tales of Ancient America, by W. W. Robinson.
Descriptions of the prehistoric animals who died when they
were caught in the deep pools of sticky black tar in what is now
the city of Los Angeles.

The Earliest Americans, by William E. Scheele.
The discovery of flints and fossil bones helps tell the story of the
first Americans and the animals they hunted.

The First Farmers in the New Stone Age, by Leonard Weisgard.
Early man stops his wanderings, settles in one place, and learns
to grow crops, tame animals, and use specialized tools.

FAR AWAY PLACES

You are about to take a trip around the world, with stops in Mexico, Africa, India, Greece, and Japan. You will read of a Mexican boy's dream, an African boy's bravery, an old Indian's most prized possession, a Japanese boy's loyalty to his grandfather, and a Greek boy's daring rescue. You will discover that people of all ages in all parts of the world face problems and dream dreams.

338

In Mexico there are many market places where people gather to sell and trade everything from beautiful jewelry to live chickens. As you can imagine, these markets are exciting and noisy places with people bargaining for the best prices and having a good time too. One day when Ramón (rä mōn'), the main character in the story, went to the village market place, he carried a dream in his heart. Before the day ended, Ramón had learned much about making dreams come true. What can you learn from Ramón?

Ramón and the Orange Bowl

The jars and bowls that Ramón's father had made were heaped high on the back of the gray burro. They almost covered him, like a peaked hut of many colors. However, the little animal had a peephole through the crockery hut he carried, so that he could see where he was going. The trail down the mountain to the small Mexican town in the valley was long and steep, but he never once stumbled nor missed a step.

Ramón's father, wearing a worn and ragged *serape*, walked beside the donkey, keeping a watchful eye on the load. Behind the donkey walked Ramón's mother and behind Ramón's mother walked Ramón.

The boy carefully carried an orange bowl in his arms and warily watched the rocky path. It would not do to slip and break his bowl, now that he and Papá and Mamá and the burro had almost reached the market!

"Ramón," his father called to him, "do you want me to put your bowl in our stall with the others and try to get a good price for it?"

"*Gracias*, no, Papá," said Ramón.

All the jars in the stall were supposed to be made by his father, Sandino.[1] Sandino, the potter, was famous in that part of Mexico for his fine pottery.

Ramón looked down at the orange bowl. It certainly was beautiful, he could not deny that. But he could not deny, either, that when it was lined up beside his father's fine wares, it would seem less beautiful. His father might have a hard time selling it at any price!

"I am not going to sell it," said Ramón. "I am going to trade it for something I want."

His mother said, "That, too, is a good way to do business at the market. Not many there have money, but all have goods to trade. What is this thing you want in exchange for one fine orange bowl?"

Ramón smiled, thinking of the thing. "It is something," he said mysteriously.

[1] Sandino (san dē´nō)

Once at the market, Ramón left his mother and father at their stall and pushed his way through the crowded market place. Gaily dressed men and women moved from stall to stall as they looked at the things laid out for sale. All at once, above the arguing about prices, and the noise of braying burros and shouting children, Ramón heard a loud, screeching voice.

"*Buenos! Adiós! Buenos días!*" screamed the voice, sawing across all the other sounds.

Ramón laughed aloud. He tried to see over people's heads to the place of the birdcages, but he could not, even though he stood on tiptoe. "I hear you, Señor Parakeet, and I'm coming to get you in exchange for this bowl I made.

"I will carry you home in your cage and teach you to say many things besides 'Hello' and 'Good-by'. I will keep you forever and everyone will know that you are Ramón's pet!"

He hugged the bowl to him and pushed on, but he could not

go very fast in that thick crowd. Once he almost stopped, for he was passing close to the merry-go-round. He saw the six wooden ponies, each painted a different color. Boys wearing sombreros and girls with flying pigtails rode merrily around on the rocking ponies. Underneath the round platform of the merry-go-round were three boys bent double. Their brown feet kicked up little puffs of dust as they ran and pushed and kept the merry-go-round whirling.

A sigh escaped Ramón. He liked the merry-go-round, but it cost one centavo to ride—and he didn't have a centavo. Maybe, if business was very good, his father would give him a centavo at the end of the day. But now Ramón had something more important to do than to ride a merry-go-round.

He moved on and at last popped out of the crowd in front of the stall of the birdcages. There must have been twenty cages there. All were empty except the one that held the parakeet.

What a beauty that bird was! It was smaller than a parrot, but it had the same strong hooked beak, brilliant green feathers, and long green tail.

"*Buenos días!*" screamed the parakeet. It tilted its head and looked right at Ramón with one shining eye.

The man who made the cages paid no attention at all to the screeching parakeet. Instead, he looked at Ramón's orange pottery bowl.

"That is a fine bowl there, boy," he said. "It is so fine that I think it must be one made by Sandino, the potter."

Ramón's dark eyes glowed with pride. "Sandino, the potter, is my father," he said. "But I made the bowl myself on my father's pottery wheel, and I mixed the color for it too."

He tilted his big straw sombrero back on his black hair. Things were going better than he had hoped. It might not be hard, after all, to trade his wonderful bowl for the parakeet in the cage.

"Your cages are very fine," Ramón said politely. "I would like to have one. In fact, for the cage and the parakeet I will trade this fine bowl."

How the man laughed! He laughed until tears came to his eyes. At last he wiped his eyes and put an arm around Ramón's shoulder.

"You do not understand about business matters," he said. "The cage took me long to make. It was not easy to trap the parakeet in the forest, and it took long to teach him the words he speaks. The bowl is a fine bowl. But it would take six such bowls to equal the value of the cage and the bird."

Ramón looked at the bowl. It was not a small bowl. But it was not large, either. And the warm orange color of it did not seem quite so beautiful to Ramón as it had before.

The man's eyes were kind as he looked at Ramón's unhappy face.

"What I would really like to have," he said, "is one of your father's tall green water jars. I would strap it on my little burro and carry water in it from the river. For one of the green jars, I will trade the cage and the parakeet."

"Thank you," said Ramón. "I will see what I can do."

He turned away without much hope. His father would never give one of the handsome green jars for a cage with a screaming bird in it.

His father was not such a poor business man as that. What Sandino, the potter, really needed was a new *serape*, to wear

as an overcoat on chilly days, and to use as a blanket at night. For such a *serape*, his father would gladly give a jar.

A firecracker of an idea sputtered and sparked in Ramón's head. His bowl once again seemed to be quite large, of a very pleasing shape, and of a color truly admirable. Perhaps— perhaps the *serape* weaver would think so too. Perhaps he would give one of his warm *serapes* in exchange for the bowl. Then Ramón would give the *serape* to his father, in exchange for a green water jar——then take the water jar to the birdcage man, and . . .

He trudged through the crowd, his bright eyes searching for the weaver. At last he saw a stack of folded *serapes* moving slowly along above the crowd. He soon came up to the weaver who didn't have a stall but carried his wares around with him like a tower on his head.

The weaver shouted with laughter when Ramón offered to trade one bowl for one wool *serape*. He would not do it.

"Not that it isn't a fine bowl," he said. "It's a remarkable bowl and I would like to have it." He gazed thoughtfully at Ramón's downcast face. "Maybe we can bargain," he said, "and here's my offer. I will take, in trade for one *serape*, your fine bowl plus twenty centavos. Twenty centavos is not much money, that's true; but then, the bowl is of an unusual orange color and is valuable to me because of that."

"Thank you," said Ramón. "I will see what I can do."

He walked away, dragging his feet. His arms ached with the weight of the bowl. He knew that there was nothing at all he could do about getting twenty centavos, in order to change the centavos and bowl for the *serape*——so that he could trade

346

the *serape* for a green water jar——and the water jar for the cage and the parakeet.

Why, he had never in his whole life had twenty centavos at one time!

"*Adiós! Adiós!*" came the piercing screech of the parakeet.

"Good-by, Señor Parakeet," Ramón answered under his breath.

He wandered on, feeling bad, and found himself by the merry-go-round. He watched the six ponies whirling, prancing as if they were alive. He would love to ride one of them. But he did not have even one centavo to pay for a ride.

Maybe, he thought, the man who owned the merry-go-round would exchange a ride for the bowl. Maybe he would exchange three rides, or five, or ten! Ramón would take them all in a row! He would ride and ride and ride until he got so dizzy that he would forget all about the parakeet! He thought of the bright eyes and shining green feathers of the bird that would never be his. He walked slowly over to the owner of the merry-go-round.

"In trade for this bowl," Ramón asked, "how many rides will you let me take on your merry-go-round?"

The man pushed his sombrero back and scratched his head. He was thinking hard, figuring . . .

"None at all," the man said, finally.

Ramón's mouth fell open, he was so surprised.

The man saw his surprise.

"It's this way," he said, speaking carefully so that Ramón would be sure to understand. "I must have centavos for my rides, because I have to pay centavos to the boys who push the merry-go-round. How could I pay them with a bowl? I would have to smash it and give each one a piece. And what good would a piece of broken bowl be to them? No good at all. No, I must have centavos for rides."

By this time a whole string of firecracker ideas was going off inside Ramón's head.

"Then I would like to push the merry-go-round," he said.

"Good," the man said. "I always need boys for pushing. Get under there and push the merry-go-round for two rides and I will pay you one centavo. With the centavo you can buy one ride."

"If you will be kind enough to keep my bowl for me, I will do it," said Ramón.

The merry-go-round came to a stop. When it started again Ramón was under it. He pushed it around and around—arms

and chest against a crossbar, feet flying in the soft dirt stirred up in a circular path under the merry-go-round.

He pushed for two full rides. When he finished, the man gave him one centavo.

Ramón dropped the centavo into his orange bowl. "I will push again," he said.

He ducked under the merry-go-round to earn another centavo.

He pushed the rest of the morning. He pushed during the *siesta* hour when everyone, except the children, was resting in the shade. It was hot. Ramón's sombrero had long ago fallen off. His hair was plastered to his forehead with sweat and his mouth was as dry as dust. But still he pushed.

"I have never seen a boy who pushed so hard and so long!" exclaimed the owner. "Rest now and treat yourself to a ride."

"*Gracias,* no," said Ramón.

Every time he finished pushing two rides, the man gave him one centavo. Ramón dropped each new centavo into his orange pottery bowl and disappeared again under the merry-go-round.

He never did take a ride!

Late in the afternoon he crawled out, covered with dust from head to foot. He picked up his bowl. There was a pleasant jingle of centavos in it. He counted them, then grinned.

"Twenty-one centavos!" he cried. "It is more than enough. I go now, but I will be back!"

He hurried through the crowd, searching for the weaver. He gave the weaver his orange bowl with twenty centavos in it. The weaver gave him a fine *serape* with bright stripes woven through it for a design.

Clutching the *serape*, Ramón started for his father's stall.

350

While still some distance off, he shouted, "Papá! Look what I have, to trade for a green water jar!" He waved the *serape* before his father's astonished gaze.

Ramón told his story and his father gladly made the trade. "You have done better business than I have today," he said, as he slipped his head through the slit in the *serape*, thus turning it from a blanket into a handsome overcoat. "Help yourself to my finest green jar, son!"

The jar was almost as big as Ramón, but he managed to get his arms around it and to lug it to the place of the cages.

He was puffing as he carefully set the jar down on the ground before the man who made birdcages. He straightened up and said, "Here is a green water jar made by Sandino, the potter. In trade, I will take the cage with the parakeet in it."

"It's a trade," the man said. He took the cage down and handed it to Ramón, who walked away with it in his arms.

A little later Ramón arrived at the merry-go-round. He handed the man his last centavo. "Now I'd like to buy a ride," he said.

"But I have no pushers. Everyone is packing up to go home, as you can see. Market day is over!" the man exclaimed. Then he added, "But it's a shame that such a hard-working pusher as you should get no ride.

"I'll push you myself!"

The space under the merry-go-round was small, but the man doubled himself into it. Ramón climbed up on a pony. In one hand he held the cage with the green bird in it.

As the merry-go-round started going around faster and faster, the excited parakeet clung to one of the bars of his cage and screamed at all the people as he whirled by, *"Buenos! Buenos días! Buenos días!"*

Yes, Señor Parakeet, it is a very good day." Ramón laughed aloud as he rode the rocking pony around and around and around. "A very good day, indeed!"

——*Barbara Ritchie*

352

THINKING IT OVER

1. What was Ramón's plan when he went to market? Why do you think he would not answer his mother when she asked what he wanted in exchange for his bowl?

2. Think about the birdcage seller, the weaver, and the merry-go-round owner. Which man do you think was the most understanding of Ramón's problem?

3. Why do you think Ramón wanted the parakeet and cage so badly?

THOUGHTS AT WORK

1. "If at first you don't succeed, try, try again." How does this saying apply to the story?

2. Down the left side of your paper, list all the people Ramón traded with. Beside each name, write what Ramón gave that person and what he received.

3. Find four different ways the author told you that the story took place in Mexico.

4. Tell how Ramón felt about his bowl at first. Then tell how he felt about it after talking with the birdcage seller.

5. Read each sentence below, and write the words you think are the most interesting. Why are they interesting words?
   a. Ramón trudged through the crowd.
   b. He popped out of the crowd.
   c. The man gazed at Ramón's downcast face.
   d. His hair was plastered to his forehead with sweat.
   e. A firecracker of an idea sputtered and sparked in Ramón's head.
   f. His bowl was of a color truly admirable.

6. What were the "firecracker ideas" that went off in Ramón's head?

7. At the end Ramón said, "Yes, Señor Parakeet, it is a very good day." Why did the day turn out better than Ramón expected?

The bullock is a powerful, slow-moving mountain of an animal. In India it is used to pull carts and plows, and it draws its heavy loads with the unhurried ease of a giant. This story too moves at the slow, steady pace of the bullock. But trouble is not slow in India or anywhere. Read with care, and look about for every clue. Trouble is only waiting its chance.

THE BULLOCK

In the vast and varied land of India there is a part known as the Great Gangetic[1] Plain. It is flat country fed by the waters of the Ganges[2] River—the Ganga[3], as some call it—flat country a thousand miles long and two hundred miles wide. Some of it is very dry indeed, but thousands of little farms dot the land where water can be had. And on one of these little farms lived an old man and his wife.

[1] Gangetic (gan jet'ik)   [2] Ganges (gan'jēz)   [3] Ganga (gung'gä)

They were not rich — far from it! They had to work hard to live at all. And when they had produce to sell — carrots or peppers, lentils or beans — the old man had to start in the middle of the night on the long journey to market. At dawn he would reach the place. All morning he would sell his vegetables and, with the money paid him, buy a few things for himself and his wife — wheat and sugar. Then he would take the long journey back, and reach his home as darkness came again.

One thing they had which made them very proud — a great white bullock with golden horns, the very one that pulled the cart to market and brought it home again. Of course, his horns were not really made of gold. One special day the old man had brushed four strokes of golden paint down each great curved horn. From every side the bullock looked magnificent.

The old man's wife went hunting for food for the bullock each day. By this time she knew just where to find the best grass — the greenest, sweetest grass along the paths and roads near the farm. She would go out with a sickle in her hand, and return with a huge pile of grass on her head.

On cold days the old man would cover the bullock's back with a quilted cloth, to keep him from getting a fatal chill. For both the old man and his wife knew that, but for the bullock, they might never have wheat to eat.

While they were very thin from hard work and little food, the bullock was big and strong. His sides stood out almost as far as the sides of the cart he pulled to market. His skin was like a great white coat that lay on his body in handsome folds. And it was a pretty sight to see this huge white beast in the rosy dawn, horns glistening in the light, pulling the old cart loaded with bright orange carrots and long red peppers and plump green beans to market, the old man in gray-white *khadi*, sitting toward the front of the cart, day-dreaming his way along.

On the night that this story begins, the old man and his wife had loaded the cart, and now the wife was making a lunch for the old man to eat on the way. In it she put some *chapati* and *dahl*.

"If he wants a carrot," she said to herself, "he can always reach for it; and he can stop for tea on the road," —as if she had not done and thought all of this many times before!

She tucked the little lunch box down in the front of the cart. Then she stuffed a sack of grass into a nest of carrots in the cart. For the bullock had to have his lunch, too, and grass was not always handy, with so many travelers competing for it.

Meanwhile the old man had dressed in his gray-white *khadi* that had seen so many seasons. Then he went to get the bullock. Two shining eyes led him to the right spot. The bullock had been standing as though expecting the trip. The old man led him to the cart and, backing him into position, fastened the harness.

The wife smoothed down one side of the bullock with her hand.

Then she said to the old man, "Your lunch is there and the grass is there."

"Good," he said. "I must be going."

"You are remembering sugar?" she asked.

"Sugar and wheat," he replied. "Sugar if I sell all the carrots."

"You will drive slowly on the bridge?" she asked, for both knew how shaky and old that bridge was.

"Oh yes," he said. "How else?"

"You will be careful at the crossings?"

"If I have any sense at all," he answered. "Don't worry."

"Watch the bicycles. Watch the cars," she said.

"Yes, yes," answered the old man, and thought to himself, "not many cars and bicycles in the middle of the night."

He took a long, thin stick, with which he could send messages to the bullock, and mounted the cart. With a touch of the stick the bullock jerked the cart to a start. He did not need the reminder, so many times had the old man and the bullock traveled together.

"God be with you," called the wife, and she watched until the gray figures had melted into the darkness, and the creak of the cart and sound of heavy steps were no longer audible. She would go into the house and light a little candle for a safe journey.

The old man talked to himself on the long trips to market and back, and to the bullock too.

"If I sell all the carrots," he said, "I'll not only get sugar. I'll get her a little present. It's a long time since she had a little present."

Soon they came to the creaky old bridge. "Careful," said the old man to the bullock. "This is older than both of us put together, and weaker than either. Gopal's[4] bullock put a hoof through a board on the other side, remember. Gently, gently."

Cautiously, as though he understood every word, the bullock stepped across the bridge, while the bridge and cart creaked a duet.

"There," said the old man, as they left the bridge, "there, now. Nothing wrong with that."

[4] Gopal (gō′päl)

Presently they overtook Gopal and his bullock, his cart loaded twice again its height with wood, and Gopal on top of it all.

"Someday your bullock will drop dead from a load like that," called the old man. "Not only that—the bridge won't hold you."

"And yours," replied Gopal, "will eat everything you have. Wait till you see what I bring back. Rocks! I'm through with mud walls that melt in the monsoons and flake with the wind."

The old man chuckled. It was true that his bullock had it easy, but Gopal's bullock had nothing but ribs and neglect. Too bad to treat a good animal like that. So expensive, too, in the long run.

The old man's bullock easily passed Gopal's, and on they went alone.

"Yes, I'll get her a little present," said the old man. "I wish it could be a *sari*, but it will have to be a sweet. One she likes very much."

"Of course," he thought, "she'll scold if it's something she can make herself. I'll have to look around."

The bullock shook his head as though he knew how hard it is to please a thrifty wife, but actually he was discouraging some flies which had settled around his mouth.

As the cart approached a crossing, the old man listened carefully. He could hear nothing. He looked in either direction. Far to the right he could see eight shining discs—the eyes of Ram's four bullocks.

"See that?" asked the old man of the bullock. "We're way ahead today."

Little happened before dawn. Some jackals stared from the side of the road as the cart passed, their eyes pinpoints of light. Later the old man could hear their haunting yelps and cries as they hunted and fought in the dark.

When the rosy light fanned the sky and finally caught the figures on the road, the warmth of its color tinged the grays with pink, reddened the orange carrots, and lent fire to the glistening golden horns. The first heat of another dazzling day beat upon the cart as it reached the market. One of the reasons the old man came so early was to find a shady spot for the bullock to spend the day. In fact, people coming to market learned to expect to find the old man on the north side of a stall, and beside a spreading tree. The stall gave shade all morning, and by afternoon, if the cart was still there, the tree gave shelter from the full force of the sun.

This morning they were early enough, and the bullock had his favorite spot. The old man gave him a handful of grass from the sack.

While the bullock munched, a camel strolled up to the tree and began to eat the lower leaves. His master had him kneel so that the huge baskets on either side of his back could be unloaded.

"Glad it isn't carrots," thought the old man, as he looked at the sacks of onions piled up on the ground beside the camel.

Of course, he knew more carrots would be coming. Now many farmers came with their fruits and vegetables, while men with tea and *pan* and *bidi* and *masala* and *chapati* and sweets set up little tables to sell food to the farmers and the people who came to buy.

Now the buyers came, some with bullocks and carts, many with little horses and carts, some with carts which they pulled themselves, some with bicycles on which they could stack amazing loads, some on foot, prepared to carry their purchases in a big sack on their heads. The selling began, and the bargaining began.

"Your carrots look dry. Too big. Too tough," the buyer would say. "If they look dry now, how will they look when I try to sell them in my shop? They aren't worth much, but I am an old customer of yours. Out of consideration

for you, I shall take a chance. I will pay . . ." and then he would offer far too little.

The old man would name a higher price.

"Sprinkle a little water on the carrots and they will look fine," he said. "I dug them only yesterday and brought them fresh this morning. The sun has scarcely touched them."

And so it would go.

By noon the old man had not sold his carrots for his first price. He had to reduce the price on the remaining carrots in order to sell them at all. Now all were sold, and the old man could look for wheat and sugar.

"I think the wheat is rough," he said to the seller. "It is not fit to eat." But because the government had fixed the price, his protest made no difference. However, he did get wheat and a little sugar. There was not enough money for a present for his wife.

"Next time," he said to the bullock, as he drank his tea and chewed his cold *chapati*. "Anyway, she's in no mood for presents when the selling is so poor."

What with bargaining and lunch and chatting with acquaintances, it was four o'clock before the old man could start back. Before his cart was well out of town, cyclists were weaving home, cars were tooting around them. children were scampering out of the way, and little horse-drawn *tongas* were intruding between the cars and the cycles.

"It is worse every time," said the old man to the bullock. "Watch it. Watch it." But he himself was so exhausted from the long hours, the midday heat, and the exertion of bargaining, that he could scarcely keep his eyes open. The reins became loose in his hands and his chin eased down to his chest.

Trouble seemed to have been waiting for the old man to sleep. Ahead of the bullock some boys were playing. As the bullock approached, one boy pushed another, who fell backward into the road. The swaying broad side of the bullock cushioned his fall, propelling him back whence he came. The boy turned and looked in surprise.

The old man stirred, his eyelids fluttering. "Watch it," he mumbled to the bullock and, in spite of his best intentions, dozed again.

A cyclist shot out of a driveway into the road. The bullock's bulging eye caught sight of him. The great head turned just enough. The man's sleeve was softly brushed by the bullock's nose.

A buffalo was lying half out into the road, its dark

body scarcely visible in the retreating light. The bullock moved steadily onward, swerving with deliberate steps. The wheel of the cart cut a trail in the dust just past the buffalo's tail.

And so, as drivers of cars and *tongas* and bicycles steered with anxious faces and tense muscles, the old man slept. The heavy traffic was left behind. The bullock and cart passed over the lonely road. Stars came out. Jackals whimpered and screamed. Still the old man slept.

When at last he awoke, he did so because everything was so quiet. The cart was motionless. As his eyes became adjusted to the gloom, he could see that the pale mass before him was the bullock standing still. Then he saw the dark outline of the bridge railing.

He stood up in the cart to get a better look. There seemed to be a quivering light on the floor of the bridge, ahead of the bullock. Now he saw that it was the light

365

on the water beneath the bridge. The bullock had stopped just short of a hole—a hole as big as a cart.

The old man's waking wits were frightened back into his head.

"Thank God," he thought. Then, "What? Who?"

He got down from the cart to inspect the hole more carefully. It was too wide to pass. He would have to take off through the meadow and cross the stream at the shallows.

He looked through the hole to the stream below. He could see the back of a bullock half-submerged in the water—the side of a cart—a broken wheel.

Suddenly he sensed that something was beside him. He jerked his head and sucked in his breath.

"Gopal!"

"Yes, I am Gopal, and there is my load of rocks. If I had been asleep as you are half the time, I would be dead. I jumped off just in time."

The old man did not have to ask about the cart or the bullock. A fortune, in poor men's terms, had gone through the hole in the bridge.

"I can get something for the carcass. The cart will take some days to put together. Will you lend me your bullock tomorrow?"

The old man looked down at the hole in the bridge, then up at the strong body, the shining eye, and the glistening horns of his bullock. He didn't say yes. He couldn't say no.

"Come, I'll take you home," was all he said.

Now, for an Indian reader, the story is finished. But if you do not know India, you may have questions.

Did Gopal get his rocks? Surely he kept trying. Did he learn to be kind? Not with so many wishes for himself.

Did the old man lend him his bullock? Surely you know he did. And you are right to suppose he would go along to see that all went well.

Did the wife get her present? Of course, every time. Sometimes a sweet, but best of all—the old man's and the bullock's safe return.

And so it goes, and not alone in India. There are those who have so little and want so much that they can think only of themselves. There are some who live for others. There are some who give as good as they get. And there are some who meet each day with kindness and hope.

——Constance M. McCullough

THINKING IT OVER

1. Choose one of the names listed below to answer each question, and then give a reason for your choice.

   the old man   the wife   the bullock   Gopal

   a. Which character was hopeful and kind?
   b. Which one thought and worked only for others?
   c. Which one thought only of himself?
   d. Which one was steady and always faithful?

2. What does this sentence from the story mean: "A fortune, in poor men's terms, had gone through the hole in the bridge"?

3. What will happen to Gopal and the old man in the future?

THOUGHTS AT WORK

1. Pretend you are the old man describing your day at the market. Tell about the people, the traffic, and the bargaining and selling.

2. Tell the differences between the way the old man and Gopal cared for his bullock and cart.

3. What did the old woman do that showed she cared about her husband and the bullock?

4. What did the old man say to Gopal on the way to market that prepared you for what happened at the end?

5. The author used many Indian words that create a feeling for the country. Choose the correct word from the list below to finish each sentence.

   khadi   tongas   sari   chapati   masala   dahl   pan

   a. The old man wished to buy a new _____ for his wife.
   b. The old man was dressed in his gray-white _____.
   c. Tables of _____ and _____ were at the market.
   d. For lunch the old man had some _____ and _____.
   e. Horse-drawn _____ were driven through the traffic.

6. Many things happened as the old man dozed on his way home. Name them in order. Which was the greatest danger to him?

O CRAB

Sitting on the stone, O crab,
Move a little,
From the stone, O crab.
Let me plough the field, O crab,
Move a little,
From the stone, O crab.

——*Pullayas of Kerala (India)*

In the heart of Africa, in an area now called the Republic of the Congo, there lives a group of people called Pygmies. They possess amazing skills necessary for living in the jungle. The Pygmies are small in size but this story will show you that they are "tall" in other ways.

Okapi Belt

Sleetan[1] had never seen bright sunlight. This may sound queer to you, for he was born and had lived all of his life on the equator where, as everyone knows, the sun beats down fiercely every day of the year. However, Sleetan lived deep in the great jungles of the Congo, and the only treeless strips of land he had ever seen were the narrow paths used by the forest animals and his own tribesmen. High overhead the boughs of giant forest trees tangled with long,

[1] Sleetan (slē′tən)

370

strong vines to form a green canopy. Vines, trees, and bushes shut out every hint of direct sunlight. Sleetan lived by day in a cool green twilight, and by night in inky darkness. He went to sleep with the birds, and it is doubtful if he ever saw a star or the moon shining through that dark canopy of trees and vines.

He had looked up the tall straight trunks of many trees, but he had never seen a tree standing all by itself—trunk, branches, and topmost shoot—out in the sunlight.

The sides of Sleetan's home were made of bark stripped from tree trunks, and the roof was made of leafy branches laid across sticks. There was no need to build a sturdier home, for Sleetan's father and mother never stayed in one spot more than three or four days—and besides, it was never cold! In fact, Sleetan was ten years old, but he had never worn a stitch of clothing in his life, except the rope of bark fibers over one shoulder and under the other arm. This rope held a quiver of arrows slantwise across his back.

Sleetan's father wore a belt made of okapi skin. Okapi skin belts were important to the Pygmies, for okapi skin was a badge of manhood.

Sometimes, but these occasions were rare, Sleetan's father, or one of the other men of the tribe, came hurrying into camp to say that the hunters had killed an okapi. Then everyone left his little brush and bark shelter, moved to the spot where the dead okapi lay, and made a new camp. This was much simpler than one might think, for no man in the tribe owned anything but the pair of little bark aprons he wore, his weapons, and his okapi skin belt. It was much simpler to move the tribe than it was to move a dead animal!

Especially was this true when the animal was an okapi, the largest of the deep jungle creatures. The top of Sleetan's head would come just about to an okapi's knees; and his father might stand upright under an okapi's stomach, that is, if an okapi would ever let him! Of course, that was because Sleetan and his father and his mother belonged to a tribe of Pygmies who were never more than four feet tall.

Even so, the okapi was a big animal, almost as tall as a giraffe. It was so shy that men could seldom get close to one. It could stand so still, and its legs were so crisscrossed with light and dark markings like trunks of saplings, that a Pygmy could pass within a few feet of one and not know it was there. It was clever enough to hide its calf away so that even the best tracker in the tribe could not find it. It was so strong that it could break a good-sized sapling in two with one bunt from its bony head. Or, that failing, it could whirl about and smash a trunk as large as its knee joint with one kick from its hoof. Lastly, it was absolutely fearless and when cornered, it would charge any number of men. When that happened, there was always great sorrow in the tribe, for then at least one man met his death.

Sleetan's father said that whoever ate enough okapi meat would undoubtedly become brave and clever and strong like the okapi. Whoever wore a belt of okapi skin would surely command the respect of the other jungle animals and birds and snakes. No one man could ever kill an okapi by himself; therefore, the skin always belonged to the tribe. A council of the oldest men cut the hide up into lengths suitable for belts and decided who among the tribe most deserved them. Whenever Sleetan looked at his father's okapi belt, he hoped that someday he too would deserve one. He knew he would never inherit his father's, for when his father died, his belt would be buried with him.

Sleetan's father made him a blow gun and taught him how to make his own darts. The boy practiced by the hour, shooting at a toadstool or a bit of lichen on an old log so he would neither lose nor break his darts. It was not long before the boy could puff up his cheeks, like a squirrel with a mouthful of nuts, and pop a leaf from its stem far over his head.

Older hunters carried little bags of poison. A pinch of that on a dart and the small animal whose hide it pierced would die within a few seconds. No more than three or four darts were needed to kill the feared and coveted okapi. So quickly did this poison kill an animal that it did not spread through the body. After a little bit of flesh had been cut away from around the wound, the rest of the flesh was used as food.

One day Sleetan's father had been standing on the banks of the great river that flowed into the west. He came back to the tribe and said, "I have seen three full-grown okapis standing on the opposite shore!"

This river was so broad that the tribe had never tried to build one of its hanging bridges across it. But three okapis all at once! The next day every hunter in the tribe hid in the trees along the banks and silently waited. Along in the afternoon several okapis came down to the opposite shore to drink. And the next day it was the same! Across that broad and turbulent river there was plenty of meat. Good fine okapi meat! But how could they ever reach that other bank? Half of the tribe went upstream, half journeyed downstream, both searching for a narrower channel where a hanging bridge of vines could be slung. Many days passed before anyone reported the least success. Even then, the old ones doubted that the only possible place found was narrow enough.

Now everyone set to work cutting long slender vines, big vines to use as cables, little vines for ropes. The boys borrowed the men's hunting knives, cut down hundreds of saplings, trimmed them smooth, and chopped them into even lengths. The young men climbed the tallest trees and examined their branches until they found a limb that was high enough, big enough, sound enough, and far enough out over the river.

Then they fastened a good long vine to the branch, and one of the men got ready to swing across the river. Before he leaped out of the tree on which he was standing, he must hold fast to the vine and high enough so he would not hit the water. If he did hit the water, his bones might be broken. Or he might be jerked loose and swept away with the current.

The oldest men most skilled in bridge building squinted this way and that, measuring heights and distances and lengths in their minds. At last when they had chosen a spot on the vine, a tribesman grasped it at that exact place and gave a mighty leap, shoving his body as far out as he could.

Down! Down! Down he swung, clearing the water by about two heights of a man. But now up! Up! Up in a great lazy arc the man on the vine swung. And then down and up again, back onto the branch returned this human pendulum.

"I missed the opposite tree by two lengths of a man," he said. "Perhaps if I hold a little lower on the vine, I can reach out and grasp the twigs on the other side. I can curl my body up in a ball when I am over the water."

It was a brave thing for him to offer, but it was for the good of the tribe. They accepted it in silence which he knew meant respect. Again he swung—down! Down! Down! And up! Up! Up! And then down! Down! Down! Down! And up! Up! Up! Back onto the same limb on the same side of the river. This time he made no remark to the tribe but grasped the vine a little

lower, and before anyone could protest, swung out over the river again.

"It's no use," he spoke sadly, at last, from his perch on the limb. "My nostrils caught the spray of the rapids—but my fingers only brushed the slenderest twigs." He opened his clenched hand and bits of torn leaves floated to the ground. This plan had failed.

That evening Sleetan found it difficult to sleep. He could not get the long vine, hanging motionless now, out of his mind. In the haze between sleeping and waking, it reminded him of a snake dangling from the branch. A long slender body wrapped around a limb with the equally long tail dangling from the branch. Sometimes that tail wrapped itself around an unwary animal or a careless Pygmy. A long tail wrapped around a boy? Sleetan chuckled deep down in his throat. He had the answer!

The next morning Sleetan told his father. He would wrap the vine around his own body up to the point the old men had considered safe at first. Then he would hold on with both hands until he was across the river. On the upswing he would let go and unroll his body to the end of the vine. If that were tied around his waist, he would have both hands free with which to grasp the branches opposite.

Sleetan's father called the old men together and told them of his son's idea. They listened carefully. Finally one spoke. "It is an old man's thought in a child's body," he said.

378

A dozen young men leaped forward. "Sleetan is a child. This calls for strength. Let me do it!"

"Let me!"

"Let me!"

"Choose me!"

"Do you understand the risk?" another old man asked the eager youths. "If you let go of the vine entirely and unroll too fast, the jerk when you come to the end may injure you badly. If you unroll to the full length of the vine and do not catch onto the tree opposite or do not get a good hold and are torn loose, you will be dashed into the rapids below."

"I would try it!"

"And I!"

"And I!"

Sleetan choked down a sob. It had never occurred to him, either last night or this morning when talking to his father, that he would not be the one to try out his scheme. But he was only a small boy, no taller than an okapi's knee; and of course it would not be proper for him to voice his disappointment, much less question a decision of the old men. He watched his father and the other men fasten the vine around the lucky young man's waist and wind him up in it.

The young man drew a deep breath and leaped. Down! Down! Down he swept. Even the birds were quiet. Every eye strained as they saw his hands loosen their grip on the vine when he began the upswing. Slowly, slowly he let his body unroll and then held out his hands to grasp the branches which he was dashed against. For a second he was lost to sight. Leaves came fluttering down. The outer twigs quivered.

Was his grasp secure? Was he uninjured? Or would he fall? The long vine, swinging in an arc high over the rapids, began swaying up and down, and a shout of joy arose from the tribe on the bank. He was safe! He was tying the vine, the first cable on their bridge, to the trunk of the tree.

In a few minutes they heard the young man shout that he had finished his work. Then Sleetan's father tied a vine around his waist and started across on the first vine—hand over hand, high above the river. Another man followed him. And another! And another! By early afternoon a frail-looking but really strong bridge swayed between the two giant trees on opposite sides of the bank. The whole tribe—old men, warriors, women, and children—crossed the river.

That night they slept near the bridge. Early the next morning the young men and warriors went down the river in search of okapi. It was not long before word came that there had been a kill, and the women and children moved on.

When they came up to the warriors, Sleetan noticed that, although the okapi had been skinned, no belts had been cut out of its hide. Sleetan eyed it with longing. Every Congo Pygmy boy eyes an okapi skin with longing, as the sign of manhood—the badge of merit awarded by the old men of the tribe. The wise

380

ones would burn a skin, precious as it is, rather than have a scrap of it fall into unworthy hands. Sleetan wondered who would receive belts cut from this hide. Undoubtedly the young man who had risked his life swinging across the river. He had done a good job and deserved honor.

Then the chief took his knife and began cutting out a belt. This was always a tense moment for the men and boys, and everyone watched carefully. Sleetan caught his lip between his teeth. The chief's knife had slipped. The strip he had cut off was too short. It would never go around a man. He was embarrassed for the chief and glanced at him pityingly.

But the chief was looking at Sleetan and smiling. And so was the young man. And so were they all!

The chief fastened the belt around Sleetan and then made a little speech to him and to the tribe. Sleetan could not be sure just what he said. It was something about wise thoughts in a youthful body, and strength and bravery being good things, but not enough. Sleetan was not quite sure what he said or what he meant. His heart beat too hard, and his pulse pounded in his ears. He clenched his hands into little hard fists so he could not finger his okapi belt while the chief was speaking. And he held his body so straight he must surely have reached at least half an inch above a full-grown okapi's knee.

——*Louise A. Stinetorf*

382

THINKING IT OVER

1. During this story, did Sleetan reach a milestone in his life? Explain your answer.
2. Both Ramón and Sleetan had problems. Describe each problem, and tell how it was solved. Which problem do you feel was harder to solve?
3. If you had been the chief, would you have given Sleetan an okapi belt? Why? Would you have given an okapi belt to anyone else? Why or why not?

THOUGHTS AT WORK

1. Tell what you learned about the Pygmies' homes, clothing, food, and weapons. Explain why they live as they do.
2. On page 372 find three ways the okapi protected itself.
3. What was Sleetan's scheme for getting the vine across the river? Do you think it was fair that Sleetan wasn't chosen to try out his plan? Explain your answer.
4. The author compares unfamiliar things to things we know. Think of words that will finish each sentence below.
   a. The okapi was almost as tall as a _____.
   b. The okapi's legs were crisscrossed with light and dark markings like _____.
   c. The boy could puff up his cheeks like a _____.
   Now make up a comparison of your own about something in the story.
5. Tell about an experience you've had when, like Sleetan, you stood very straight, your heart beat too hard, and you had to keep still.
6. The Pygmies thought the okapi belt would help protect them from the wild animals. What lucky pieces, like the okapi belt, do we treasure?

Some sixty miles from the Japanese capital city, Tokyo (tō′ kē ō), Mt. Fuji (fü′ jē) rises majestically above the fields. Since ancient times, the Japanese have considered this mountain a symbol of beauty. Each year thousands of people climb its difficult slopes, and those who reach the peak at sunrise are rewarded by a spectacular sight. In this story Mt. Fuji becomes especially important to a boy named Fujio (fü′ jē ō) and his grandfather, and at the same time they become very important to each other. You will find out why.

THE FUJI STICK

Fujio pushed his bowl of rice away from him and put down his chopsticks, his dark eyes thoughtful. The evening meal was usually a happy time in the Toyama[1] home. The family sat on the *tatami* covered floor around a low table and Mama-san served the rice from a large wooden bowl. The tea was strong and hot, and the talk around the table was good. Usually. But today Fujio's forehead creased in a frown—today there was something wrong.

[1] Toyama (tō yä′ mä)

He looked around the table. Mama-san smiled her same gentle smile as she ladled rice into their bowls and poured the tea. Papa-san sat straight and proud, smacking his lips as he enjoyed the rice in his bowl. Obaa-san[2] sat primly, as a grandmother might, nibbled her rice and sipped her tea in silence. And small sister Michiko,[3] with her bobbed black hair and impish black eyes, pushed the rice around in her bowl with the ends of her chopsticks. Now and then she giggled at the way the tiny bits of rice skidded around the slippery china and found their way down the front of her flowered kimono.

[2] Obaa-san (ō'bä-sän)   [3] Michiko (mē chē'kō)

At last Fujio's glance fell upon his aged grandfather. His dark eyes narrowed. That was where the trouble was! Ojii-san[4] wore his old, mended kimono instead of his newest one. He sat with his balding head bowed to his chest. His rice sat untouched in his bowl. The bitter green tea he usually loved cooled in the cup in front of him. Fujio scowled. What was the matter with Grandfather? Couldn't the others see that the honored one was acting strangely?

At last Grandfather raised his head and looked around. His black eyes seemed narrower than usual. Then he raised his gnarled hands to command the attention of his family. Immediately everyone was silent.

"My birthday is two days from now," he announced. "Seventy-two years have come upon me swiftly. There is much I want to do before my tired bones stiffen. One wish I have is very strong. That is to climb to the top of the great mountain." Now his eyes seemed to hold a vision. Fujio felt his own heart thump faster at Grandfather's words. He leaned forward to hear the old man. "I want to stand proudly at the top of Fuji-san and greet the sunrise as my own honored father once did. I wish to look down upon my beautiful country and see the blue lakes and the green valleys and the mountains."

Fujio's own eyes widened as he watched the effect of his grandfather's words upon Mama-san and Papa-san. "You are too old to climb so high," Papa-san said. "Climbing is for the young man."

[4] Ojii-san (ō'gē-sän)

The old man shook his shiny head. "Some of the pilgrims who climb the sacred mountain are as ancient as I. If they can do it, I can do it!" His jaw was set in determination. Fujio watched his grandfather shake his head indignantly. "I have listened too long now to my honored friends talk about climbing the mountain," the old man said. "And too many times I have had to look upon the seals of Fuji-san on their walking sticks. Soon I will be much too old to climb. I must do it now!"

Grandmother nodded and smiled in agreement. Fujio found himself nodding too. Surely the family would understand Grandfather's wish. It was very clear to him.

But no more was said about it then. Silence fell over the table like a cloud. When the meal had ended, Grandfather placed his cushion-like *zabuton* on the floor in front of the television and prepared to watch an American western. Fujio sat on his heels beside the old man. He felt a tingle of excitement go up his back as he spoke.

"Ojii-san . . . I wish to talk to you about your dream to climb Fuji-san." He spoke as quietly as he could. "I have this same dream. Some of my older friends have already seen Lake Kawaguchi[5] from the top of the mountain. They make fun of me because I have only seen the lake from the foot of the great mountain. They say I am too small to climb—a baby! I have been thinking. We could climb to the top together. We would

[5] Kawaguchi (kä wä gu'chē)

show everyone that you are not too old — and I am not too young."

He sat back, waiting breathlessly for his grandfather's reply. The old man stared at the bright television screen for a long time. Fujio rocked on his heels, frowning. Hadn't his grandfather heard him? He opened his mouth to repeat his words, but his grandfather nodded.

"I think your idea is good, Fujio. You were named for the great mountain. It is right that you climb to the top while you are young. Yes . . ." he nodded again. "It is a good idea. We will help each other and enjoy the climb together. The family will see our dreams come true when we show them the seals of the great mountain on our walking sticks." He sat taller. "We must make our plans. Perhaps it can be a secret journey." A smile spread over his wrinkled face. "Do you think so?"

Fujio bounced on his heels, holding back a shout of joy. "Oh, yes! We will climb to the top the very day of your birthday. Tomorrow we will plan what clothes to wear on our journey up the mountain."

Grandfather slapped his knee in happiness. "We will need strong walking sticks — and a camera to take many pictures."

"And rice cakes to eat when we get hungry!" Fujio jumped to his feet, wishing he could spin around the room to show how good he felt. But this was not allowed in the house. The rice-paper walls were too easily torn.

He went out the open door to the garden. There, beside the pool, he spun around. The stones tickled his feet, reminding him that he was still in his soft cotton *tabi* and had forgotten to put on his sandals to come outside. It didn't matter! Nothing mattered now. He and Grandfather were really going to climb to the top of Mt. Fuji! The day after tomorrow! Nothing would spoil their dream now.

He stepped across the pool on the large flat stones and stood beside the stone lantern at the edge of the path. Little Michiko toddled into the garden, scuffing her wooden *geta* as she walked. She carried her favorite *kokeshi* doll clutched tightly in her small fist. When she reached Fujio, she held the armless wooden doll out to him. "See what Mama-san bought for me from the doll man on the street."

Fujio nodded, sighing in disgust. He had seen the wooden doll with the painted face endless times. He couldn't be bothered about dolls now. Now he wanted only to think about the journey to Mt. Fuji.

Michiko's small mouth pouted. "I heard," she said impishly. "You and Ojii-san will climb the mountain."

Fujio whirled to face her, his eyes showing his alarm. "It is a secret, little one."

She shook her dark head and turned back to the house. Fujio watched her go. She was little. Perhaps she didn't understand about secrets, he told himself. Perhaps if he gave her a present, she would forget. His eyes darted about the garden. What would she like? "Michiko . . ." he called softly, "come back . . ."

And as Michiko turned back, Fujio's eyes came to rest on the small cage beside the bench near the path. Of course! He hurried over to the bench and picked up the tiny cage, peering inside. "Hello, my happy singer," he greeted his pet cricket. "I think you will soon have a new master. . . ." He motioned to Michiko. "I will give you my cricket if you keep the secret."

Michiko's dark eyes looked at the insect in the cage. Her tiny nose wrinkled and she shook her head. "No! I do not want your bug!" With that, she clip-clopped over the path toward the house.

A frown creased Fujio's forehead. Now Mama-san and Papa-san would know the secret he and Grandfather shared. Would they forbid him to go on the journey up the mountain? The cricket in the cage chirped and

Fujio sighed. "I am not sure this is the time to sing, my friend."

He stayed in the garden until Mama-san's soft voice called to him. "It is time for bed, Fujio."

Fujio hung the cricket cage on a tree branch and went inside. Mama-san and Grandmother closed the sliding doors, dividing the big room in two for the night. Mama-san spread the heavy quilt-like *futons* on the floor—one for each to sleep on and one to cover with. Fujio slept in the same room as Grandfather and Grandmother. Michiko slept in the second room with Mama-san and Papa-san. There was no time to talk to Grandfather alone. No one mentioned Mt. Fuji again that night. Fujio sighed. They would have to talk about it in the morning—after breakfast, when Grandmother and Mama-san put the beds away in the cupboards,

391

opened the sliding doors, and cleaned the house. Papa-san would go off to work in the bakery. Then he and Grandfather could walk in the garden and talk. And they would know if Michiko had told their secret.

Fujio snuggled down under his quilt and stared up at the ceiling. Grandfather's snores filled the room. "How could he sleep?" Fujio wondered. In another day they would journey to the foot of the great mountain! They would start their climb! No matter what anyone said, they would get to the top! Butterflies danced in his stomach at the very thought.

The next morning when the family gathered around the table for their breakfast of soybean soup and rice, Fujio had the feeling again that something was wrong. This time he looked straight at his grandfather. Ojii-san's bald head was again bowed. The silence in the room made Fujio shudder. He looked at Michiko. She grinned impishly at him. "I have told about your journey," she said sweetly.

"We do not like the idea, Fujio. It would be too long a climb for your grandfather's tired legs—and too long a climb for your short legs." Mama-san shook her dark head.

Grandfather looked up. His dark eyes were glowing. "I *must* go up the mountain. How many more years will I be able to climb? Would you have me the only aged one in all Japan who hasn't seen the sunrise from the top of our beloved Fuji-san?"

Fujio watched his mother and father look at each

other. Papa-san shrugged his shoulders. "Honored Father, if you feel that strongly about it, you must certainly try to climb the mountain. With a strong stick, and Fujio to help you, you might reach the summit."

Fujio felt his heart speed up. "Thank you, Papa-san."

"I will drive you to the foot of the mountain tomorrow morning. It will take you all that day and night to climb. But if you tire, you must come back down. Agreed?"

Fujio and his grandfather both nodded. "Agreed!" Fujio exclaimed. And he began to count the hours until the next morning.

Early the next day Papa-san drove Fujio and his grandfather across the many miles to Mt. Fuji. He helped them adjust their packs on their backs and then said good-by.

"And much luck in your climb," he told them. As he gazed up the slope to the top of the mountain towering in the clouds, he shook his head. "You will not do it," he muttered. "It is too far to climb."

Fujio saw his grandfather straighten up as tall as his thin frame could go. "We will! You go home now, my son, and work in the bakery. Return tomorrow and you will see our seals of Fuji-san."

Fujio watched his father drive off. Then they started up the mountain. The trail wove gently up the slope and many people walked upward. Now and then Fujio saw a pair of worn straw sandals by the side of the trail. He pointed toward one of the pairs. "Someone has lost his shoes, Grandfather."

The old man shook his head. "The pilgrims who climb the sacred mountain carry many pairs of sandals. They throw them aside when they become worn and they put on a new pair." He pointed to another pair of the straw sandals farther up the slope. "They mark the trail for climbers."

Bells tinkled ahead and behind them. Fujio saw the pilgrims dressed in white. For them, the summit of the sacred mountain was a shrine, a place to visit and worship. He saw that they had bells tied to the ropes which they wore around their waists to help pull each other up the slopes. Each climber had a lantern. "I am glad we have flashlights," he told his grandfather.

Onward up the slope they walked, slowly on the uneven parts. When they reached a small temple, they bought strong walking sticks to help them on their climb. There were many climbers. Young men passed by Fujio and Grandfather. Men the age of Papa-san walked more slowly, Fujio noticed. Women climbed beside their husbands. But Fujio did not see anyone as ancient as Grandfather. And he didn't see another boy as young as himself.

Now and then they had to stop along the path to rest. Grandfather shaded his eyes and looked upward toward the summit. "It is still a long way to the top, Fujio."

How tired Grandfather sounded! Fujio's dark eyes showed his concern. "Perhaps we were wrong to come after all, Grandfather. We can turn back."

Grandfather stood tall and straight. "We will go to the very top and see the sunrise from there in the early morning."

395

Fujio slipped his pack off his back and took out the rice cakes Mama-san had packed for them. "Here. We will eat, Grandfather. Then we can go on."

As they sat beside the trail, other climbers went by them. Some sang happy songs. The people wound along the path as far up the slope as Fujio could see. He watched Grandfather eat the rice cake. Could the old man go on to the top? He sighed. Could *he* go on? Even now his legs ached. He brushed dust off his heavy shoes. He could go back down and climb again another year when he was taller and stronger. But Grandfather's bones were already stiff with age. If he went down now, he might never be able to say that he had climbed the great mountain. Grandfather would lose face with his friends and feel ashamed that he could not climb the mountain. That must not happen!

Grandfather got slowly to his feet, using his walking stick to push himself up. "We must go on, Fujio. We will almost reach the top by dark."

Fujio nodded. At least Grandfather had not given up. Up and up they went, more and more slowly with each step. Fujio found himself breathing hard. He watched his grandfather closely. Now and then the old man stopped to take a deep breath and mop his forehead. Fujio's legs throbbed from the climb. He watched his grandfather in wonder. How could one so old climb so well? What a strong man his grandfather was!

They climbed through the long afternoon and stopped again to eat. The sun began to set and the climbers put on heavier clothing and lit their lanterns. Fujio took their flashlights out of the pack to light the path ahead of them. Soon the slope was twinkling with hundreds of lights. Fujio heard his grandfather puffing. Once the old man stumbled and fell to his knees. Fujio helped him to his feet. On they went. Now Fujio put his arm around Grandfather's waist to help him along the darkened path. The old man's footsteps became slower and slower. Fear clutched at Fujio. How far could they go? "We should have listened to Mamasan and Papa-san," he thought.

At last they reached a hut near the top of the mountain. Many of the climbers went in and stretched out on the floor to sleep. Grandfather motioned Fujio inside and they too stretched out on the floor. Soon

397

Grandfather was snoring. Fujio sighed and closed his eyes. Now they were too far to return home. So of course they would go on. He smiled in the darkness. In the morning they would be standing on top of the world!

Shuffling feet and hushed voices woke Fujio. The first faint light of dawn filtered into the open doorway of the hut. Quickly he shook his grandfather. "It is almost morning, Ojii-san. We must go on."

Grandfather tried to rise, but fell back to the floor. "I cannot get up!" he moaned. "Your mother and father were right. Old bones were not meant to climb mountains."

Fujio's heart pounded. If Grandfather couldn't go up, he couldn't go down either! What would become of them? He looked anxiously at Ojii-san.

The old man looked sad. "If you want to see the sunrise, go on without me," he told Fujio.

Fujio shook his head. "I will not go on without you, Grandfather. Come, I will help you. Your dream to go to the top of the mountain will come true. It will!"

He took his grandfather's thin arm and pulled him to his feet. The old man leaned on Fujio, and on his heavy walking stick. "I will try," he said finally. And slowly they started out, up the slope of the mountain.

Grandfather's weight seemed to push Fujio down. The mountain air was thinner than that below. He puffed for breath. Each step became painful. Ojii-san's feet dragged. Often he would stop, mop his forehead,

398

and sigh. "I will wait for you here, beside the path," he said.

Stubbornly, Fujio shook his head. "No! We have come this far. We will go on together." As he spoke, Fujio tripped on a loose stone. He felt a sharp pain in his ankle as it turned. He cried out as he sank to the ground. Grandfather bent to help him to his feet. Fujio gasped, "My ankle! I twisted it."

Ojii-san pushed Fujio gently to a rock. "Then we must sit here and rest," he said. "I am afraid we have come as far as we can. This great mountain is too much for us." He rubbed his grandson's ankle as he spoke. They sat quietly, neither one speaking. The light in the eastern sky was beginning to brighten. Fujio could see the pink and gold sunlight peeking through the clouds. In just a few more minutes the sun would be up. He saw his grandfather's eyes searching the sky. How much the honored one wanted to see that sunrise! They must get to the top before the sun rose.

With an effort, Fujio got to his feet. "Come, let us go on, Grandfather. Now it is I who must lean upon you. We won't give up now. We are near the top and the sun is waking."

His grandfather nodded. He put his arm around Fujio. Suddenly his fading strength seemed renewed. Up they went. Slowly . . . very slowly. Soon they could hear chanting voices and shouts of joy ahead of them. The end of the trail was near! On they went. Fujio's ankle hurt. Grandfather moaned under his breath. But—they were there!

The sun slid out from under a cloud blanket and rose, a giant red ball in the sky. Fujio shouted a loud

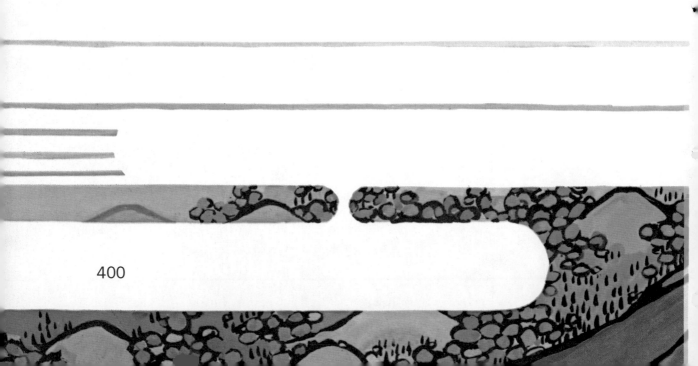

hurrah, and Grandfather's eyes filled with tears. They stood together, quietly watching the beautiful sight before them. "We have done it!" Grandfather exclaimed. "We will get a seal of the mountains to put on our walking sticks. Those waiting for us below will want to see them."

Fujio nodded. His heart throbbed with happiness. "The way down is easier, Grandfather. We can go slowly and ask for help if we need it. We will have no trouble." He sighed and breathed the clear air. It was, he thought, like standing on top of the whole world. He clutched his walking stick tightly. "We climbed well, Grandfather. And we will have the proof."

——Virginia K. Smiley

THINKING IT OVER

1. Explain why you would agree or disagree with this saying: "He who climbs Mt. Fuji once is wise; he who climbs it twice is a fool."

2. The okapi belt was a badge of manhood. What did the Fuji stick stand for?

3. What problems did Fujio and Grandfather have to solve before they could climb Mt. Fuji? How did each show his determination to succeed?

THOUGHTS AT WORK

1. Find four ways the author told you the story took place in Japan. What clues tell you that it happened in modern Japan?

2. Why do you think Grandfather hadn't climbed Mt. Fuji as a young man? Why did he feel he could not wait any longer?

3. Fujio's father said, "Climbing is for the young man." Tell why you do or do not agree with him.

4. How did Fujio get along with his sister Michiko? In what ways did she remind you of little sisters you have known?

5. Tell about a time when you were determined to do something that your family felt you were too young to try. Did you get your way?

6. Think of a word or phrase to describe how each person felt in these sentences.

   a. Butterflies danced in Fujio's stomach.
   b. Grandfather's jaw was set.
   c. Fujio's heart thumped faster.
   d. The old man's footsteps became slower and slower.
   e. Grandfather's rice sat untouched in his bowl.

7. The author says the Japanese never like to "lose face" with their friends. What does this expression mean? When did Fujio or Grandfather almost "lose face"? Tell about a time when you almost "lost face."

THE REASON
FOR THE PELICAN

The reason for the pelican
Is difficult to see:
His beak is clearly larger
Than there's any need to be.

It's not to bail a boat with——
He doesn't own a boat.
Yet everywhere he takes himself
He has that beak to tote.

It's not to keep his wife in——
His wife has got one, too.
It's not a scoop for eating soup.
It's not an extra shoe.

It isn't quite for anything.
And yet you realize
It's really quite a splendid beak
In quite a splendid size.

John Ciardi

ISLAND FOR A PELICAN

The island is a real island, Mykonos, (mē′ kê nôs), which lies off the southern coast of Greece in the Aegean (i jē′ ən) Sea. The pelican is Petros (pe′trōs), whose name means *rock* or *stone* in Greek. One day Petros came to Mykonos, and little did he realize the excitement he was to cause.

404

In the middle of the Aegean Sea there is an island. Everything on it is white. The houses are white. The windmills that flap their long sails in the wind are white. Even the stones of the narrow donkey paths are whitewashed.

For many years the island was famous for two things: its sailors and its churches. The sailors were strong and brave and daring. Their swift sailing ships went everywhere. As for the churches, they were sprinkled all over the island like dots of white icing on a cake. There were 365 of them, one for every day of the year.

The reason there were so many churches was because of the sailors. If they were caught in a storm, they said a special prayer. They would promise to build a church if they got home safely.

One shipwrecked sailor did not have much money when he got home. He could not build a big and beautiful church. So he made the best church he could. It was perfect in every way, with a dome and a door and everything. When it was finished, it was called the Cats' Church because it was just big enough to hold

a cat and her kittens. After that there were 366 churches on the island. "We even have one for leap year now," the islanders said.

Then came the time when people no longer needed sailboats. They had big steamships that went quickly from port to port. The island was forgotten, and everyone on it became very poor.

But after a while the people who traveled on the big steamships heard about the white island with the windmills and the churches, and they wanted to see it. They liked to walk through the narrow whitewashed streets. They liked to swim in the blue sea. They liked to sit at tables on the waterfront and eat fish. Most of all, artists liked to come and paint pictures of the island.

Every year more visitors came.

All the other nearby islands were jealous, especially the nearest one.

Then something happened that made the island even more famous.

It was something dropped from the skies.

Thodori[1] and Vassili[2] found it.

Thodori was a sailor. Vassili was his young godson who lived with him and helped him with his boat. Early one morning they were walking along the beach. Suddenly something moved in an odd way at the edge of the water.

They ran forward.

[1] Thodori (thə dô′rē)   [2] Vassili (väs′il ē′)

A large, strange-looking bird lay on the sand. Vassili had never seen anything like it. He was not sure he wanted to get too close—that long yellow bill made him nervous. But Thodori crouched beside it.

"It's a pelican," Thodori said, "a young one, a fledgling. From the look of it, I'd say it was too exhausted to fly south to Africa with its own kind." Vassili watched while Thodori took off his jacket and wrapped it carefully around the pelican. It was too weak to make any move of protest.

"What are you going to do with it, Thodori?"

"We're going to carry it home," Thodori said.

They carried it home. Thodori made a bed for it under the staircase and Vassili helped him take care of it. Every free moment that Vassili had he spent under the stairs, tossing little fish for the pelican to catch in its long bill, and talking to it in a low voice. After a while, it seemed to Vassili that the pelican waited for him to come home. When he arrived, it clattered its bill impatiently at him in welcome and blinked its eyes at the fish in Vassili's hands.

Then the day came when Thodori said, "That pelican is strong enough to fly again. We'll have to let it go. It's the right thing to do."

Vassili did not say anything.

Very early the next morning they carried it out to the beach. Thodori let it go. "Now fly away to Africa!" Vassili cried. The pelican flapped upward into the air. "Good-by!" Vassili called as he saw it cut a wide white circle against the sky. "And good luck to you!"

Then there was a sudden rush of air against his face and a great sweep of wings.

The pelican had come back to his side.

"Fly!" Thodori shouted, waving his cap.

It waddled toward him and nipped his leg.

"Fly to Africa!" Vassili shouted, flapping his arms to show the pelican what to do.

The pelican gave Vassili's leg a nip.

Thodori and Vassili looked at each other.

"I guess it doesn't want to leave us now," Thodori said, scratching his chin.

And so it was. The pelican had evidently decided to stay. As it followed them home along the beach, neither of them said anything, but Vassili's face shone.

They gave the pelican a name—Petros.

Petros grew big and strong. His eyes were bright and beady. His bill was like a pair of long yellow scissors. And everyone on the island said how clever Thodori was to have caught him.

Every morning Petros got up and followed Thodori and Vassili to the waterfront. He would go for a swim while they worked on the boat. Then Petros would preen his feathers and waddle as far as the fish market. He would clatter his bill until the fishermen gave him his breakfast. After that, he would play on the quay with a little white mop of a dog named Fofo. [3]

[3]Fofo (fō fō')

All day long Petros would stay on the quay, reaching out with his long bill to take tidbits off the tables. In the afternoon he would go home with Vassili and Thodori and have a nap. Then as soon as everyone came out for the evening promenade, he would be back. At night he would wait for Vassili to walk home with him.

Soon Petros was famous. The newspapers even published his picture. There was no doubt that he was the island's number one attraction. The shops sold more postcards of Petros than they ever had of the churches and windmills.

The people on the next island grew even more jealous.

"They have all those windmills and churches," they said. "And now Petros! It is too much. We must do something about it."

Every time they saw a ship pass full of tourists on their way to see the churches and the windmills and Petros, they shook with rage and jealousy.

One fine morning some fishermen from that other island were out in their boat when they saw something floating on the water. It was a large white something.

"It's not a fish," they said. "And it's not a parcel. What do you think it could be?"

But when they drew closer, they saw that it was Petros.

He had flown out to sea and was sitting on the water, resting his wings.

"This is the chance we have been waiting for!" the fishermen from the other island said. Quietly, swiftly, they rowed toward Petros. They took him aboard and sailed home in triumph.

That night when Petros did not appear on the quay, nobody thought very much of it. "He is off on a little vacation," they said. "He deserves it. He will be back tomorrow."

Vassili frowned and looked worried. Thodori told

411

him to get on with his work and not be so silly. "Petros belongs here," he said. "This is his home. He'll be back tomorrow in time for his breakfast."

But the next day Petros did not come home. And the day after that he was still missing.

Fofo moped. The tourists went back to their ships, disappointed. Vassili and Thodori worked on the boat, but Vassili was so busy thinking about Petros that he did everything wrong. Thodori must have been thinking of Petros, too, because he did not seem to notice.

Nothing on the island seemed the same without Petros. Everything was dull. Nobody enjoyed the evening promenade along the waterfront now that Petros was no longer there. It was worse than when the wind blew down the electric lines and there was no light on the island.

And then some startling news arrived.

Petros had been seen on the next island!

The waterfront buzzed.

A delegation was sent off at once to see if the report was true. There was the Chief Official of the island, the priest, and the Chief of Police. Thodori and Vassili wanted to go too, but they were told they would have to stay behind. "This is an official delegation," they were told. "You are only a simple sailor, Thordori, and Vassili is only a boy. And this is an official diplomatic mission. What's more, there's no room for you in the boat. Surely you understand, Thodori."

So Thodori went and sat outside a coffeehouse and waited.

And Vassili went off to the beach and skimmed stones across the water toward the other island and waited.

The moment the delegation landed on the other island, there on the waterfront was Petros.

But the men of the other island were waiting too.

The Chief of Police said, "We have come to take Petros home."

"That is out of the question," said the Chief of Police of the other island. "Petros stays here."

"But Petros is our pelican!" The Chief Official of the island said.

"As he came to you, so he has come to us now," the Chief Official of the other island announced. "He got bored with your island. Now he is making his home with us, here. If he wants to go back to you, let him fly back of his own free will."

The words went back and forth, loud and bitter.

Finally the priest said, "We are outnumbered. It is wiser to return to our island before any blood is shed. Once we are home, we can proceed in the proper diplomatic way."

And so the delegation that had come to rescue Petros was forced to retreat.

They returned with the sad news that Petros was indeed on the other island. Their pelican was practically a prisoner.

413

Thodori and Vassili listened. Vassili looked at Thodori, but Thodori said nothing.

That night the talk in all the coffeehouses was about Petros. Everyone made speeches, using words like "honor" and "justice." Finally it was decided to send a telegram to the next island.

"Petros must be sent back at once, or else!"

"Or else what?" came the reply, collect.

"You will see!" said the second telegram.

The men of the other island telegraphed back mockingly, "You can even go ahead and declare war if you like. Petros is here and here he is going to stay. There is no law governing the domicile of pelicans!"

The next night everyone who could squeeze into the biggest coffeehouse on the island was on hand. The islanders were holding an emergency meeting.

Vassili listened to all the talk. And he wondered what was the best way to get Petros to come back to the island of his own free will. He thought about it all the time. And he waited.

At last a night came when there was no moon. The sea was calm. Vassili said to himself, "This is the night for Petros to come home."

He waited until he was sure that Thodori was asleep. He put on dark trousers and a dark shirt. He took Thodori's dark cap off the hook and pulled it well down over his eyes. All alone, with no one to see him go, he went down to the quay and set out in Thodori's boat.

He knew better than to get the engine going. He would have to row all the way. He rowed until his arms ached. It was a long way for a boy to row. No island boy that he had heard of had ever done it all alone, and there were times when he thought he would never make it. "Maybe," he told himself, "it would be wiser to turn back." But he would rest for a few minutes on the calm sea and think of Petros. Then he would pull at the oars with new strength.

It was late when he landed. He hauled the boat onto a little beach. It was deserted. Then, light as a cat, he sprang into the darkness, a willow basket hooked over his arm.

In the town everyone was sleeping. Even the two policemen whose job it was to keep watch over Petros were peacefully snoring.

Vassili's hand dipped into the basket. A silver fish flashed silently through the black night. Petros opened one eye and caught it without a sound.

One of the policemen woke up just then.

He poked the other policeman with his elbow.

"Look at Petros. What do you think he's doing?"

Petros was slowly waddling along the waterfront, stopping every now and then to pick up a silver fish and gobble it. No one else was in sight. Everything was thick silence.

"Stop being so jumpy," the second policeman said. "There's nobody around. The harbor master would have sounded the alarm if any ship had landed. One of the fishermen must have dropped some fish. Let Petros have them if he wants them."

The policemen peered after Petros as he wandered along the quay, stopping every few feet to gobble fish. Then they got bored and turned around and dozed off again.

Fish by silver fish, and of his own free will, Petros wandered toward the little beach. There Vassili waited, silent, in the little boat.

"Petros?" Vassili whispered.

He held up the last of the fish.

Petros hopped aboard. The fish curved through the air. Petros' bill clattered. The fish disappeared.

And then once more Vassili began to row.

The next morning was Sunday. Everyone on the island was getting ready to go to church when suddenly Fofo appeared on the waterfront, barking wildly.

"What is Fofo barking about? Doesn't she know it's Sunday?" the Chief Official of the island said as he sat at breakfast.

But Fofo went right on barking. And then, when everyone came out of doors to see what was the matter, she began dashing toward the Cats' Church.

"There must be a cat inside that's just had kittens," the Chief of Police announced. He buttoned up his uniform. "I suppose I'll just have to go along to make sure."

A crowd had already gathered outside the Cats' Church when the Chief of Police arrived.

He blinked.

There, standing by the open door of the Cats' Church, was Petros.

"A miracle!" everyone cried. "Petros is back!" And they ran to tell Thodori.

Thodori was still asleep.

Vassili, from his cot in the corner of the room, saw the Chief of Police and the priest and the Chief Official of the island standing over Thodori's bed.

"What's the matter now?" Thodori asked, rubbing the sleep out of his eyes.

"Petros is back!" they told him.

Thodori sat up in bed.

"Petros?" he cried. "Back?"

"Yes," the Chief of Police said.

"He's at the Cats' Church, the Lord be praised!" the priest said.

"Come and see, Thodori," the Chief Official of the island said. "Petros must have come back all by himself."

"I said he would," said Thodori. "I said it all the time."

"Eh, Vassili," Thodori shouted when the others had gone. "Wake up. Petros is back!" He stared down at the boy. Vassili seemed fast asleep. Now all the church bells on the island were ringing. "That's funny," said Thodori. "That noise is enough to wake them as far away as Athens.[4] The boy is usually the first one up. And what's my cap doing on the floor?" He scratched his chin thoughtfully for a moment. Then he quickly lifted a corner of the blanket and saw that Vassili was still wearing his shirt and trousers.

Thodori shook his head. "But he's only a boy," he muttered in astonishment. "Who would have believed that he could do it all by himself?" Gently Thodori pulled the blanket up over Vassili and tiptoed out of the room, closing the door behind him.

[4] Athens (ath′ ənz)

And if you go to the island, you will see the white houses and the windmills and the 365 churches, one for every day of the year, and the Cats' Church for leap year, all set in the bluest sea in the world. And if you are lucky, Petros may even accept a silver fish from your hand, as he does from Vassili every day.

But you must offer it to him politely.

—*Edward Fenton*

THINKING IT OVER

1. Why did the islanders threaten to fight over Petros? Did they really like pelicans that much?

2. Compare the way the adults and Vassili behaved after Petros left the island. Which do you feel was the better way? Why?

3. Would you say Petros came home of his own free will or did Vassili steal him? Explain your answer.

THOUGHTS AT WORK

1. Why did the "official delegation" not let Vassili and Thodori go with them to rescue Petros? Do you think this was fair? Why?

2. Did the delegation report accurately when they said Petros was "practically a prisoner" on the next island? Explain your answer.

3. Did Petros like living on one island better than on another? Why?

4. Pretend you are a tourist on the island and write a letter home describing the fuss over Petros's disappearance.

5. How did Vassili plan to "rescue" Petros from the next island? Why didn't Vassili tell anyone about his plan?

6. Just suppose that the policemen watching over Petros had discovered what Vassili was doing. How would the ending of the story have changed?

7. An author can write interesting descriptions by using (1) comparisons, (2) exaggerations, or (3) color words. Read each description below and tell which of the three the author used.
   a. "That noise is enough to wake them as far away as Athens."
   b. ". . . the churches . . . were sprinkled all over the island like dots of white icing on a cake."
   c. ". . . light as a cat, he sprang into the darkness. . . ."
   d. "His bill was like a pair of long yellow scissors."
   e. ". . . the bluest sea in the world."
   f. "A silver fish flashed silently through the black night."

THE SUN THAT WARMS YOU

Is it not so, brother?

The sun that warms you

warms me,

The fate that forms me

forms you,

The irk that frets you

frets me,

The rain that wets me

wets you,

The hour that tries you

tries me,

But the sun that dries me

dries you.

It is so, brother.

——Eleanor Farjeon

❧ BIBLIOGRAPHY ❧

The Cave Above Delphi, by Scott Corbett.
Two American children join their Greek friends in a search for an ancient ring hidden in Greece.

A Stranger in the Spanish Village, by Anita Feagles.
Two Spanish boys fear that the tall, pale American is not really a man, but a man-eating monster in disguise.

Ninji's Magic, by Elisabeth MacIntyre.
A New Guinea boy does many things wrong at the strange new school, but finally he does something right and makes his family proud of him.

Ramu, A Story of India, by Rama Mehta.
Playing hooky from school causes all kinds of trouble for a young boy of India.

Shaun and the Boat: An Irish Story, by Anne Molloy.
If the new *curragh* was not ready in time to enter the boat race, it would be no one's fault but Shaun's.

Isfendiar and the Wild Donkeys, by Bronson Potter.
An Iranian village boy sets off alone across the desert, determined to find the mysterious donkeys.

My Name Is Pablo, by Aimée Sommerfelt.
Being arrested and sent to a boy's reformatory for not having a license to shine shoes is only one of a Mexican boy's many troubles.

In-Between Miya, by Yoshiko Uchida.
What would it be like to live in Tokyo in a beautiful house and never have to worry about money? A Japanese village girl gets a chance to find out.

ALPHONSE, THAT BEARDED ONE

by Natalie Savage Carlson

The longest story in the book has been saved for last. It tells about a time more than two hundred years ago in the wilds of Canada. Then French soldiers often did battle with the Indians. Once when a war was threatened, a French settler decided he did not want to join the army. What happened as a result makes this story perhaps the tallest as well as the longest tale in the book.

In a forgotten time when Canada was New France, a settler named Jeannot Vallar went hunting in the wilderness that lay around his cabin. He did not have to go far to find an old she-bear digging at a rotted stump.

"*Bien!*" exclaimed Jeannot to himself. "This fat one will keep me in grease until next winter."

He shot the bear, pinched her fat sides, then lifted her over his shoulders with many a puff and a grunt. As he started away, almost bent double under her weight, he heard a whining sound in a nearby tree.

He looked up and saw a little bear cub clinging to a branch and trembling with fright.

"The old one can wait here for a time," said Jeannot. "She is in no hurry anyhow."

He dropped the dead bear to the ground and pulled the cub from the tree.

"Game can be shot any day," said the settler to the cub, "but it is not every day that I can catch such a pet as you. I will call you Alphonse."

He brought the cub back to his cabin. All the way there, the little bear cuddled close to him, for here was something warm and living even if it had a strange smell.

Alphonse soon became used to this smell. It belonged to the rude cabin to which Jeannot brought him and to the Indians and trappers who dropped in for short visits.

It was especially strong when the grizzled woodsman, Arsine Jolicoeur, crossed the threshold one day and squatted by the hearth to mold some lead balls for his long, long gun.

"So ho!" said Arsine to Jeannot. "You may not have much longer to live in this snug cabin. The Iroquois are beginning to cause trouble again. The governor's men will be looking for strong ones like you who have seen service with the army. Your gray hairs will be no excuse."

After the visitor had left, Jeannot climbed to the loft. He whistled to Alphonse to follow. Then he pulled the cobwebs away from the old chest in the corner and lifted the lid. He peered at the contents.

He pulled out a musketeer's jacket and looked back and forth from it to the bear. He held up a dented helmet and looked first at it then at the bear's furry head. Next he laid a rusty sword across his knees. He stared from it to the bear's long claws. Then he neatly returned all these things to the chest and closed the lid tightly.

He smiled slowly and thoughtfully.

"Alphonse," he told the cub, "you have many things to learn."

Jeannot made a little suit of tanned hides for Alphonse and taught him to dress himself and to understand a great many things. Alphonse learned quickly. When there were things that he could not understand, he would swing his head and roll his eyes, *çà* and *là*, *çà* and *là*, for that is the spirit of a bear.

When Alphonse was as big as he was going to get, Jeannot opened the chest again. He took out the helmet, the jacket and the sword. The jacket was too small for Alphonse, so Jeannot let out a tuck here and put in a gusset there until it would go all the way around him. He cobbled a sturdy pair of jack boots, and these boots were the only part of the outfit that fit Alphonse properly.

The bear was taught to march to the beat of a drum, to shoulder a gun and to handle the sword well. And of all these things, Alphonse was best at marching and never lost a chance to show off before strangers. For that is the spirit of bears as well as of men.

On a late afternoon, Jeannot had him dress in battle array and gave him his last lesson.

"Alphonse," he said, "this is the oldest and most important rule for a soldier: Keep your eyes open, your mouth shut, your powder dry and do not volunteer for anything."

The bear listened intently. He rolled his head and his eyes a little, *çà* and *là*.

There was a sudden rat-a-tat on the cabin door. Jeannot put his finger to his lips. He motioned Alphonse to climb up and hide in the loft. The bear quickly obeyed, but he crouched close to the landing above the top rung and peeked down, for it is the spirit of a bear to be as curious as a boy.

Jeannot opened the door. There stood a corporal with a document in his hands. He was a great moose of a man with a pulled-out chin and a squashlike nose flattened over his moustache. Beside him stood a leftover piece of a fellow with pale blue eyes and a bouquet of hair on his chin. Both carried knapsacks on their backs and long, long guns.

"Duty calls, Jeannot Vallar," said the big man. "I am Corporal Pagot and this is the common soldier Genest."

Jeannot bowed and invited them inside.

"I have always wanted to fight the Iroquois and become a hero," he said, "but I am no longer young. I suffer from ague and I see spots in front of my eyes. Sometimes my ears ring, and I get mad spells when I believe that I am the king of France. Perhaps it is better that I send my brother in my place. He is a big, strapping fellow—not unlike yourself, my corporal, although shy of talk—and he has had some military training."

The corporal studied the document in his hands.

"That should be agreeable with my captain," he said. "Better a strong wife than a weak ox to pull the plow. Where is your brother?"

Jeannot walked to the ladder leading to the loft and whistled through his fingers. In no time at all, Alphonse came lumbering down.

The soldiers stared in amazement at his long, furry nose and fiery little eyes. Pagot's eyes were pulling from their sockets. At last he found his voice — such a weak, little one for a man his size.

"But, m'sieu," he protested, "your brother looks like a bear to me."

Jeannot Vallar turned an insulted look on his visitor.

"Is that politeness, my corporal?" he asked. "Does my brother say that you look like a moose?"

"Many of his men do," offered the little soldier, speaking for the first time.

Pagot glowered at him.

"If your long ears listened to orders instead of gossip, my little one," he said, "you would be something more than a common soldier in the ranks."

"You see," said Jeannot, "everyone has a right to his own opinions but it is not politeness to carry this thing too far."

"But he has fur all over his face, and paws instead of hands," insisted Corporal Pagot. "And just now he growled."

Jeannot clucked his tongue.

"*Hélas!*" he sighed. "It was a great tragedy for us that time the bears stole little Alphonse from his cradle. You have heard of such things surely, my corporal — a baby carried off by a she-wolf or a lynx and raised as its own. Is it any wonder our Alphonse still carries the mark of his life with the bears? It was only two years ago that I found him in a trap and dragged him back home, snarling and biting. Poor Alphonse!"

The corporal was not sure of this.

"I think that you made a mistake, Jeannot Vallar," he said. "I fear that it is one of the bears that you brought home. Your Alphonse must still be in the woods. Perhaps we might search for him a bit. I am in no hurry to get back to the war and my captain."

Jeannot shook his head.

"There can be no mistake about this being my brother," he declared. "About face, Alphonse. Bend over." Jeannot flipped out the stub of a tail. "You see! A pompon on the end of his backbone. Our Alphonse was so marked. This is absolute proof, my corporal. Have you any more questions?"

Corporal Pagot doubled up his fist and beat it against his forehead as if to stir up his brains.

"It is most extraordinary," he admitted. "You must be correct, m'sieu. But it will take quite a bit of explaining to put this thing in the right light before my captain. Luckily he is nearsighted."

"Then there will be nothing to explain," said Jeannot, "and I can promise you that Alphonse will keep his silence about the whole matter."

Still the corporal had a doubt left.

"Don't bears have pompons on the end of their backbones?" he asked.

As the corporal spoke, Jeannot's whole appearance changed. He haughtily stretched to his full height, raised his chin in the air and tossed his long gray hair over his shoulders. He pulled a greasy rag from his pocket and daintily flicked it at the soldier.

"And who questions the king of France?" he demanded. "Away, peasants, varlots, knaves! And take this bearded one with you. My Majesty will have no more of this insolence."

The two soldiers turned limp. The little Genest made a tight bow to Jeannot Vallar, and Corporal Pagot fell on his knees.

"Forth to battle!" shouted Jeannot. "The enemy is at the palace gates!"

Alphonse marked time in his tall boots. Pagot rose to his feet. Both soldiers fell into step with Alphonse. Left, right, left, right, left, right the trio marched out the door and down the trail that led to the fort.

So in this way, a bear from the wilderness marched forth to join the army of New France.

Left, right, left, right, left, right the soldiers marched down the trail as if in step to the beat of a drum. Alphonse was in the lead because neither man wanted to walk in front of him.

The sun shone on his breastplate and helmet. His short legs seemed all boots as he plodded on. The same sun shone on Corporal Pagot and the little Genest. It drew beads of sweat out of their smooth-shaven cheeks.

Deeper into the forest wriggled the trail. The trees hid the three soldiers. On they marched and marched and marched. The men were beginning to weary but Alphonse pushed tirelessly on.

"I'm hungry," Genest complained.

Alphonse turned and looked at him. He licked his chops.

"It isn't time yet," replied the corporal. "The shadows are still short. Let us talk about something that will take our minds off food. The wild boar forgets acorns when the huntsman's horn fills his mind with other thoughts."

"*Bon!*" agreed Genest. "Let us talk about what we will do when we leave the army. What are your plans, my corporal?"

Pagot fell into a jaunty swagger. Alphonse kept on licking his chops as if the conversation had not been changed.

"I shall return to Normandy and seek an easier life," said the corporal. "Perhaps some fine nobleman will take me into service as his lackey. I will have nothing to do all day long but open and close carriage doors. What are your plans?"

"I am going to become a cook in some prosperous inn," said the other. "I shall cook pigs' trotters and hare smothered in butter and—"

"Enough of that," scolded Pagot. "Perhaps we should give the subject a turn. Think of the village fêtes and fairs! I saw my first juggler at one, and a little white pig that danced to a pipe."

Alphonse began to drool over his breastplate.

"And once I climbed the greased pole to the very top," boasted the corporal. "What did you do at the fairs, Genest?"

"I sat under a tree and ate sausages and cheese."

"Think of the puppet shows," urged Pagot, "and dancing on the grass with the pretty maidens in their ruffled white bonnets. Did you dance much, Genest?"

"No," confessed the common soldier. "I was afraid that if I set my sausages and cheese down somebody might steal them."

Alphonse stopped and turned around. He pointed appealingly to his mouth, for it is the spirit of bears to get very hungry—as any woodsman knows.

"So, so, Alphonse, we will eat right away," promised Pagot. Under his breath he said to Genest, "This wild man looks as if he is ready to make a meal of us."

"There is a stream at the next turn of the trail, if I remember rightly," said Genest. "Let us stop there and catch some nice fish for supper."

The path turned from the woods and there was the stream.

"Halt!" ordered the corporal. "Here is our supper waiting to be caught."

The men made themselves busy fashioning three fishing poles from willow branches and knotting bits of string. Alphonse watched them closely.

"Dig some worms for us, Alphonse," ordered Pagot. "Your long nails should be good for that."

Alphonse dug worms out of the wet bank as he had so often done for Jeannot Vallar. Pagot baited three hooks. He held one pole out to Alphonse, but the bear pushed it away.

"All right, my fine friend," said Pagot. "Those who won't hold a pole get no fish for supper. You can go hungry."

Pagot and Genest squatted on the bank and flipped their lines into the water. Alphonse lumbered over and sat down beside the corporal.

The sun sank low as the men waited for a bite. But the fish did not seem to be as hungry as they. Nothing nibbled at the bait. Then to their astonishment, Alphonse plunged his paw into the water and splashed a big fish onto the bank. He swallowed it—bones, tail and all.

The men kept on fishing but had no luck. Alphonse

435

frisked a second fish out of the water, then a third and a fourth. The men watched the fishtails disappear into his big mouth.

Genest leaned over to Pagot.

"Let me put a flea in your ear, my corporal," he whispered. "I'm sure this bearded fellow is a bear. And that pompon on the end of the backbone doesn't prove anything to me."

"*Chut!*" warned Pagot, finger to lip. "This Alphonse must be a man when we get back to the fort or it is the pillory for both of us."

When it began to grow dark, they gave up the fishing and scattered to collect wood. Soon they had a cheery bonfire going. Alphonse pulled up a big log and the three sat on it. Pagot and Genest munched the cold, dried, salted army food from their knapsacks.

As the little Genest buckled his knapsack, he remembered something.

"We have only two blankets among us," he said. "Someone will have to sleep with 'Phonse."

"I appoint you to sleep with the bearded one," said Pagot.

"No, no," refused Genest. "You sleep with him."

"Not I," said the corporal.

"Nor I," added the other. "I'll sleep on the bare ground by myself."

The black night crept closer about them, brightening the flames of the fire. Across the stream an eerie light played over the marshland.

"Look!" Genest pointed at it. "The *feu follet!*"

Pagot stiffened but Alphonse sleepily dropped his head between his knees.

"It is truly the wicked goblin with his little light out to make mischief," said Genest moving closer to Pagot.

The forest seemed to come to life. From its depths a wolf howled. An owl hooted among the treetops. This chorus was swelled by the wild cry of a loon.

Alphonse lifted his head and wriggled about restlessly.

Then a sudden gust of wind shrieked through the trees.

"Hark!" cried Pagot, hand to ear. "It is the *chasse galerie.*"

"Y-yes," Genest whispered through chattering teeth. "The ghostly hunter rides through the sky tonight. Hear

437

the baying of the hound and the cries of the hunter? It means bad luck."

Alphonse smelled the wind. He growled deep down in his chest.

The strange cries came closer. A circle of hostile, shining eyes surrounded the little group by the fire.

"Indians!" cried Genest. "Put out the fire, 'Phonse."

"Wolves!" bawled Pagot. "Build up the fire, Alphonse."

Alphonse did neither. He growled furiously. He rose in his boots and strode toward the eyes.

"Gr-r-r-r-r-r-r-r!" he growled. "Gr-r-r-r-r-r-r-r!"

The eyes disappeared and furry paws ran away in all directions.

Alphonse gave a last mighty growl, then returned to the log. For it is not the spirit of a bear to fear any other beast in the forest.

The two men sat in silence for several minutes. Genest spoke first.

"I have changed my mind," he said. "I will sleep with 'Phonse after all."

"Ho, ho!" exclaimed Pagot. "You are too late. I changed mine before you did. *I* will sleep with Alphonse."

The dispute was settled by the three sleeping together, with Alphonse in the middle.

So in this way, the bear from the wilderness gained the respect of his two fellow soldiers.

III

The left, right, left, right of the soldiers had covered their boots with dust by the time they reached the fort in the woods.

Pagot was now in the lead with Alphonse last because an armed column should have strong protection from the rear. Between them was little Genest, like a fly crawling between two beetles.

The high palisade of the fort rose before them. It was made of great logs turned on end. Over it flew the white flag of France with its golden lilies.

A guard peered out of a loophole over the gate. He pointed the muzzle of his long, long gun at the approaching party.

"Halt!" shouted the guard. "Who goes there?"

"Corporal Pagot and party," answered the big man.

"Advance and give the password."

Pagot stepped nearer the gate.

"Arquebuses and brassarts," he replied.

There was a pause.

"That was the password last week," retorted the guard. "You can't come in unless you know this week's password."

Pagot clenched his long, long gun.

"Charlot Bonnet," he bellowed, "you know me well. Open the gate and let us in."

"Not without the password, my corporal," grinned Bonnet. "Those are my orders."

Pagot's nose grew purple. Alphonse's head began to sway and his eyes to roll, *çà* and *là*.

"Bonnet," shouted Pagot. "I will have you put in the pillory. I will have you thrown in irons."

"You have to get in first," the guard saucily reminded him. "And you need the password for that."

Then Alphonse stepped forward and pulled back his nose.

"Gr-r-r-r-r!" he growled angrily, for it is the spirit of bears to get cross when they are tired and hungry.

"Ah, now that's it," said the guard. "*Gruau!* Groats. We had them for breakfast. Open the gate, you Henri down there."

The heavy gate swung open. The three soldiers marched through.

There were log cabins along the inner sides of the fence. Soldiers were loitering about in the square. They wore shiny new shoulder-belts and some of them made fine style with their big hats dripping with plumes.

"*Pouah!*" snorted Pagot. "The new lace-cuffed soldiers with their frills and *frou-frou* have arrived from France. Perhaps this explaining about Alphonse won't be so hard after all, eh my little friend?"

"We are in luck," agreed Genest. "These swallow-flies straight from France will believe anything."

The soldiers quickly gathered around the newcomers.

"Why is this bear dressed up so funny?" asked one

440

of them, a foppish lad with golden curls and round blue eyes. "Is bear-baiting the latest sport in New France?"

"This is no bear, my simpleton," retorted Pagot. "Have you never seen a man from the wilderness?"

"But he has fur all over him," said another mincing soldier.

"Ha! Ha! Wait until you have spent as many winters in New France as this fellow," said Pagot. "You will grow fur all over you, too."

"With that long snout, he looks like a bear," insisted the first.

"Is that what passes for manners in the king's guard now?" demanded the corporal. "Does my comrade say that you look like a pussycat?"

And all the while they talked about him, Alphonse rocked his head *çà* and *là*.

A third soldier found his tongue.

"I have heard the stories told by my father whose grandfather sailed with Jacques Cartier," he offered. "He said that to the west of New France is the kingdom of Saguenay. In it are great lakes full of sea serpents so large they can swallow a canoe. The land is covered with gold and rubies. Strange men live there, some of them having only one leg—unipeds he called them."

"This bearded one is from there," said Pagot. "He is one of the long-nosed men covered with fur."

The soldier with the curls sneered.

"The kingdom of Saguenay was a myth," he scoffed. "There is no such place."

Pagot saw that Alphonse was growing impatient with the spirit of a bear that wants to be somewhere else.

"Stand aside, my fine lace cuffs," he ordered. "We must report to the captain."

The elegant new soldiers opened an aisle for the three. But as Alphonse marched past, the pussycat of a soldier blew his lips out with a disrespectful sound like a cow pulling its hoof from mud.

"That fancy young truffle needs salting," remarked Pagot.

He stalked manfully to the captain's desk and made a deep flourish. The captain squinted at him.

"Corporal Pagot reporting with the new conscript," said the corporal.

"Where is the conscript?" asked the officer, blinking his eyes and turning his head from side to side like an inquiring rooster.

442

Pagot pulled at Alphonse.

"Here he is, sir," he said. "Alphonse Vallar, sharp of wit and sound of body."

The captain blinked and squinted more than ever.

"Alphonse Vallar," he repeated. "He looks like a bear to me."

Then Pagot forced a loud laugh.

"Ha! Ha!" came out Pagot's false laugh. "What a wit you are, my captain! Now that you mention it, this conscript *has* the look of a bear. Let us hope that he can fight like one. Ha! Ha!"

The captain laughed too. He tossed his gray hair. Then he swallowed his laugh.

"We have quite a score to settle with the Iroquois," he said, "but we don't have to wait much longer now that reenforcements have arrived from France. You may go."

The three soldiers turned on their heels and walked out.

"Genest," said Pagot as they crossed the square. "I have a little matter to settle with Charlot Bonnet. He is not a featherhead like these new soldiers. I think it best to enter into a little plot with him. I will not punish him for his waggishness if he will keep his mouth shut about our new conscript."

Corporal Pagot hurried to the gate and climbed the ladder that led to the landing near the top of the palisade.

"You might as well come into the barracks and get

rid of those tortoise-shells," Genest said, pointing to Alphonse's armor. "None but pikemen and canoneers wear them any more."

As they were about to enter one of the log cabins, their path was blocked by the pussycat soldier and his companions.

"Regard the man from the Saguenay kingdom," taunted the youth. "He has the outmoded armor of a soldier and the nose of a bear."

The becurled soldier pulled a small jeweled box from his pocket. He daintily flipped the lid and took a pinch of snuff. He sniffed it first into one side of his nose then into the other.

Sniff! Sniff!

Alphonse leaned over and looked into the little box.

"Have a sniff, my bearded gentleman," invited the soldier. He pushed the box under the bear's nose. "Take a deep breath. It will clear that big furry head of yours."

"Don't do it, 'Phonse," warned Genest. "You will be sorry."

Alphonse took a deep breath. Sno-o-o-of! His head cleared like an exploding blunderbuss. Achoo-o-o-o-o! Achoo-o-o-o-o!

The bear shook his stinging nose. Then he let out a terrible roar. He stepped forward and gave the owner of the snuffbox such a cuff on the right cheek that the man fell to his knees. As he tried to rise, Alphonse gave him a cuff on the left cheek that sent him sprawling in the dust.

The soldier sprang up angrily. He whipped out his sword. Alphonse pulled out the rusty blade that Jeannot had given him.

Bong! Cling! Clank! There was a flash of steel in the sunlight. The two figures jumped this way and that way with toes turned out. They furiously struck at each other.

Bang! Cling! The fighters stepped forwards and backwards and sideways. Twice the French soldier's blade struck Alphonse but the steel of his breastplate blocked it. The bear fought like a hero, but it was easy to see that he was no match for this swordsman from France.

Corporal Pagot came sliding down the ladder.

"Stop!" he shouted. "Stop this instant!"

No one heard him. All the soldiers were busy watching the duel. Backward, backward stepped Alphonse's boots until they were against the logs of the palisade. Then his enemy lunged forward. With a twist of the wrist, the man sent the bear's sword spinning through the air.

Alphonse snarled furiously. He reached out and grabbed the man's blade in his tough paw. He pulled it away from the soldier and threw it over the palisade.

With a thundering roar, he seized the frightened soldier in his paws. He pulled him into the grip of his powerful arms and began to squeeze him to his chest. For it is the spirit of a bear to fight to win, not to uphold honor.

The man's eyes started to bulge. Pagot grabbed Alphonse's shoulder and shook it roughly with his own powerful arm.

"Enough, Alphonse!" he cried. "Atten*tion!*"

Alphonse released his victim. He dropped his paws to his sides and raised his nose in the air.

The defeated swordsman slunk away to the jeers of his comrades.

"At ease!" Pagot ordered Alphonse. "Company dispersed!"

The bear gave a last sneeze. Ah-choo-o-o-o!

Wild cheering rose from the crowd.

"Hurrah for Alphonse!"

"Long live Alphonse, that bearded one!"

The hero lumbered over to where he had so recently had his back to the palisade. He slowly scratched his back against the logs.

So in this way, the bear from the wilderness gained the respect of all his comrades-in-arms.

Next morning a great *fla* and *ra* of drums awoke Alphonse. He sat up in the narrow bunk and scratched his ears.

Pagot, wearing all his equipment, came dashing over to him.

"The croak-notes are playing the tune that calls everyone out for something important," he cried. "Into your clothes and don't forget your sword."

Alphonse dressed slowly, shaking his head *çà* and *là* from time to time. Genest tried to stop him when he clamped the breastplate over his chest. But the bear pushed him away and finished his dressing by donning the dented helmet. Jeannot Vallar had always demanded that this armor be worn when the drum sounded, and it is not the spirit of a trained bear to change the routine of his tricks.

The soldiers were drawn up in long lines in the square. The captain saluted them with his sword.

"Brave soldiers of New France," he began, "we are ready to march against our Iroquois enemies. All we need is some knowledge of their strength and their plans. Who will volunteer to get this information? Step forward two paces, brave volunteer."

No one stepped forward. Rather each man stepped back two paces. Each *man*, that is, but not Alphonse. He did not move one way or the other. He just stood in his best at-attention pose, his nose high in the air.

Looking back and forth, the nearsighted captain caught sight of the blurred form of Alphonse two paces ahead of the line.

"The new conscript!" exclaimed the officer. "What a brave one!"

At this Genest jumped out of the ranks and pulled at the bear.

"Back, 'Phonse," he warned. "Back up. You are stepping into a trap."

Then Pagot must join Genest to help save Alphonse.

448

The captain was full of admiration.

"*Three* volunteers!" he cried. "This is a proud day for New France. Company dispersed. Brave volunteers come with me."

In his office, the captain began thumbing through maps and drawings. Pagot peered over his shoulder fearfully.

"Just what is our mission, my captain?" he asked.

"You are to be spies," answered the officer. "Sergeant Besette here will help you with your disguises. You are to pose as Indian warriors. Go to the Iroquois village. Mingle with the Indians and learn all you can."

Sweat broke out on Pagot's heavy face. Genest grew pale. Only Alphonse showed no fear.

"You will leave immediately," said the officer. "There is no time to lose."

Sergeant Besette went to work on the disguises. He helped Pagot and Genest take off their clothing. He handed them breech-cloths and blankets and moccasins.

He cut off Pagot's moustache and Genest's chin whiskers. He shaved their heads, leaving only one short scalplock on each, which had something of the look of the pompon on the end of Alphonse's backbone. Then he fastened an eagle feather to each pompon.

He mixed little pots of paint and slopped and daubed like an inspired artist, for he had been a sign-painter in Paris before he joined the army.

First he gave each man a blue nose. He smeared

black over their eyelids and cheeks, and red over the rest of their faces. The upper parts of their bodies he painted with stripes of every color in the pots. Then he jumped back and looked at them with pride.

"Ah, I am a great artist!" He kissed his fingers. "Regard my masterpieces."

He turned to the bear.

"Now," said Sergeant Besette, "it is Alphonse's turn. What shall we do with Alphonse?"

For any third rank fool could see that Alphonse was going to be a difficult subject for this painter. He had taken off his armor and clothes and stood in his own fur coat, waiting to be made into an Iroquois.

The three men studied him from every angle. They scratched their heads. They bit their fingernails. They beat their foreheads.

"I fear that I do not have enough talent for this," sighed the painter. "But I will paint his nose and nails red just to show that I am not one to shirk his duty."

Sergeant Besette made Alphonse's nose into a beautiful red strawberry and daintily painted his nails.

"Perhaps we will think of something on the way," said Pagot. "Come, Alphonse, let us get this unpleasant business over as soon as possible."

All the way out of the fort and through the woods, the two men argued about what to do to make Alphonse into an Iroquois.

"I have it!" exclaimed Genest as they crossed the last ravine. "We will pretend that 'Phonse is a bear."

Pagot beamed upon him.

"Sometimes I think that you have something in your head other than sausages and cheese, my little soldier," he glowed. "That is perfect. I have seen Indians carrying a deer home from the hunt. It was tied to a pole by its hoofs. Just before we reach the Iroquois village, we will fix Alphonse so."

"With those red nails and that nose," added Genest, "it will look as if we had a fierce struggle with him. We shall play the brave hunters."

"Don't let us try to make this thing too good," warned Pagot. "A few herbs flavor the soup but too many turn it bitter."

When they came to the edge of the Indian cornfields, Alphonse was told to play dead. They tied his paws together with buckskin thongs and lashed them to a long pole. Then the two false Iroquois bravely strode toward the gate of the Indian palisade. Between them hung the limp form of Alphonse, so cleverly disguised as a bear.

The gate of the Iroquois village was open because many Indians were returning. As they entered, they saw the long houses fanned around an open yard.

An Iroquois painted like the Frenchmen stepped beside them. On his head were elk antlers and the unlucky elk's teeth hung in a necklace around his neck. He pushed his blue nose within a few inches of Pagot's.

"Ough," grunted the Indian.

"Ough," Pagot returned.

"Ough, ough," croaked the little Genest.

Pagot glared back at him.

"Don't be so talkative," he warned out of the corner of his mouth. "You will give us away."

The Indian seemed satisfied. He led the men toward a big pot steaming over a fire and motioned them to lay Alphonse down. As they did so, Pagot untied the thongs binding him to the pole.

"You are in a ticklish situation," he whispered into the bear's ear, "but stay dead as long as you can."

Alphonse did not understand him, but he was sleepy and the fire felt warm. He lay quietly with his eyes closed.

Then a terrific racket broke out behind one of the bark houses. A group of Indian warriors in full war paint and feathers came dancing into the yard. They waved gourd rattles and tomahawks. Deer hoofs dangled from their knees and kicked into the air. Tomtoms thumped.

The dancers formed a circle, stamping along on their heels and raising and lowering their bodies in time to the tomtoms. As they danced, they chanted and made hideous faces.

"Ough?" invited Pagot as he pulled Genest into the dancing circle.

The two soldiers fell into step with the Indians. They stamped, howled and flung their arms about in imitation of their fellow dancers.

Hi-yah! Hi-yah! Stomp, stomp, stomp! Boom, boom, boom!

From his place by the fire, Alphonse opened one eye. His little ears raised. One hindpaw began twitching to the beat of the tomtoms. Then both hindpaws began kicking in rhythm.

He stood up and started marching toward the dancers, left, right, left, right. For it is the spirit of a trained bear to want to show off every time he gets the chance.

At sight of what they had supposed to be a dead bear coming to life, the dancing Indians froze in their steps.

"*Oh, là, là!*" cried Pagot. "This ends the fête."

Both men ran toward Alphonse. Pagot grabbed his paw and spun him around.

"Come, Alphonse," he cried. "Run for your life!"

The sudden turn of affairs threw the Indians into confusion. They went running into their houses and into each other. All was spill and tumble. By the time they had recovered from the shock, the three spies were out the gate and halfway across the cornfields. A delayed whistle of arrows blew them into the woods.

Moccasins and paws went so fast they hardly touched the ground. Huh, huh, huh panted Pagot and Genest. But Alphonse was fresh as a moosebird because he had had a nice rest by the fire.

Pagot thought that it was better not to take a straight cut to the fort or the Iroquois might overtake them. So they broke away from the trail and went into the thick underbrush.

Night found them hopelessly lost in the woods. They

slept on the ground and this time the two blankets shared were the ones that Pagot and Genest had worn as part of their costumes.

All the next day, they wandered through the forest. Pagot and Genest were full of despair. But Alphonse was happy as a finch because it is the spirit of a bear to feel more at home in the forest than under a roof.

It was he who finally led them to a cave among the rocks. It was getting dark again and the men were overjoyed to find shelter.

They went into the cave, stumbling over rocks in the darkness. Weary and footsore, they huddled together and fell fast asleep. The cave was filled with snore echoes.

So in this way, Alphonse learned that a soldier's life is not all drums and marching and cheers.

When Pagot woke up, he had to go outside to find out if it was morning yet. The sun was shining and the birds twittering.

The corporal gathered an armful of brush and twigs. He carried them into the cave and started a fire with his flint.

Soon the flames were crackling cheerily. They showed an irregular chamber strewn with rocks. Roots hung down from the ceiling and water slowly dripped from them. *Three* bears were sleeping in a row.

Pagot let out a shriek that loosed new echoes in the cave. He reached for his sword but his hand touched only skin garments.

"Genest! Alphonse!" he cried. "Wake up!"

The little soldier sat up and rubbed his eyes. Alphonse sat up and scratched his ears. The two strange bears rose to their haunches and bared their long fangs.

Genest squealed and ran to Pagot. The two bears got to their paws and shuffled toward the men, snarling and growling. Then Alphonse added his own growls to the uproar and the whole cave was turned into a bear garden.

The bears began grunting and rubbing noses. For Alphonse realized that he was among those of his own spirit. What one bear tells another no one knows, but soon the two wild bears stopped growling at the men. One of them even licked Genest's cold, white face.

When he was able to speak, Genest pointed to the new companions.

"Look!" he cried. "Those pompons on the end of the backbone. They have those birthmarks, too."

"Genest," said Pagot. "I have had a flea in the ear about this Alphonse from the very first. There is no longer any reason for us to make the dunces about him. What is more, it looks as if we are now bears also."

Genest's face brightened.

"Why can't 'Phonse and his countrymen catch some fish for us?" he suggested.

Pagot ordered Alphonse to do this very thing. The bear shook his head *çà* and *là*. Then Pagot gave him a push toward the entrance of the cave. Alphonse grunted to the other bears to follow him.

Outside the cave, he stood and shook his head some more, *çà* and *là*. He did not know what the men wanted him to do. Then his little eyes brightened. He broke three branches off a willow tree.

He nudged the other bears to rise on their hindlegs. He gave each one a branch and showed him how to carry it over his shoulder.

Then he started marching back and forth, for this seemed to be the thing that men expected of bears.

"Ouf, wouf, ouf, wouf," grunted Alphonse.

The other bears fell into step behind him. Ouf, wouf, ouf, wouf they marched back and forth.

Alphonse was the only one out of step when Pagot and Genest came from the cave to see if the bears had caught any fish yet.

"That is what comes of sending a bear to do a man's job," said Pagot. "Oh, well, perhaps we can help with this."

Pagot joined in the lesson. He taught the wild bears to mark time and stand at attention. He even taught them how not to volunteer. He lined them up with Genest.

"Now who will volunteer to go to the Iroquois village and steal a haunch of venison?" he asked. "No, no, you in front. Do not look me straight in the eye. Never look

me straight in the eye when I ask for volunteers. It draws my attention to you. Alphonse—" But Alphonse had already stepped back two paces because it is not the spirit of a bear to be caught in the same trap twice. "And you, Genest, stop scratching your neck."

"I can't help it," replied Genest. "I feel like somebody is watching us. I can feel eyes crawling all over my neck."

The bears began looking over their shoulders. They sniffed the air and growled. The hair on their shoulders stood on end. For through the leaves of the bushes appeared hideously-painted faces.

Alphonse and the bears dropped on all fours and streaked for the cave. The two men almost beat them there.

"Close the entrance," directed Pagot. "Alphonse, you and your bears push that great boulder into it."

Alphonse grunted and pushed with all his might, but the wild bears were no help at all. They crouched in the back of the cave with an I-told-you-so look gleaming in their eyes.

As the boulder shivered and slowly moved under the force of the Indian onslaught, the men and Alphonse piled more and more rocks against it. Genest even tried to outpush the Iroquois.

"Now we have made a snug fort," announced the corporal at last. "It is a poor badger that can't dig some kind of a hole."

They sank to the ground, panting and exhausted.

"Huck! Huck! Our fire is making a lot of smoke," coughed Genest.

Shuddering, Pagot pointed toward their wall of rocks.

"It isn't coming from the fire," he groaned. "Look!"

The smoke was pouring in through the cracks.

"*Hélas!*" he moaned. "The Iroquois are trying to smoke us out. Ba-hup! Ba-hup!"

"I'm not—huck, huck, huck—going out," choked Genest.

"Huck, gr-r-r-r-huck, huck," coughed the bears.

At last they had to pull the stones away from their doorway. They staggered out into the fresh, biting air. And as they came out, one by one, the Iroquois seized them.

When the captives reached the Indian village, they were greeted by a noisy and curious crowd. They were led into one of the long houses and securely bound. The wild bears snarled and bit at the thongs that held them. Alphonse whined and shook his great head *çà* and *là*.

Then the boom, boom of drums shook the smoky air in the house. The Indian warriors left.

"We are cuckoo eggs hatching in a hawk's nest," sighed Pagot. "A council is being called. Our fate will be decided."

Alphonse showed no interest in their talk. All of his attention was given to the beating drums.

"I wonder what will happen to 'Phonse," mused Genest.

Pagot looked at the bear sadly.

"Good old Alphonse," he said. "They will surely get him into the cook pots this time, peace be to his broth!"

As the soldiers brooded over the possible fate of the bearded one in order to forget their own, the Iroquois men returned from the council.

The captives were roughly dragged out before a screaming, scowling mob. Pagot and Genest were fastened to two stakes set in the middle of the square.

Alphonse and the wild bears were carried to the edge of a blazing fire where the cook pots waited. But the Iroquois women were too excited about the doomed men to waste any time on bears at the moment.

All the Indians were intently watching the hapless Pagot and Genest. Some were piling firewood around them. Others shook tomahawks at them and made horrible faces. All the while the drums beat impatiently.

Boom, boom, boom!

Only one little Indian boy took any interest in the bears. He stood staring at Alphonse, a small tomahawk held in his brown hand. The bear's paws were twitching to the beat of the drums. His head was straining from side to side, *çà* and *là*.

Alphonse stared back at the boy. He lifted his shackled paws to him in a beseeching manner.

The little Indian looked at the sharp edge on his tomahawk. Then he pressed his tongue between his teeth and began cutting the leather thongs that held Alphonse. At last the bear was free.

461

He rose to his hindlegs and shook his fur coat. Again he held his paws out beggingly. Delighted with these antics, the boy handed him the tomahawk.

Alphonse swung it over his head and let out a roar that drowned all the other noises and sent the little Indian crawling under a wolf skin. Clumsily he hopped upon one hindpaw then the other.

Gr-r-r-r-rh-rh! Yee-ai-ai-ai-ai!

Alphonse was doing the war dance which he had been kept from performing at the last Indian fête.

Gr-r-r-r-r-rh-rh! Yee-ai-ai-ai-ai!

Alphonse growled and squealed as he raised and lowered his furry body on his stamping hindpaws. He waved the tomahawk wildly and bared his long, sharp fangs in a terrible snarl.

The Indians were rooted to the ground like the trees of their own forest. Only their black eyes moved as they watched Alphonse's war dance.

Around the stakes he danced four times.

Gr-r-r-r-r-rh-rh! Yee-ai-ai-ai-ai!

Then he sat down on his haunches with his nose in the air and waited for cheers of "Long live Alphonse, that bearded one!" But the Iroquois were struck dumb with astonishment and Genest had fainted.

At last the chief broke the spell. He was so old that his skin was brown and wrinkled as a dried tobacco leaf, but his step was as sure as that of a lynx. He walked to Alphonse with savage grace. He put his hand on the bear's head.

462

"Friends and relatives," shouted the chief to his tribe, "it is a sign. The bear chief warns us that all the bears of the forest will war against us if we kill these white men."

The Indians started murmuring and shifting about uneasily.

"This is no ordinary bear," agreed one. "With our own eyes we saw him teaching his brothers the white man's walking war dance."

"Yai! Yai!" remembered another. "Our own eyes have also seen him come to life beside our campfire once before."

"Through magic he has broken his strong bonds this time," added yet another. And it did not seem likely that the Indian boy hiding under the wolf skin would dispute his words.

"The Frenchmen have outwitted us again," shouted the first speaker. "They have made allies of the bear tribe. The very forests will be peopled with our enemies. This war is bad medicine for the red man."

"Another council," demanded the chief. "A peace council! Build up the fire under the great oak. Release the captives."

Pagot and Genest, who had come out of his faint by this time, were cut loose from the stakes. But as soon as the wild bears were freed, they raced for the palisade and quickly scrambled over it. Alphonse longingly watched their pompons disappear from sight.

The old chief stretched his arm out to Alphonse.

"Chief Dancing Bear shall have the place of honor at the council," he decreed. "Through him, we shall make peace with the white men."

So in this way, a bear from the wilderness ended a war before it was well begun.

Alphonse might have become a great general, but it is not the spirit of a bear to want to command armies. He received high honor, it is true. Even the king of France rewarded him.

"For great bravery, Alphonse Vallar is granted a seigneury of fifty square miles of land. In return he must build a mill, gather dependents, level forests, clear fields and make two blades of grass grow where only one grew before," wrote the king of France in his own fancy hand.

Alphonse yawned when his grant was read to him, for it is not the spirit of a bear to turn forests into fields. But Pagot and Genest were full of plans.

"Let us stay in the New World," Pagot urged Genest. "We shall become the dependents of this new seigneur."

When they returned to the cabin in the wilderness, Jeannot Vallar approved of this plan. He grabbed the axe from the corner and pressed it into Pagot's big hand. A mad light came into his eyes.

"Off to the battle of the trees!" he commanded. "And take the peasant Genest with you."

When the dependents had left, he turned to Alphonse with a laugh.

"Ha! Ha! My heroic brother," he said. "With these stupid servants to work for us, we shall live like noblemen."

Alphonse unbuckled his breastplate and threw it into a corner. The helmet was banged on top of it. He tore off his ill-fitting garments and threw them on top of the breastplate. Lastly he kicked off his worn boots.

Then dropping on all fours he marched down the trail one, two, three, four, one, two, three, four to join the other bears. For it is not the spirit of a bear to want servants and the life of a nobleman.

—— *Natalie Savage Carlson*

THINKING IT OVER

1. Tell about the times when Alphonse saved his companions from danger. Was he behaving like a bear or like a soldier?
2. Do you think Corporal Pagot knew a great deal more than Genest? Why?
3. Which episode or happening did you think was the funniest? Explain your answer.

THOUGHTS AT WORK

1. Find several places in the story where the author speaks of "the spirit of the bear." Why do you think she added these comments?
2. The Indians thought that Alphonse had gotten loose through magic. Why didn't the little Indian boy tell them the truth?
3. When the men were tied up by the Iroquois, Pagot sighed, "We are cuckoo eggs hatching in a hawk's nest." Tell in your own words what he meant. Skim pages 433 and 452 to find more of Pagot's wise sayings. Put them into your own words.
4. Tell whether you liked or disliked Jeannot, Alphonse's master.
5. Several happenings taught Alphonse that a soldier's life was not all drums, marching, and cheers. Tell about two of these happenings.
6. Why do you suppose Alphonse threw off his soldier's uniform and marched down the trail to join the other bears? How do you think Jeannot felt when he left?
7. Many French words such as *bien* were used in the story. Find several of these words and see if you can guess their meaning. Then check them in the glossary.

Pronunciation Key

The symbols and key words listed below will help you tell which sounds to use in reading the words in the glossary.

a	hat	e	let	o	hot	u	cup
ā	age	ē	be	ō	go	u̇	put
ã	care	ėr	term	ô	order	ü	rule
ä	far	i	it	oi	oil	ū	use
		ī	ice	ou	out		

ch in child   th in thin   ə *represents:*   a in about   i in April

ng in long   ŦH in then   e in taken   o in lemon

sh in she   zh in measure   u in circus

Abbreviations

n. noun   *v.* verb   *adj.* adjective   *adv.* adverb   *interj.* interjection

The pronunciation system and key are from *Thorndike, Barnhart Junior Dictionary*
© 1968 by Scott, Foresman and Company

GLOSSARY

A

ac quaint ance (ə kwänt′ns), a person one knows, but not as well as a close friend. *n.*

adi ós (ä′dē ōs′), a Spanish word for *good-by. interj.*

ad vise (ad vīz′), to give advice to; to say what should be done. *v.*

ague (ā′gū), a fit of shivering; also, a fever with chills and sweating. *n.*

al ly (al′ī), a person, state, or nation joined with another for a special purpose. *n.*

al tar (ôl′tər), 1. a table or a raised platform in the most sacred part of a church or temple. 2. a raised place for offerings or sacrifices. *n.*

an tic (an′tik), a funny or silly act; an amusing or silly trick. *n.*

anx ious (angk′shəs), 1. uneasy about something; worried. 2. desiring very much; eager: *He was anxious to learn to swim. adj.*

ar ea (ãr′ē ə), 1. ground space or floor space; any flat surface. 2. the size of a space. 3. a region: *the eastern area of the country. n.*

ar que bus (är′kwə bəs), a very heavy gun used long ago. *n.*

ar ray (ə rā′), clothes worn for some special occasion. *n.*

as so ci ate (ə sō′shē āt), to join as a friend, companion, or partner. *v.*

au di ble (ô′də bl), loud enough to be heard: *His words were barely audible. adj.*

awe (ô), a feeling of great fear or dread, mixed with wonder. *n.*

B

barbed wire (bärbd wīr), a wire with barbs, or sharp points, twisted every few inches. along its edge. *n.*

bar na cle (bär′nə kl), a small, shelled sea animal that fastens itself to rocks, wharves, and the bottoms of ships. *n.*

be drag gled (bi drag′ld), wet and limp, as from being dragged through water or wet grass. *adj.*

be hold en (bi hōld′n), in debt, as for a favor or act of kindness. *adj.*

bel low (bel′ō), to roar; to shout in an angry way. *v.*

be seech (bi sēch′), to ask for in an earnest or humble way; to beg. *v.*

bi di (bē dē), in India, a name for a kind of cigarette. *n.*

bien (byeN), (N means the vowel has a nasal sound), a French word for *good* or *well. adj., interj.*

boar (bôr), a wild hog or pig. *n.*

bob sled (bob′ sled′), a long sled with two sets of runners. *n.*

bon (bôN), (N means the vowel has a nasal sound), a French word for *good. adj., interj.*

bore (bôr), to make tired by dullness; to weary: *He was bored with the game. v.*

bore (bôr). (Past tense of the verb **to bear**). 1. carried: *The train bore many passengers.* 2. put up with; endure: *She bore her sorrows with courage.* 3. brought forth; produced: *The tree bore good fruit.* 4. moved towards; pressed on: *The runaway horse bore down upon the crowd. v.*

borne (bôrn). (Past perfect of the verb **to bear**): *The woman had borne only one child. v.*

bo tan i cal (bə tan′ə kl), having to do with botany, the science of plants and plant life. *adj.*

brace (brās), 1. to make firm, strong, or steady; to give support to. *v.* 2. something used to give support. *n.*

bras sart (bras′ərt), armor; a protective covering for the upper arm. *n.*

breech-cloth (brēch′ klôth′), a cloth, tied around the waist, to cover the lower part of the body. *n.*

brin dle (brin′dl), gray or tan with dark streaks and spots. *adj.*

bron to saur us (bron′ tə sô′rəs), a huge plant-eating dinosaur, 65 feet long, 12 feet tall. *n.*

brood (brüd), to think anxiously about something for a long time. *v.*

brow (brou), 1. the forehead. 2. the eyebrow. 3. the top or upper edge of a slope: *a tree on the brow of a hill. n.*

Bud dhist (bud′ist), having to do with Buddhism, a religion founded long ago by Buddha in Asia. *adj.*

bue nos (bwā′nōs), a Spanish word meaning *good, adj., interj.*

hat, āge, cãre, fär; let, bē, term; it, īce; hot, gō, ôrder; oil, out; cup, pút, rüle, ūse; ch, child; ng, long; sh, she; th, thin; ŦH, then; zh, measure; ə represents *a* in about, *e* in taken, *i* in April, *o* in lemon, *u* in circus.

bue nos días (bwā'nōs dē'äs), a Spanish phrase meaning *good day* or *good morning.*

bulge (bulj), something that swells outward, usually from a surface. *n.*

bunt (bunt), a push or shove with the head or horns. *n.*

bur dock (bėr'dok'), a tall weed with broad leaves and prickly flower heads or burrs. *n.*

bu reau (byur'ō), a chest of drawers, usually used to hold clothes. *n.*

C

cà and là (sä and lä), a French phrase for *to* and *fro*; *up* and *down.*

ca ble (kā'bl), a strong, thick rope or wire. *n.*

cal i co (kal'ə kō), cotton cloth, often printed with a colorful pattern. *n.*

cane brake (kān' brāk'), a growth of cane plants with long, jointed stems. *n.*

can o py (kan'ə pē), a covering that gives shade or shelter. *n.*

car cass (kär'kəs), body of an animal. *n.*

cat a logue (kat'l ôg), a list of names or articles; also, a book that contains such a list. *n.*

cav ern (kav'ərn), an underground hollow place; a large cave. *n.*

cel e brat ed (sel'ə brāt'id), well-known; famous. *adj.*

cen ta vo (sen tä'vō), a Spanish word for a coin. About 7 centavos equal 1 cent in American money. *n.*

cess pool (ses'pül), a pool or hole into which waste material empties. *n.*

chal lenge (chal'ənj), 1. to invite to take part in a contest, battle, or game. 2. to doubt; to question. *v.*

chal lis (shal'ē), a lightweight cloth usually with a flower design. *n.*

cham ber (chām'bər), any enclosed space; a room. *n.*

cha pati (chə pät'ē), in India, a round, thin bread, like a pancake, made of wheat flour. *n.*

chasse ga le rie (chäs gal rē'), a French Canadian term for a ghostly night rider or hunter. *n.*

chry san the mum (krə san'thə məm), a plant with round flowers that have many petals. *n.*

chut (shut), a French word for *hush*; a call for silence. *interj.*

civ il (siv'l), courteous; polite. *adj.*

clam ber (klam'bər), to make one's way by climbing, often using both hands and feet; to scramble. *v.*

com pli cat ed (kom'plə kāt'id), not simple; complex; not easy to explain. *adj.*

con ceit ed (kən sēt'id), having too much pride in oneself; vain. *adj.*

con demn (kən dem'), to declare guilty of wrongdoing or a crime; to sentence to punishment. *v.*

con fi dence (kon'fə dəns), 1. faith in one's own ability, power, or judgment; trust or belief: *We have confidence in our friend.* 2. boldness; certainty: *His confidence helped him get the job.* 3. a secret told to another: *She told me in strict confidence. n.*

con scious (kon'shəs), 1. awake to one's feelings: *He was conscious for only a short time.* 2. knowing; aware: *He was conscious of a noise in the room. adj.*

470

con script (kon′skript), a person forced to join the army or navy. *n.*

con sid er (kən sid′ər), 1. to think over carefully; to ponder. 2. to be thoughtful of others and their feelings. *v.*

con sid er a ble (kən sid′ər ə bl), large in amount; much. *adj.*

con spir a tor (kən spir′ə tər), a person who plans secretly with others to do something. *n.*

con tra dict (kon′trə dikt′), 1. to disagree. 2. to deny the truth of what someone said. *v.*

con vert (kən vėrt′), in football, to turn a try for a point into a score by kicking or rushing the ball over the goal. *v.*

coo lie (kü′lē), an unskilled worker in China and other parts of Asia. *n.*

cor al (kôr′əl), the hard pink or white substance made from the many skeletons of very small sea animals. *n.*

corn dodg er (kôrn doj′ər), a hard flat bread, made of corn meal. *n.*

cor ral (kə ral′), a pen or enclosed place for keeping animals. *n.*

cov et (kuv′it), to desire something very much. *v.*

cow er (kou′ər), to crouch or shrink down, as from fear or shame. *v.*

cred it (kred′it), 1. the time given for payment of something bought. 2. one's reputation in money matters: *to have good credit.* 3. a source of honor or praise: *He is a credit to his country.* 4. trust; belief: *There is credit in what you say.* 5. acknowledgement of something done: *You received full credit for your work. n.*

crest (krest), the top part of a hill or wave; peak; summit. *n.*

crim son (krim′zn), a bright, dark-red color. *n.*

crouch (krouch), to stoop or bend low like an animal ready to spring, or a person in hiding. *v.*

crude (krüd), not expertly done; roughly made: *a crude drawing. adj.*

cu bic yard (kū′bik yärd), the volume of a cube whose edges and depth measure a yard. 1 cubic yard = 27 cubic feet. *n.*

cun ning (kun′ing), 1. clever; skillful. 2. sly; tricky: *a cunning thief.* 3. pleasing in some way; attractive: *a cunning kitten. adj.*

D

dahl (däl), a kind of dried pea often used for soup in India. *n.*

dan gle (dang′gl), to hang in a loose way with a swinging motion. *v.*

daub (dôb), to spot or smear; to paint in small patches. *v.*

de cree (di krē′), to order or settle something with authority. *v.*

del e ga tion (del′ə ga′shən), a group of persons with the authority to act or speak for others. *n.*

del i ca tes sen (del′ə kə tes′n), a store that sells prepared foods, such as cooked meat and cheese. *n.*

de scend (di send′), 1. to come down from a higher to a lower place. 2. to make a sudden attack: *The enemy descended upon the town. v.*

---

hat, āge, cãre, fär; let, bē, tėrm; it, īce; hot, gō, ôrder; oil, out; cup, pu̇t, rüle, ūse; ch, child; ng, long; sh, she; th, thin; ŦH, then; zh, measure; ə represents *a* in about, *e* in taken, *i* in April, *o* in lemon, *u* in circus.

di lap i dat ed (də lap'ə dāt'id), partly ruined; falling apart. *adj.*

dip lo mat ic (dip'lə mat'ik), having to do with diplomacy, the official business between nations. *adj.*

dis perse (dis pėrs'), to separate and go in different directions. *v.*

dis po si tion (dis'pə zish'ən), the natural or usual way of acting toward other persons: *a sunny disposition. n.*

dom i cile (dom'ə sīl), the house or place in which one lives; one's home. *n.*

don (don), to put on, as clothing. *v.*

dor mi to ry (dôr'mə tô'rē), a building usually at a school or college that has many rooms for sleeping. *n.*

dor sal (dôr'sl), on the back. *adj.*

drake (drāk), a male duck. *n.*

dra ma (drä'mə or dram'ə), exciting real happenings that seem like events in a play. *n.*

draw (drô), a ditch or gully, dug out by water. *n.*

dy nam ic ten sion (dī nam' ik ten'shən), a force that pulls or stretches against something to create movement or power. *n.*

E

ear nest ness (ėr'nist nis), firmness and seriousness of purpose. *n.*

ed dy (ed'ē), to move with a twisting or whirling motion, as air or water does; to move in circles. *v.*

ee rie (ir'ē), mysterious; weird. *adj.*

ef fect (ə fekt'), power; force: *His words had no effect on him. n.*

el e gant (el'ə gənt), showing good taste, as in manners; refined. *adj.*

emerge (i mėrj'), to come into view; to appear. *v.*

en dure (en dùr'), to put up with; to stand, as pain or trouble: *He had to endure much pain. v.*

en vi ous (en'vē əs), feeling discontent or jealousy at the good fortune of another, meanwhile wishing to have the same good fortune. *adj.*

ev i dence (ev'ə dəns), proof which shows whether or not something is true or real. *n.*

ex er tion (eg zėr'shən), use of energy or strength to do something; effort. *n.*

ex haust ed (eg zôs'tid), tired out; worn out. *adj.*

ex ist (eg zist'), 1. to live: *Man must have air to exist.* 2. to be real: *Do ghosts exist or not? v.*

ex pe di tion (eks'pə dish'ən), a journey for a certain purpose, such as for discovering something or exploring. *n.*

ex po si tion (eks'pə zish'ən), a public display; an exhibition. *n.*

ex tinct (eks tingkt'), no longer living; having no living members left alive: *Dinosaurs are extinct animals. adj.*

F

fal ter (fôl'tər), to speak with a hesitating or unsteady voice. *v.*

fa tal (fā'tl), causing death; deadly: *You might get a fatal chill. adj.*

fau cet (fô'sit), a device for regulating the flow of water or other liquid coming from a pipe or tank; a tap. *n.*

fawn (fôn), to show affection, as a dog does, by crouching, licking, and wagging the tail. *v.*

fête (fāt), a festival; a certain time of feasting or celebrating. *n.*

feu fol let (fü fō′lā), a French term for will-o-the-wisp; an eerie, moving, fiery light that appears over marshy places at night. *n.*

fil ter (fil′tər), to pass through something and as a result be strained or changed: *The light filtered through the leaves. v.*

fledg ling (flej′ling), a young bird that is just beginning to fly. *n.*

fleece (flēs), the coat of wool that covers a sheep. *n.*

floun der (floun′dər), to move in a confused or clumsy way: *He floundered through the deep snow. v.*

flour ish (flėr′ish), to grow in a healthy way; to thrive. *v.*

fop pish (fop′ish), like a fop, a man who is very vain about his looks or clothes; a dandy. *adj.*

foul (foul), very unpleasant or disgusting in looks or smell. *adj.*

friz zle (friz′l), the piece of steel struck by the flint in a flintlock gun. *n.*

frou-frou (frü′ frü′), 1. a French word for a rustling or swishing sound. 2. frilly trimming on clothes that makes a rustling sound. *n.*

fu ton (fü ton), in Japan, a thick quilt used for sleeping on the floor. *n.*

G

gap (gap), 1. an open space; empty place. 2. unknown parts; blanks: *a gap in our knowledge. n.*

gap-toothed (gap tütht), having wide spaces between the teeth. *adj.*

gape (gāp), to open widely, as the mouth of a cave or a hole in the ground. *v.*

gen er os i ty (jen′ər os′ə tē), 1. willingness to share what one has with others. 2. a generous gift or act. *n.*

ges ture (jes′chər), to move the body, to express an idea or feeling. *v.*

ge ta (gā tä), in Japan, wooden clogs worn outdoors. *n.*

glare (glār), 1. to stare in an angry way. *v.* 2. a fierce, angry look. 3. a strong, unpleasant and blinding light. *n.*

gnarled (närld), covered with hard, rough lumps; twisted. *adj.*

gnash (nash), to strike or grind together: *He gnashed his teeth in anger. v.*

goad (gōd), a stick with a sharp point used for driving cattle. *n.*

good-na tured (gùd′nā′chərd), of a kindly and pleasant nature; cheerful. *adj.*

gouge (gouj), to dig or scoop out. *v.*

gra ci as (grä′sē äs), a Spanish word for *thank you.*

gru au (grü′ō), a French word for a fine wheat flour often used to make a cereal like oatmeal. *n.*

gul ly (gul′ē), a ditch made by rain. *n.*

gun ny sack (gun′ē sak), a bag or sack made of gunny, a strong cloth. *n.*

gus set (gus′it), a piece of material added to a garment, to give more width or strength. *n.*

hat, āge, cãre, fär; let, bē, tèrm; it, īce; hot, gō, ôrder; oil, out; cup, put, rüle, ūse; ch, child; ng, long; sh, she; th, thin; ŦH, then; zh, measure; ə represents *a* in about, *e* in taken, *i* in April, *o* in lemon, *u* in circus.

H

hack a more (hak′ə môr), a halter; a strap for leading, tying, or training an animal, especially a horse. *n.*

haugh ty (hô′tē), very proud of oneself and scornful of others. *adj.*

haunt (hônt), 1. to come to mind often. 2. to linger; to visit often. 3. to visit as a ghost or spirit. *v.*

heir (ãr), a person who has the legal right to receive property or a title after the one holding it dies. *n.*

hé las (ā′läs′), a French word meaning *alas;* an exclamation of sorrow, pity, or regret. *interj.*

helms man (helmz′mən), the man who steers a ship. *n.*

herb (ėrb *or* hėrb), a plant whose leaves are used for flavoring or medicine. *n.*

hid e ous (hid′ē əs), very unpleasant looking; horrible; frightful. *adj.*

hoar hound (hôr′hound′), candy flavored from the leaves of the horehound plant. *n.*

hoop skirt (hụp *or* hüp skért), a full skirt worn over a hoop to make the skirt stand out. *n.*

hop per (hop′ər), a box, usually funnel-shaped, for passing on material, as into a machine. *n.*

hos pi ta ble (hos′pi tə bl), generous and friendly in welcoming and entertaining guests. *adj.*

hur tle (hėr′tl), to move or rush in a sudden or violent way. *v.*

hy e na (hī ē′nə), a wild animal about the size and shape of a large dog. *n.*

I

im age (im′ij), a likeness of a person or thing such as that seen in a mirror or clear water. *n.*

imp ish (imp′ish), full of mischief; naughty. *adj.*

im pres sion (im presh′ən), the mark or imprint made by pressing or stamping an object onto a surface. *n.*

in dig nant (in dig′nənt), angry because of a mean act or unfair treatment of oneself or another person. *adj.*

in form (in fôrm′), 1. to give information to; to tell. 2. to tell tales about another; to tattle. *v.*

in her it (in her′it), to receive something from a person, often a relative, when he dies. *v.*

ini ti ate (i nish′ē āt), to admit someone into a group or club by a special ceremony or activity. *v.*

in so lence (in′sə ləns), speech or behavior that is very impolite, rude, or insulting. *n.*

in ten tion (in ten′shən), a determination to act in certain ways; plan. *n.*

in ter fer ence (in′tər fir′əns), in football, clearing the way for the ball carrier or the passer by blocking would-be tacklers. *n.*

in trude (in trüd′), to force or thrust something in or upon. *v.*

J

jab (jab), poke with something pointed: *I will jab a stick into the hole.* v.

jack al (jak′ôl *or* jak′l), a wild dog about the size of a fox. n.

jaun ty (jôn′tē), gay and lively. *adj.*

jeal ous (jel′əs), feeling envy toward someone more successful. *adj.*

jos tle (jos′l), to push roughly. v.

K

kha di (kä dē), in India, a coarse, off-white, handwoven cloth. n.

kin dling (kin′dling), small pieces of wood used to start a fire. n.

knave (nāv), a man who is tricky, deceitful, or dishonest; a rascal. n.

ko ke shi (kō ke′shē), in Japan, a painted wooden doll with just a stick for the body and a ball for the head. n.

L

lack ey (lak′ē), a man servant; a footman. n.

la dle (lā′dl), to dip out: *to ladle soup from a kettle to a bowl.* v.

lance (lans), a long-handled spear with a pointed end. n.

lanky (langk′ē), tall and thin. *adj.*

lar der (lär′dər), a place where food is kept; a pantry. n.

len til (len′tl), a plant of the pea family with small seeds in pods. n.

li chen (lī′kən), a tiny flowerless plant that looks like dry moss and grows in patches on rocks. n.

loft (lôft), an upper room of a building just under the roof; an attic. n.

loi ter (loi′tər), to waste time; to linger. v.

loom (lüm), to appear suddenly in an unnaturally large form or in a way not clear to the eye. v.

lure (lur), to tempt or attract by offering something that is especially desirable; to bait. v.

M

mag is trate (maj′is trāt), a government official with the power to enforce the law. n.

mar row bone (mar′ō bōn′), a bone with marrow, a soft tissue that fills the hollow part of bones. n.

ma sa la (mə sä′lä), in India, a spicy sauce. n.

mile stone (mīl′stōn′), 1. a stone that has been set up on a road to show the distance in miles to a place. 2. an event that marks a certain time in a person's life or in history. n.

mince (mins), to talk or act in an unnaturally refined or polite way; to put on airs. v.

mis er a ble (miz′ər ə bl), very poor; wretched: *a miserable hut. adj.*

hat, āge, cãre, fär; let, bē, tėrm; it, īce; hot, gō, ôrder; oil, out; cup, pút, rüle, ūse; ch, child; ng, long; sh, she; th, thin; ŦH, then, zh, measure; ə represents *a* in about, *e* in taken, *i* in April, *o* in lemon, *u* in circus.

mock (mok), to make fun of; to laugh at in a scornful way. *v.*

mois ture (mois′chər), a slight wetness; dampness. *n.*

mon soon (mon sün′), a seasonal wind in southern Asia causing heavy rain from April to October. *n.*

mood (müd), the way one feels. *n.*

mope (mōp), to be silent, gloomy, and out of spirits. *v.*

mor sel (môr′sl), a small bite. *n.*

m'sieur (mə syė′), a shortened form of *monsieur*, a French word meaning *Mr.* or *sir. n.*

muse (mūz), to think about something in a quiet or dreamy way; to ponder. *v.*

mus ky (mus′kē), like musk, a substance that has a strong smell. Musk comes from a gland in a male musk deer. *adj.*

N

neg lect (ni glekt′), failure to care for or to give proper attention to. *n.*

nov el (nov′l), 1. a story often about imaginary things and events, long enough to fill a book. *n.* 2. of a new kind; strange; *a novel idea. adj.*

O

oath (ōth), a serious promise, made in the name of something revered, that one speaks the truth or will keep a promise. *n.*

on slaught (on′slôt′), a fierce and furious attack: *The onslaught of the enemy drove them back. n.*

out mod ed (out mōd′id), out-of-date; old-fashioned; no longer used. *adj.*

P

pa le on tol o gist (pā′lē on tol′ə jist), a person who studies paleontology, the science that deals with life that existed long ago. It is based on the study of fossil animals and plants. *n.*

pal i sade (pal′ə sād′), a high fence of strong wooden stakes, used as a defense. *n.*

pal let (pal′it), a small bed, usually made of straw. *n.*

pan (pän), in India, a mixture of lime and spices wrapped in the leaves of the betel-nut plant, and used for chewing, like chewing tobacco. *n.*

pan icky (pan′ik ē), feeling or showing panic, a sudden terrifying fear. *adj.*

par af fin (par′ə fin), a white or colorless substance like wax, often used to cover objects to protect them from the air. *n.*

peer (pir), to look closely or curiously. *v.*

pen du lum (pen′jə ləm), a weight hung from a fixed point in such a way that it is free to swing to and fro. *n.*

per se cute (pėr′sə kūt), to do harm to; to treat badly again and again. *v.*

pil lo ry (pil′ə rē), a wooden frame with holes in which a person's head and arms were locked. It was once used as a punishment. *n.*

pom pon (pom'pon), a ball often made of feathers or wool, worn on clothing as an ornament. *n.*

pre serve (pri zėrv'), to protect; to keep from change or destruction. *v.*

pret zel (pret'sl), a hard, brittle crack-er, made in the form of a knot, and glazed and salted on the out-side. *n.*

prim (prim), very fussy about one's ap-pearance and behavior. *adj.*

prod uce (prod'üs or pro'dūs), the yield: *Vegetables are a farm's produce. n.*

pro file (prō'fīl), a side view, especially of a head. *n.*

prom e nade (prom'ə nād'), a walk for pleasure, show, or exercise. *n.*

proph e cy (prof'ə sē), something told about the future; a prediction. *n.*

prow (prou), the forward part of a ship; the bow. *n.*

pter o dac tyl (ter'ə dak'tl), a large, extinct fly-ing reptile with wings like a bat. *n.*

pub lish (pub'lish), 1. to prepare and offer for sale printed material, such as newspapers, books, or magazines. 2. to make generally known; to an-nounce publicly. *v.*

Q

quay (kē), a landing place for ships often built of stone; a wharf. *n.*

quiv er (kwiv'ər), 1. a case for holding arrows. *n.* 2. to shake with a trem-bling motion; to shiver. *v.*

R

race (rās), a group of persons, animals, or plants that have something in com-mon: *an ancient race of trees. n.*

range (rānj), 1. a series of things in a row or line, such as mountains. 2. an open space of land where horses or cattle may graze. *n.*

rap ids (rap'idz), the part of a river where the water flows very fast. *n.*

rare (rār), 1. not often found; scarce: *rare jewels.* 2. thin; not dense: *Air at high altitudes is rare.* 3. not com-pletely cooked: *a rare steak.* 4. un-usually good: *Animals have a rare sense of smell. adj.*

rare ly (rār'lē), not often; seldom: *He rarely went outside. adv.*

ra vine (rə vēn'), a narrow valley, usually with steep sides. *n.*

reed (rēd), 1. tall grass with a hollow, jointed stem, that grows in wet places. 2. a pipe or hollow tube made from the stem of a reed. *n.*

re luc tant (ri luk'tənt), unwilling; not eager to take action. *adj.*

re sent (ri zent'), to feel hurt and angry at: *I resent being left out. v.*

re tort (ri tôrt'), to make a sharp or witty reply; to answer back. *v.*

row el (rou'əl), a small pointed wheel on the end of a spur used to prod a horse. *n.*

hat, āge, cãre, fär; let, bē, tėrm; it, īce; hot, gō, ôrder; oil, out; cup, put, rüle, ūse; ch, child; ng, long; sh, she; th, thin; ŦH, then, zh, measure; ə represents *a* in about, *e* in taken, *i* in April, *o* in lemon, *u* in circus.

rude (rüd), roughly or poorly made: *He came upon a rude cabin. adj.*

runt (runt), an unusually small person, animal, or plant. *n.*

S

san (sän), a Japanese word used with a name to show respect; also used after names within the family: *papa-san.*

sap ling (sap'ling), a young tree. *n.*

sa ri (sä'rē), a long piece of material, wound around the body with one end often draped over the head. *n.*

sau cy (sô'sē), showing lack of respect; impolite. *adj.*

scalp lock (skalp lok), a long bunch of hair left on the top of the shaved heads of warriors of some tribes of American Indians. *n.*

scheme (skēm), a plan of action. *n.*

scoff (skôf), to make fun of; to show a lack of belief; to jeer. *v.*

scorn ful (skôrn'fəl), showing that one feels that something is not worth noticing or bothering with. *adj.*

scowl (skoul), to look angry or displeased by lowering the eyebrows; to frown. *v.*

scrim mage line (skrim'ij lin), in football, the place on the field where the ball is stopped by the opposing team; also, the place where the teams line up to start the next play. *n.*

se dan chair (si dan' chãr), an enclosed chair attached to poles and carried by two men. *n.*

seign eury (sān'yə rē'), the property of a French lord or gentleman. *n.*

seize (sēz), 1. to take hold of suddenly; to grasp. 2. to take possession of something by force. 3. to take advantage of. *v.*

self-con fi dence (self'kon'fə dəns), a firm belief in one's own ability, judgment, or power. *n.*

se ñor (sā nyôr'), a Spanish title of courtesy, meaning *Mr.* or *sir. n.*

se ra pe (sə rä'pē), a brightly colored woolen blanket often worn over one shoulder. It can also be used as a blanket. *n.*

shack le (shak'l), to put metal bands around the legs or wrists to prevent them from moving freely. *v.*

shag bark (shag'bark'), a hickory tree with rough bark that can be peeled off in strips. *n.*

sha man (shä'mən, or sham'ən), a priest of an ancient religion; also a medicine man; a magician. *n.*

shank (shangk), any thing, like a leg or stem, that connects one part with another. *n.*

shin (shin), the front part of the leg below the knee. *n.*

shirk (shėrk), to avoid doing what one should do. *v.*

shod (shod). (Past tense of the verb **to shoe**: *A well-shod horse. v.*

shud der (shud'ər), to tremble or shake as from fear or cold. *v.*

shuf fle (shuf'l), to drag the feet. *v.*

478

si es ta (sē̯ es′tə), in Spanish, a short rest or nap, taken at noon or in the afternoon. *n.*

sloth (slōth), a slow-moving animal that lives in trees, hanging upside down from the branches. *n.*

smite (smīt), to strike; to hit hard. *v.*

so ber (sō′bər), 1. serious; quiet; solemn: *He had a sober look on his face.* 2. calm; sensible: *They wore sober clothes.* 3. showing self-control; moderate: *He behaved in a sober way.* 4. not drunk. *adj.*

so ber ness (sō′bər nis), seriousness. *n.*

sooth say er (sūth′sā′ər), a person who claims to be able to tell the future. *n.*

spec i men (spes′ə mən), a part of something taken to show what the whole is like; a sample. *n.*

spec tac u lar (spek tak′yə lər), showy; attracting attention by unusual display. *adj.*

stern (stèrn), the back end of a ship or boat. *n.*

stout (stout), 1. brave and bold. 2. fat; fleshy. 3. strong and firm: *a stout building. adj.*

strait (strāt), a body of water, such as a narrow channel, connecting two larger bodies of water. *n.*

stud (stud), to set or decorate with things that stick out, such as nail-heads or jewels. *v.*

sulky (sul′kē), sullen; in a bad mood. *adj.*

sum mit (sum′it), the highest point; the top. *n.*

sur vive (sər vīv′), to remain alive; to continue to live. *v.*

T

ta bi (tä bē), in Japan, a heavy cotton sock, with a thick sole and a separate part for the big toe. *n.*

tack le (tak′l), in football, one of two players who knocks down or tackles opposing players. *n.*

tangy (tang′ē), having a sharp taste, flavor, or smell. *adj.*

ta ta mi (tä tä′mē), in Japan, a thick, straw matting, fitted together to cover the entire floor. *n.*

thresh old (thresh′ōld), the piece of stone or wood set under a door. *n.*

til ler (til′ər), the handle used to turn the rudder in steering a boat. *n.*

tim ber (tim′bər), trees; forests. *n.*

tinge (tinj), to give a slight color to; to tint. *v.*

tin gle (ting′gl), to have a thrilling or prickling feeling, such as that caused by excitement or cold. *v.*

ton ga (tong′gə), a two-wheeled cart, drawn by bullocks or ponies. *n.*

touch hole (tuch′hōl′), a small opening in old-time cannons and firearms, through which the gunpowder inside was set on fire. *n.*

tow (tō), yarn from the coarse and broken parts of hemp or flax. *n.*

trace (trās), one of the two straps, ropes, or chains by which an animal pulls a carriage or wagon. *n.*

---

hat, āge, cãre, fär; let, bē, tèrm; it, īce; hot, gō, ôrder; oil, out; cup, put, rüle, ūse; ch, child; ng, long; sh, she; th, thin; ᴛH, then, zh, measure; ə represents *a* in about, *e* in taken, *i* in April, *o* in lemon, *u* in circus.

tread (tred), to step heavily on. *v.*

trick le (trik'l), a small flow of something, such as water. *n.*

trow el (trou'əl), a small tool used to dig up plants or loosen dirt. *n.*

trudge (truj), to walk wearily or with effort. *v.*

tur bu lent (ter'byə lənt), full of violent movement. *adj.*

tur moil (ter'moil), a great disturbance; a noisy moving about. *n.*

ty ran no saur us (tə ran'ə sô'rəs), the largest flesh-eating dinosaur. *n.*

U

up start (up'stärt'), a person who has a high opinion of himself; one who feels very important. *n.*

ut ter (ut'ər), speak; to make known. *v.*

ut ter ly (ut'ər lē), totally; completely: *He was utterly alone. adv.*

V

var mint (vär'mənt), a very unpleasant or offensive person or animal. *n.* [*Informal or Dialect.*]

var si ty (vär'sə tē), in a school, the most important team in a sport. *n.*

ven i son (ven'ə zn), the flesh of a deer used as food. *n.*

ven ti late (ven'tl āt), to change the air in a place; to drive out stale air and let in fresh air. *v.*

ver te bra (ver'tə brə), one of the bones of the spinal column, or backbone. *n. Plural:* ver te brae (ver'tə brē).

W

wag gish ness (wag'ish nis), being fond of making harmless jokes. *n.*

wal low (wol'ō), to roll about, as in mud. *v.*

ware (wār), pottery; earthenware. *n.*

war i ly (wār'ə lē), with caution; carefully. *adv.*

wash out (wosh'out'), a ditch made by water washing away the earth. *n.*

whence (hwens), from where; from what place: *He returned from whence he came. adv.*

whim per (hwim'pər), to cry in low, broken sounds. *v.*

whit tle (hwit'l), to cut small pieces from wood with a knife. *v.*

wince (wins), to draw back suddenly, as from a blow; to flinch. *v.*

woodsy (wùd'zē), in pioneer days, a man who lived in the woods by hunting, fishing, or trapping; a woodsman. *n.*

Y

yield (yēld), to provide; to give. *v.*

yoke (yōk), 1. to fasten two animals together with a wooden frame. *v.* 2. the frame used to fasten two animals together. *n.*

Z

za bu ton (zä'bü ton), in Japan, a large square cushion used to sit on. *n.*

ABCDEFGHIJK 765432
PRINTED IN THE UNITED STATES OF AMERICA